THE GUINNESS BOOK OF ROYAL BLUNDERS

Geoffrey Regan

GUINNESS PUBLISHING

For Lindsay and Richard

Published in Great Britain by
Guinness Publishing Ltd
33 London Road, Enfield, Middlesex EN2 6DJ

"Guinness" is a registered trademark of
Guinness Publishing Ltd.

First published 1995

10   9   8   7   6   5   4   3   2   1   0

ISBN 0-85112-671-5

A catalogue record for this book is available from the
British Library

Designed by Cathy Shilling
Picture Editor: Alex Goldberg
Typeset by Ace Filmsetting Ltd, Frome, Somerset

Printed and bound in Great Britain by
The Bath Press, Bath

Front cover illustration: *The Royal Libertine Reclaimed* a caricature
depicting George IV and Queen Caroline, *c* 1820 (ME)

Picture Acknowledgements
The Publishers wish to thank the following for permission to
reproduce pictures in this book:
Anne Ronan/Image Select (AR/IS)
Hulton Picture Library (H)
London Features (LF)
Mary Evans Picture Library (ME)
Peter Newark (PN)
Popperfoto (P)
Rex Features (RF)

CONTENTS

INTRODUCTION

One might be excused for thinking that a book that contained details of people who believed they had swallowed grand pianos, or had given birth to pillows, or who awarded medals to chickens must be a report from the Board of Bedlam, London's first mental institution. Surely the cases of men who employed clothes-testers in case their clothes were poisoned, or tried to eat their servants or suffocated their dinner guests with rose petals must have originated from a psychiatric conference. And how was it that the story that the navy had been directed to abandon its normal duties to collect cooking ingredients at the whim of a very important person was not raised in the House of Commons? The truth is that those responsible for each of these eccentric actions had one thing in common: they were all royal and as such were able to insist that their fantasies were indulged. In this way they qualified for inclusion in this book of 'Royal Blunders'.

Throughout the book I have concentrated my attention less on the political blunders of royalty and far more on the domestic, ceremonial, social and personal ones. This seemed essential in order to differentiate between the 'royals', who reigned as well as ruled, and those who simply ruled, often maintaining themselves in power by force. Clearly twentieth-century dictators have been as autocratic as any of the monarchs in history, but none was ever hedged round with the mystique of monarchy, and it is this peculiar element that I wished to investigate.

The book is divided into six sections, dealing first with the fitness or otherwise of kings and queens to occupy their thrones. There can be no other 'occupation' known to man that has suffered so much from the effects of mental illness. As I attempt to show this was frequently the result of inter-marriage between close relations. The dangers of this process were well known by the fifteenth century and yet the needs of diplomacy outweighed the inevitable and tragic human consequences. I have demonstrated these consequences in pictorial form, believing that the propagation of such pitiful specimens in the name of dynastic ambition was one of the most unforgivable of all royal blunders.

The pomp and ceremony of the royal 'industry' has always been part of the essential process of maintaining the royal image. However, coronations and weddings have been subject to mishaps – some farcical and some even tragic. Few brides would want to forget their 'happiest day' more readily than Princess Ena, granddaughter of Queen Victoria, whose wedding snaps taken in Madrid, in 1906, included the carnage and mayhem of an assassination attempt. Nor would the unlucky brides of the Grand Duke Peter of Russia, or Henry IV of Castile or the Duke of Calabria remember their wedding nights with any affection. Yet some royal weddings have contained as much humorous material as – and probably far more than – any television sitcom and it is with this in mind that they are included in these pages.

Royal marriages have generally been arranged by the parents of the young couple and, at least in the past, little consideration was given to their wishes. As a result, many royal marriages were unhappy and held together by the strong mortar of duty rather than the thinner daub of love. Sexual incompatibility was a prominent factor in marital discord,

The antics of George IV's wife, Caroline of Brunswick (far left of the stage), made her a popular target for contemporary satirists, particularly after she returned from her travels with her Italian paramour, Bartolomeo Bergami. Always referred to as 'Queen' Caroline, she was in fact never crowned. (H)

and the inability of a princess or queen to produce an heir to the throne was viewed as a supreme failure on her part. However, as I have demonstrated, the failure was frequently the result of impotence on the part of the male. This inability to breed – by either prince or princess – viewed only as a misfortune among ordinary folk, constituted a supreme 'royal' blunder.

Even where there was no sexual discord, marriages could be bitterly unhappy. The

Empress Elizabeth of Austria felt she had found her handsome prince in Franz Josef, but instead he placed duty before love, something she was never able to do, and as a result both lived lives of bitter frustration and tragedy. One senses a similar problem in the marital breakdown between the Prince of Wales and Princess Diana. On a more comical level, the marriage of the Prince Regent and Caroline of Brunswick was doomed from the start on the grounds of mutual incompatibility. The fact that Prince George was already married might be seen to constitute another objection.

To be born a prince or princess may once have been every child's dream. However, in Chapter Four, I have examined just what it was like to be born into a royal family and to be brought up to be a member of the exclusive 'royal club'. Few monarchs have been good parents and the lives of royal children have been blighted by ineptitude in fostering them. From Queen Victoria onwards, British royal mothers have shown an almost uncanny ability to produce deeply flawed and unhappy heirs to the throne as a result of distant, loveless 'mothering'. Even this, however, has been preferable to the treatment meted out to heirs to the throne in Russia, Germany and Turkey. In these states there have been numerous occasions when the ruler has actually murdered his eldest son.

In this book death is not quite the last chapter. Even this most final of royal actions has been accompanied by farce. Death has often visited palaces and castles less than decorously, so that George II was whisked away by the Grim Reaper while in the privy, and Queen Caroline of Ansbach literally split her sides while laughing at one of her surgeons, whose wig had been set alight by a candle. The darkest comedy was reserved for King Edmund Ironside, whose death by treachery might have graced an episode of Rik Mayall's *Bottom*.

During his visit to Chile in 1968, Prince Philip was introduced to Dr Allende, soon to become president of his country. It was an official function and Allende was wearing a lounge suit instead of white tie and tails. Prince Philip asked him, 'Why are you dressed like that?' Allende replied, 'Because my party is poor and they advised me not to hire evening dress.' 'If they told you to wear a bathing costume,' snapped the Prince, 'I suppose you'd have come dressed in one.'

In the final 'Royal Miscellany' I have examined a number of aspects of royal life that have generated blunders of one kind or another. In her royal travels Queen Elizabeth II has been subjected to various types of reception, none, presumably, more symbolic and less welcoming than a Maori 'twenty-one bum salute' in New Zealand. In terms of maintaining the modern image of royalty, few events have done more harm than Prince Edward's 'It's A Royal Knockout' in 1987. Well-intentioned though this charitable frolic obviously was, it chipped away at the 'mystique' of monarchy, revealing the younger royals as a group of 'Hooray Henrys', no more palatable to the general public for the knowledge that they were living off public funds through the Civil List. Littered additionally throughout the book are various royal gaffes, an alarming number of which originated from Prince Philip, the Duke of Edinburgh.

In conclusion, this writer has been forced by the sheer weight of adverse evidence to reflect on the notion of a hereditary monarchy, which is certainly one of the most curious of all human institutions. From ancient times when tribesmen made the logical choice of the wisest or the strongest in battle to lead them, how did a system evolve that has resulted in rule by families like the Habsburgs, Wittelsbachs, Romanovs and Windsors?

To get the best answer one should perhaps ask an American. They have never had any royalty of their own, but they love everybody else's and travel thousands of miles just to see them. In this they are at odds with one of the most famous and respected of their founding fathers, that grand old Virginia gentleman Thomas Jefferson, who took a decidedly jaundiced view of royalty. He remarked in 1787, 'No race of kings has ever presented above one man of common sense in twenty generations.' Next year he was no better pleased: 'There is not a crowned head in Europe whose talents or merits would entitle him to be elected a vestryman by the people of any parish in America.' Probably the best day in American history was when George Washington resisted the invitation to become King George I of the United States. Instead he became president and every four years thereafter the president had to stand for re-election. And if he was out of favour he was out of office. How many kings one wonders would have gained re-election after four years?

But then, how many tourists would come to Britain to watch the House of Commons in action? Or a president in a dark lounge suit travelling in a bullet-proof limousine? And does 'Presidential Blunders' have quite the same ring – or the variety of material – as 'Royal Blunders'?

William of Orange, later William III of England, was noted for his stoop, which gave him the impression of being a hunchback. On one occasion, a doctor from Amsterdam passed William, who was dressed in farmer's clothes. The doctor greeted him as 'Your Majesty'. William asked him how he recognized him in his 'disguise' and the doctor replied, 'I recognize you by your hump.'

THE ROAD TO RUIN: RASPUTIN AND THE ROMANOVS

There are few if any parallels in the histories of the great European powers to the rise of Grigory Rasputin. Probably it could only have happened in Russia, a country that combined a deep religious mysticism with the extremes of wealth and poverty. Perhaps the image of Mahatma Gandhi in his loin cloth and sandals taking tea with King George V and Queen Mary at Buckingham Palace is the closest the British mind could get to understanding what it must have been like for a Russian peasant to find favour with the Tsar and his family. Yet for all the splendours of the Winter Palace or Fabergé's fabulous eggs, Russia had the thinnest veneer of civilization of any of the European powers in 1914.

The name 'Rasputin' means 'dissolute' in Russian and Grigory kept the nickname he had earned as a boy either as a sign of deep penitence for his sins or, more likely, as a badge to demonstrate his contempt for convention. He was, in fact, born Grigory Efimovich, son of a farmer at the village of Pokrovskoe, in western Siberia, in 1872. As a young man he was a ruffian and a wastrel, rarely able to keep his eyes or his hands off the local girls. If they failed to run away at the first sight of him he would try to pull their clothes off and rape them. Not surprisingly Grigory received many a beating from husbands and fathers, if not from the sturdy village girls themselves. He found an outlet for his libidinousness in a Christian sect called the Khlysty, which held the view that it was possible to worship God through sexual encounters. This appealed strongly to Grigory and he joined them in their sado-sexual orgies in the forests around his village. At the age of twenty he married a peasant girl who, in spite of all that happened to her husband in the next twenty-four years, stayed faithful to him and brought up his four children at home.

But Rasputin was not cut out for a life of toil, and one day he announced to the rest of the village that he had been called to go on a pilgrimage. The villagers were not convinced. They knew him for a lazy and worthless poltroon. Yet Grigory surprised everyone by walking two thousand miles to the monastery on Mount Athos in Greece, from which he returned two years later a changed man. The profligate Grigory had become a man of God, or so he claimed. Wearing verminous clothes and curbing his previous debauched habits, Rasputin the mystic healer was about to reveal himself to an unsuspecting world. His reputation as a preacher spread quickly and soon he began to make contacts with prominent St Petersburg families, who took him at his own valuation. Instead of locking up their daughters and kicking Grigory down the steps and into the street, they entertained him in their houses, apparently accepting his filthy clothes and dirty habits as a sign that he was genuine. Yet as his star rose and he was welcomed into higher social circles, the peasant mystic began to adapt his image. His rough clothes gave way to coloured silk shirts, velvet trousers and soft leather boots. The private Rasputin began to experience the thrills of the big city, the wining, dining and whoring that passed as the good life for Russia's upper classes. Mystic by day, Rasputin became a debauchee by night.

But Rasputin was looking for more than a few frolics and a bit of fun. He wanted the security of belonging to a social class that, but for his monk's habit and his crucifix, would have kicked him into the gutter and spat on him. He needed friends in high places who could protect him if necessary from the many enemies successful men always make. And who could protect him better than the royal family? Chance, and his gift as a healer, was to come to his aid.

Rasputin's introduction to Tsar Nicholas II and his family occurred in a way that gave him his best chance of making a lasting impression on them. The Tsarevitch Alexis, heir to the throne, suffered from the royal disease haemophilia, almost certainly passed on to him from his great-grandmother, Queen Victoria of Great Britain. The first crisis caused by the disease occurred when the boy was just three and a half. He fell while playing in the garden and his face swelled quickly, closing both his eyes. Alexis was soon screaming with pain and the royal doctors were unable to do anything to stop the internal haemorrhaging. In despair the Tsarina Alexandra Feodorovna asked her close friend and confidante, Anna Vyrubova, for advice and she, already aware of Rasputin's reputation as a healer, suggested that he should be called. Rasputin hurried to the palace and entered the sick room. He knelt and prayed by the child's bed and then spoke to him. 'Don't be afraid,' he told Alexis, 'everything will be all right. Your pains will go.' By the next morning the swelling had gone down and the Tsarevitch had recovered. How exactly Rasputin achieved the cure has never been made clear – hypnotism has been suggested – but whatever he did, it worked. Two years later Rasputin achieved another such 'miracle' when the boy's leg swelled from bleeding into the knee joint. It was this capacity to help the young Tsarevitch that enabled Rasputin to establish so tight a hold on the Tsarina's heart and mind.

Rasputin's success with the Tsarevitch soon made his name famous in St Petersburg and no doors were closed to him. It became fashionable among wealthy hostesses to invite Rasputin to their houses for seances and other mystic gatherings. Yet Grigory never lost the rough habits of the peasant and his crude table manners were regarded as quite shocking. He was frequently seen to 'plunge his dirty hands into his favourite fish soup'. Yet oddly it was

The Russian 'holy man' Grigori Rasputin with a group of mainly female admirers, c. 1914. Rasputin exploited his position with the Russian royal family to widen his sexual conquests and live a life of debauchery. (ME)

precisely the crudity of the man that appealed to so many society ladies, who found his rough manners a refreshing change from the effete manners of their courtier husbands.

Rasputin's sex appeal was something on which there is general agreement. Women apparently found him irresistible and upper-class ladies as well as actresses and common whores took pleasure in the arms of the 'mad monk'. Part of the answer lay in Rasputin's ability to convince women that by submitting to his lust they were redeeming themselves from sin. It was a continuation of his Khlysty beliefs. Yet Rasputin was no redeemer. He was merely exploiting his monkish garb to satisfy his inordinate sexual drives. Incredibly husbands even gave blessing to their wives as they submitted themselves to him. In cafés and restaurants throughout St Petersburg Rasputin enjoyed a full nightlife, entertaining young women and leading them to a vacant bedroom, which he referred to as the 'Holy of Holies', for their salvation.

Whatever the public felt about Rasputin's morals, the Tsarina Alexandra had absolute confidence in him. He was entertained frequently at the palace and often visited the children's nursery. Claiming that he wished to see the four young grand duchesses pray before they went to bed, he sometimes hung around their bedrooms and often sat on their beds while the girls were in their nightgowns. The girls' governess, Mademoiselle Tiutcheva, was horrified at the liberties this 'peasant' took with her young ladies. On one occasion, she found Rasputin seated on the end of the bed of the fourteen-year-old Grand Duchess Olga, stroking her bare feet. She complained to the Tsarina about Rasputin's behaviour, but Alexandra was furious at her for doubting the integrity of a 'Man of God'. The Tsar took a more realistic view of the monk's behaviour and ordered him to stay away from the children's rooms. Nevertheless, the Empress had her way in the end and the governess was dismissed. Afterwards she took her revenge by spreading malicious rumours that Rasputin was being allowed to bathe the grand duchesses.

By 1911 St Petersburg began to divide into warring camps, between pro- and anti-Rasputin factions. Significantly, the battle lines could almost be drawn on a sexual basis, with the majority of women siding with the monk and most men mistrusting him. In that year, Rasputin almost overreached himself by committing sacrilege in trying to rape a nun. This would have ended the career of anyone less formidable than Rasputin, yet in the end it was the support of the Empress Alexandra that saved him. Nevertheless, the Prime Minister, Peter Arkadyevich Stolypin, was determined to end the unhealthy influence that Rasputin wielded at the palace and ordered an investigation into the monk's activities. He presented his report to the Tsar but Nicholas refused to accept it. So Stolypin acted on his own authority and ordered Rasputin to leave St Petersburg. Rasputin humbly undertook a pilgrimage to the Holy Land, during which he wrote frequent mystical letters to the Empress. When she learned of Stolypin's actions, Alexandra was furious at the way that her friend had been treated. Even Tsar Nicholas himself was angry to find his authority usurped. But there was to be a mysterious reckoning. On a visit to Kiev, in September 1911, Rasputin was suddenly heard to call out in a loud voice, 'Death is after him [Stolypin]! death is driving behind him!' The following night at the theatre in Kiev, Stolypin was assassinated in the presence of Tsar Nicholas by an anarchist. How Rasputin could have known of the approaching assassination is a mystery, as he was not known to have been connected with the assassin or his group.

In spite of the protection he received from Empress Alexandra, Rasputin now came under enormous pressure from a newspaper smear campaign which accused him of every sort of crime. Even though Tsar Nicholas ordered the press to desist on pain of fining or imprisonment, the campaign continued. The monk was accused of sleeping with the Empress and with her friend, Anna Vyrubova, as well as having raped all the grand duchesses. Their nursery, it was said, was now Rasputin's harem where the girls, mad for love of him, fought to be next in his bed. More seriously, Rasputin was accused of being 'a cunning conspirator against [Russia's] Holy Church', and part of the 'dark forces near the throne'.

Tsar Nicholas now felt that he had no alternative but to allow the Duma President, Michael Rodzianko, to carry out a new investigation of Rasputin's character and behaviour. But Rodzianko found himself facing obstruction orchestrated by a very important personage – the Tsarina herself. Even though he completed his report he was told

that the Tsar was not prepared to grant him an interview to present it. It was clear now that Rasputin's power had grown very great within Russia. Even though he was under attack by the press, the Church and the Duma, his person was inviolable as long as he kept the support of the Empress. Although Rasputin had no interest in political power as such, he enjoyed his life of debauchery and needed the Empress to protect him from police harassment. And if that meant interfering with the government of the country he was quite prepared to do so.

The outbreak of war in July 1914 provided Grigory Rasputin with a new opportunity to consolidate his hold on the royal family. The Tsarevitch Alexis was taken by his father on an inspection of Russian troops on the Galician front. The boy suddenly fell ill. He was suffering from a cold and heavy catarrh in his head which had set up a bad nose bleed. The army doctors were unable to stop the bleeding and so the decision was taken to return to St Petersburg. When the Empress was informed of the crisis by telephone she immediately called in Rasputin. By the time the Tsar and his son arrived at the palace Alexis was more dead than alive and all the doctors had given up hope. But when Rasputin entered the sick room he simply made the sign of the cross over the boy's bed and told the kneeling parents, 'Don't be alarmed. Nothing will happen.' Then he simply turned and walked out. Alexis fell asleep and by the next morning he had recovered. It was a miracle – at least for all those present in the Tsarevitch's bedroom. Whatever efforts he might make to find a rational explanation for what had happened, the Tsar found it easier to accept his wife's sublime faith in Rasputin as a great healer sent from God. From this moment onwards, Rasputin's power went almost unchallenged and Russia was condemned to suffer a spreading gangrene at the heart of her affairs.

Rasputin now began to use his power over the Empress to remove those in high places who were most opposed to him. He began with the Grand Duke Nicholas, Commander-in-Chief of Russia's army. He told Alexandra that the Grand Duke was no longer to be trusted. He was planning to kill him, Rasputin, as a hated 'man of God', and afterwards he would overthrow the Tsar. It was the purest nonsense but Alexandra believed every word. She began to bombard her husband with letters critical of his uncle's handling of the war. The letter she sent to the Tsar on 16 June 1915 shows how effective Rasputin's lies had been:

> I have absolutely no faith in N. – know him to be far from clever and having gone against a Man of God, his work can't be blessed or his advice good. Russia will not be blessed if her sovereign lets a Man of God sent to help him be persecuted, I am sure. You know N.'s hatred for Grigory is intense.

Acting on his wife's suggestion, the Tsar dismissed his uncle and took over the command of the Russian armies himself. It was a disastrous decision. Not only was the Grand Duke a far more able soldier, but the loss of the Tsar at the helm of affairs allowed Alexandra and Rasputin to exercise a stranglehold on the government of the country while Nicholas was away at the front, five hundred miles from the capital. In addition, the Tsar's ministers warned him that from now on military defeats would be blamed on him personally, which would result in an inevitable decline in the popularity of the royal family. But the Tsar refused to listen and placed his faith in his wife and her mystical advisor.

Meanwhile, the magician – for that is what he seemed to be to his opponents – was still up to his tricks. Late in 1915 the Empress's best friend, Anna Vyrubova, was involved in a train crash. She was so severely injured that she was given the last rites of the church and left to die. But Rasputin visited her sick room and called to her, 'Annushka!' On the third call Anna opened her eyes for the first time and attempted to get out of bed even though both her legs were crushed. Rasputin turned to the watching Empress and told her, 'She will recover, but she will remain a cripple.' He then walked out of the room before falling to the ground, overcome by a wave of nausea. Whatever powers he had used had so drained him that it was days before he recovered. Nevertheless, he was right. Anna Vyrubova did recover. Although she remained a cripple, she lived until 1964.

Alexandra and Rasputin now purged the government of anyone who opposed them. In the mind of the Empress her 'Man of God' became a symbol of Russia, a nation not of lazy aristocrats but of sturdy peasants and righteous Christians who fought for their Motherland and for their Tsar. With her husband at the front fighting the Germans and Austrians, she believed that Rasputin must become the man who would guide Russia's government through the crisis. After all, he had proved himself worthy of this role by saving the life of the Tsarevitch.

While the Tsarina was entertaining such worthy thoughts the saintly man of her vision was becoming the font of all patronage and corruption. Everyone who needed favourable consideration by the Tsar, on appointments, legal cases, money matters and every kind of speculative intrigue, came to see Rasputin. Once they had obtained his backing they knew that the Tsarina would look on their petition favourably. Rasputin took bribes in money from men and in 'favours' from the more attractive women. Once satisfied, he simply wrote the words 'My dear and valued friend. Do this for me. Grigory' and passed it on to Alexandra. Rasputin's merest wish became her command. Sometimes queues of cars waited outside Grigory's apartment and people stood for hours on the stairs for an interview with him. Some of the requests were absurd. One elegant socialite, who must have 'tickled Grigory's fancy', received his support for a request to admit her as a prima donna at the Imperial Opera. Alexandra's powers were great but, unfortunately, she had no control over God-given talent. On the other hand, some women were shocked when they found out the price Rasputin was charging for his services. Several fled from his room in some distress and headed off to the police station to accuse the monk of attempted rape. The desk officer yawned; he had a thick dossier on Rasputin's sexual offences, but nothing was ever done about them.

Rasputin by now had become a marked man and a number of attempts were made to murder him. Irate husbands and fathers frequently beat on his doors demanding the return of their wives and daughters. Once two men with guns burst into his apartment and ran up the stairs demanding to know where their wives were. However, Rasputin was forewarned and as the husbands broke down the door he just had time to hustle their wives out of a window and down a fire escape. Police records reported nightly affrays *chez* Rasputin. He was usually drunk, often violent and sexually outrageous, regarding anyone in a skirt as his by *droit de seigneur*. Only the Empress still believed in him and refused to hear a word said against him. Nothing the police reported made an iota of difference: he had saved the Tsarevitch and he would save Russia. Even the infamous Yar incident in April 1915 failed to change her view. Rasputin was in Moscow and one evening attended the luxurious Yar restaurant which, in spite of wartime privations, still provided

A caricature depicting Rasputin, with the Tsar Nicholas II and Tsarina Alexandra as submissive and obedient children. The influence of the 'mad monk' on the Russian royal family was so strong that even before the outbreak of war in 1914 he played a major part in determining national policy. (ME)

the best food in Russia and was frequented by wealthy foreign visitors. While the diners enjoyed their lavish dishes downstairs, a violent fracas broke out in an upstairs room. Screams were heard along with the sound of breaking glass. While the waiters rushed upstairs to see what was amiss, the manager summoned the police. It was Rasputin, drunk and in a fiery mood. When the police arrived and saw who it was they refused to arrest him. Eventually, the manager had to telephone the Minister of the Interior for permission to arrest Rasputin. Meanwhile, Grigory was exposing himself to the female diners and boasting that they should think themselves lucky if he chose to sleep with them. After all, he crowed, this was the way he treated all the Tsar's family and he could do what he liked with 'the Old Girl', by whom he meant the Tsarina.

A full report of the incident was sent to the Tsar by General Dzhunkovsky and everyone assumed that that would be the end of Rasputin. Nicholas interviewed Grigory personally. The monk cunningly excused himself by claiming that as a poor peasant he was innocent, having been tricked into drinking too much by evil-minded men. Unconvinced, the Tsar banished him from St Petersburg. But when the Empress heard of what had happened she demanded that Dzhunkovsky be dismissed and Grigory allowed to return. Weakly the Tsar complied with her wishes. Yet again Rasputin had won and now there was no way of stopping him except by assassination.

During 1915 Russia endured catastrophic defeats on the battlefield, suffering casualties numbered in millions. Soldiers and workers looked forlornly to their government for salvation, but all they saw was an Empress – who was German herself – and a sex-mad monk, who indulged himself in debauchery while the people died of wounds or starvation. It was a formula for revolution. Meanwhile, Alexandra and her 'Man of God' hired and fired ministers according to Rasputin's whim. Anyone who had ever opposed him was dismissed and some of his new appointments were risible. One evening at a restaurant Rasputin met a fellow-debauchee, a court chamberlain named Khvostov, who was deep in his cups. When the gypsy band began to play and sing, Rasputin was dissatisfied, complaining that the basses were feeble. Seeing Khvostov, obviously drunk, Rasputin patted him on the back and told him to join in the song. Surely anyone as fat as Khvostov could sing bass. Curiously enough

Khvostov was a good singer and proceeded to demonstrate as much at a prodigious volume. Rasputin was impressed and decided that this was just the man to become the new Minister of the Interior. Khvostov's appointment was confirmed only days later.

By the end of 1915 the Tsar's ministers had tried to warn him of the danger Russia faced from Rasputin and the Tsarina. In retaliation the vengeful Alexandra marked her opponents down for destruction. In the next twelve months four prime ministers, five ministers of the interior, four ministers of agriculture and three ministers of war all fell victim to Alexandra and Rasputin's prejudices. In February 1916, on Rasputin's recommendation, an elderly 'third-rate' and 'double-faced' politician named Boris Stürmer became prime minister. Alexandra informed her husband, 'He very much values Grigory, which is a great thing.' On the other hand, Polivanov, the Minister of War, was dismissed because, in Alexandra's words, 'he is our friend's enemy.' The truth was even worse. Polivanov had in fact discovered that Stürmer had provided Rasputin with four War Office cars that were too fast for the police to catch when the monk went on his nightly rampages. Polivanov had been going to inform the Tsar but Alexandra was too quick for him, telling Nicholas, 'Get rid of Polivanov, any honest man better than him. Luvvy, don't dawdle, make up your mind.' Polivanov was sacked accordingly. It was a crushing blow for the Russian army, for Polivanov had been an able administrator. His replacement, Shuvaiev, was an amiable dullard, committed to the Tsar, of whom it was said he would jump out of a window if the Tsar suggested it.

Polivanov had in fact left a legacy of great importance for Russia. He had ensured that for 1916 the armies would have the artillery and supplies for a major offensive and this was duly undertaken on the Austrian front by the able General Brusilov. The results of the 'Brusilov Offensive' were astounding. Within weeks the Austrian army had been driven back in a rout and Russia was achieving her greatest victories of the war. And then Rasputin intervened. He had now taken on the role of new military strategist and had convinced the Empress that she must intervene with the Tsar and stop Brusilov's offensive. Of all the damage that Rasputin did to Russia this was probably the worst. Brusilov had offered Russia her last lifeline. Once the offensive ground to a halt, the Germans swiftly bolstered up their faltering Austrian allies. The vast Russian losses that could only have been justified by victory were now perceived as just another part of the government's failure to conduct an effective war on the Austrian front. Brusilov was furious. The great general had been betrayed by those he had sought to serve. It is hardly surprising, a few years later, to find him leading the 'Red Army' in the civil war against the 'Whites'.

Two years of war had brought only defeat and hardship for the Russian people and already they had found scapegoats. Most prominent was the Empress herself, the 'German woman' as she was called. Spy fever swept Russia and along with Alexandra, Rasputin was also accused of being in the pay of the Germans. The prime minister Stürmer, who had been appointed by the Tsarina and had a German-sounding name, was yet another suspect. In view of Rasputin's reputation, it was generally assumed that he and the Tsarina were lovers and that the Tsar was being cuckolded in his own palace. The popularity of the royal family was fatally damaged during this period. This undoubtedly contributed to the decision to execute them after the Tsar's abdication in 1917, in the wake of the March Revolution. But first Rasputin had to be removed.

The murder of Rasputin by a group of aristocrats led by Prince Felix Yussupov and the Grand Duke Dmitri Pavlovich, has taken on a legendary quality. By 1916 the man seemed almost to be more than human. Even the manner of his death – he was first poisoned, then shot several times in the body, then kicked and beaten with a heavy club, and finally drowned under the ice of the frozen river Neva – revealed the extraordinary physical resilience of Grigory Rasputin. But his death brought no relief for Russia's suffering people. In spite of wild celebrations in St Petersburg at news of Rasputin's murder, both Tsar Nicholas and his wife attended the funeral and the grand duchesses each scattered flowers on the coffin. The names of the murderers were known to everyone, yet how could the Tsar order their arrest when they were acting in all good faith for the welfare of Russia? To have executed or imprisoned Yussupov and his friends, with their close links with the royal family, might have shattered the already fragile hold that the Tsar still had on Russia. In any case, the damage was already done. Rasputin's death had come several years too late. A mother's desperate search for help when her child was suffering had been answered in the shape of a man from God. But the mother was also an empress who could not divorce private needs from public obligations. Alexandra's fatal blindness to Rasputin's true nature and her willingness to fall in with his personal prejudices and petty intrigues cost Russia the services of many able men and inflicted on her a number of corrupt and inefficient politicians. It was a royal blunder of the most tragic sort, which would cost the Tsarina not only her life but the lives of all her family as well.

The resemblance between King George V and Tsar Nicholas II was so remarkable that numerous instances of mistaken identity occurred. Probably the worst was at the wedding of the then Prince of Wales to Mary of Teck in 1893. At the reception Prince George was mistaken for Tsar Nicholas by one of the guests who asked him if he had come to London on business or simply for the wedding. Prince George replied that as it was his wedding he felt he should attend.

CHAPTER 1: UNFIT TO RULE

Royal Insanity

It may seem redundant to assert that the worst thing that can happen to any state is to be ruled by a madman. Yet history demonstrates that so many monarchs have been either mad or mentally disturbed, that royal insanity can hardly be regarded as an aberration. Furthermore, royal consorts, children and more distant relations appear to have shared this mental insecurity. And to compound the felony the problem was kept in the family for generation after generation as a result of the practice of royal cousins marrying one another. Germany, the land of Goethe and Beethoven, thereby served as a breeding ground for crop after crop of blighted princes and princesses suffering from serious psychiatric disorders, ranging from manic depression to complete and permanent mental dysfunction. Inter-marriage between ruling families such as the Habsburgs and the Wittelsbachs meant that defective genes played trick or treat with proud parenthood. For every stunning beauty like the Empress Elizabeth of Austria there was a whole army of mental cripples like the nineteenth-century Princess Alexandra of Bavaria, who spent her life in anxious seclusion, convinced that she had once swallowed a grand piano made of glass. Another princely ruler believed himself to be made of butter and therefore feared that he would be melted if he went out in the sun, while yet another feared to urinate in case he might inundate his entire castle.

The royal disease

For British readers King George III is undoubtedly the most famous of mad rulers, though whether he really talked to a tree believing it to be the king of Prussia is open to some doubt. Nevertheless, his case has attracted much attention from historians eager to identify the roots of the king's malady and assess to what extent it may have contributed to the most notable British blunder of the late eighteenth century, British policy towards the American Colonies, culminating in the American War of Independence. Certainly Britain's policy throughout bears the taint of insanity, yet if this is true one would have to conclude that not only the king but all his ministers too were barking mad. The facts paint a different picture. George III's bouts of insanity occurred in three separate periods, all of them well after the catastrophic American imbroglio, although one is tempted to suggest that early manifestations of the malady, perhaps during the 1770s, may have gone unnoticed – particularly in a member of the Hanoverian dynasty, where eccentricity was never far from the surface. Recent research suggests that George's bouts of madness, manic depression or porphyria, whichever is eventually shown to be the case, were confined to a period of six months in 1788-9, three months in 1801, and four months in 1804. His mental collapse after 1810 may have been the result of senile dementia and have no more serious a cause than old age. Nevertheless, though George's periods of

George III of Britain suffered from bouts of porphyria, a hereditary disease of the metabolism causing periods of extreme mental disturbance. 'Farmer George' was by nature a kind man, but his influence on national policy – particularly towards the American colonies – was disastrous. (PN)

'madness' are far shorter than the public imagination may credit, they were influential on British policy, if for no other reason than that they brought into the spotlight that deplorable wastrel, the Prince of Wales and later Prince Regent, George Augustus Frederick or 'Prinny'.

During 1788 King George's physical health deteriorated as a prelude to the collapse of his mind. He began to experience fantasies that rendered him quite incapable of dealing with his ministers. Overriding all others was the belief that London had been overwhelmed by a cataclysmic flood and that in order to help rescue the survivors he must go there in his yacht. While his family tried to come to terms with his affliction he became fixated about one of the queen's ladies-in-waiting, Lady Pembroke, and insisted that she was his wife. Whether the good lady regarded this as a compliment or not is not recorded, but George certainly told his real wife, Queen Charlotte, that she was mad and should be locked up. He sometimes believed that he had given birth to a pillow case, which he named Prince Octavius, and in celebration knighted a number of his pages and servants. He also tried to 'plant' some beefsteak believing that it grew on trees. When sent some grapes by the long-suffering Queen he enquired as to which queen had sent them. Was it Queen Esther? Or the Queen of Hearts? Some of his imaginings were so witty that one might almost echo Polonius in seeing 'method in his madness'. He once told his doctor, the hated Francis Willis, that he had devised a new Trinity, composed of himself, the good doctor and Lady Pembroke. But there was a darker side to George's mental instability. He was sometimes violent and on such occasions shouted vile oaths at his family. From time to time he had to be straitjacketed. A famous anecdote from this period reflects the hatred he had for the Willises, father and sons, who supervised him in his illness. When first meeting Dr Willis the elder, King George observed, 'Sir, your dress bespeaks you of the Church. Do you belong to it?' 'I did formerly,' replied the good doctor, 'but latterly I have attended chiefly to Physick.' 'I am sorry for it,' the King went on, 'you have quitted a profession I have always loved, and you have embraced one I most heartily detest.' 'Sir,' insisted the doctor, 'our saviour himself went about healing the sick.' 'Yes, yes,' said King George, 'but he had not £700 a year for it.'

The harsh treatment the King received was a reflection of the general treatment of the insane in eighteenth-century England. Once his mind had gone he received few special favours from the Willises. Consequently it is pleasing – if mischievous – to rejoice when his jailers got a 'taste of their own medicine'. Once, when straitjacketing the king, the doctor released his arm to feel his pulse, whereupon King George punched him in the head and knocked him to the ground. Free for a moment the king lifted his chamberpot and emptied it on the doctor's head, saying 'Arise, Sir George, knight of the most ancient, most puissant Order of Cloacina, Goddess of Privies.'

Driller killer

Frederick William I of Prussia, known as the 'Sergeant-Major' king, introduced a new kind of mental disability into Europe during the eighteenth century: military mania. His own obsessions were well described by his soubriquet, but his malign influence on such rulers as Tsars Peter III and Paul I of Russia was uniquely harmful to that country.

Frederick William could not resist tall soldiers and he eventually created a regiment of giants, which he kitted out in extra-large uniforms, helmets and boots. He provided them with muskets, pikes and swords which other soldiers found it difficult even to lift. They looked magnificent in their blue and scarlet uniforms and were led on to parade by a large bear as a mascot. Frederick William's interest soon became a fixation and he scoured Europe looking for tall men to join his regiment, bribing landowners to send him particularly tall farmworkers and giving bonuses to parents who would surrender the taller of their sons. It is said that Peter the Great sent him fifty Russian giants and the Sultan of Turkey almost as many. Frederick William even resorted to kidnapping 'giants' when they could not be induced to join voluntarily and was known to have taken priests by force from their monasteries. He purchased one man in Holland who stood 6 feet 4 inches tall, describing him as 'a phenomenon as rare and as extraordinary as the passage of a comet'. He located a shepherd just as tall in Mecklenburg but found that he could not be persuaded to accept a career in the military. Frederick William commented, 'Persuasion has no effect on him. But a couple of officers and a pair of reliable NCOs can make off with him soon enough, when he is alone in the fields tending his sheep.' He even introduced a breeding programme similar to the one operated by the Nazis 300

Frederick William I of Prussia, nicknamed the 'Sergeant-Major king' on account of his obsession with military matters. A strict Calvinist with a violent temper, he was notorious for his ill-treatment of his son, the future Frederick II, and bequeathed to Prussia a baleful tradition of militarism. (ME)

years later. However, whereas the Nazis were concerned with the superior qualities of the 'master race', Frederick William was only interested in height. His attempts to mate very tall men with similar women often produced pitiful physical specimens and simple-minded oafs who had no future except as village idiots. However, Frederick William was undeterred. After all, the regiment was for show only; he had no intention of risking such fine specimens in battle. Frederick William earned his nickname from his habit of drilling his troops himself as if he were a mere sergeant.

If Frederick William's obsession seems as comical as Uncle Toby's hobby-horses in Laurence Sterne's *Tristram Shandy*, it should not be allowed to obscure the truth, which was that the 'Sergeant-Major' king was a brutal psychopath, willing to execute men for the slightest indiscretion and to torment others for the sheer pleasure of seeing them suffer. Apart from the cruel upbringing that he inflicted on his sensitive son, which we will consider elsewhere (see p. 125), he loved to persecute his court historian, an amiable and harmless old man named Jacob Paul von Gründling. Frederick demanded that Gründling attend what he called his 'Tobacco Parliament', which was a nightly gathering of his friends and cronies, who wined and dined and then smoked to their heart's content. Once everyone was thoroughly merry they indulged in what they enjoyed most: bullying. Gründling was a natural victim for Frederick William and his thugs. The King sent anonymous articles to learned societies attacking Gründling's work. When they were printed, he made the historian read them aloud to the 'Tobacco Parliament' and enjoyed watching him squirm. When they had bored of this particular prank, they indulged in some 'rough-and-tumble' which on one occasion involved setting the old man on fire. One evening they brought in a monkey dressed in Gründling's clothes, telling him that he was his long-lost son and forcing him to embrace the monkey and own him as his son. Even the death of the old man in 1731 did not stop the king's fun. He decided to deny Gründling a conventional Christian burial. Instead he pickled him in a wine cask and buried it in the castle grounds at Potsdam. Frederick William I died in 1740, having spent the final years of his life trying to stamp out the cultural influences that his wife was bringing to bear on his son, Frederick. He failed in this, his son turning out to be the greatest of Prussia's kings, not only on the battlefield but in the salon. Frederick won battles but also composed symphonies. The old madman Frederick William would never have understood. He played at war; his son fought it – and grew to hate it for the waste that it was.

The regiment of giants, incidentally, had no future under Frederick the Great. The huge soldiers proved pathetically clumsy and were easy meat for enemy cannon balls.

No hiding place

Sultan Abdul Hamid II of Turkey was one of the most paranoid rulers in history. His life consisted of little more than an attempt to preserve himself from imagined plots and assassination attempts. He did nothing that was not directed towards his own preservation, viewing everything and everyone as a potential hazard. When Kaiser Wilhelm II and his wife visited Turkey in 1898 Abdul Hamid's face paled markedly when he noticed the words 'Bombe Glacée' on the menu prepared by his master chef. The word 'bomb' was illegal in Turkey, at the orders of the Sultan, and the chef was sacked on the spot.

Abdul Hamid II had succeeded the lunatic Sultan Abdul Aziz in 1876 (see p. 34).

However, whereas Abdul Aziz had enjoyed life to the limit, his successor knew no peace. He believed – with some justification – that the Ottoman empire was seething with revolutionaries and assassins who would try to kill him, probably by poison. Thus Abdul Hamid had every article of his clothing inspected before he wore them, in case they had been coated with a poison that could penetrate the pores of his skin. His boots might contain poisonous spiders or snakes and his hat might be full of explosives. He always wore chain mail under his shirt, as well as a steel-lined fez. While food-tasters have been a regular feature of the courts of autocratic rulers throughout history, few of these took their obsessional fears as far as Abdul Hamid. The latter employed 'clothes-testers', who were required to 'try on' the attire the sultan wore each day.

Once he was up and dressed, the sultan was ready to begin his day's work, looking through the documents that had been received from the various government departments. However, in case these had been poisoned each had to be baked in an oven and then thoroughly disinfected before he handled them. To avoid being poisoned by water or milk, Abdul Hamid had his private well patrolled day and night. He also kept his own personal cow, which he milked himself.

Dissatisfied with the security arrangements at the traditional Ottoman palace of Dolomabache, Abdul Hamid built a new palace, containing state-of-the-art security systems. He was often to be seen on the palace roof with a powerful telescope scanning his surroundings for signs of danger. His habit of carrying a gun with him at all times led to numerous accidents. Once while walking in the gardens of the palace a gardener bending to tend some flowers stood up to acknowledge his Sultan. Abdul Hamid shot him through the forehead. On another occasion, as a dare, a young concubine unwisely crept up behind Abdul Hamid. The crack-shot sultan drilled her between the eyes. Abdul Hamid even had two pistols in holsters attached to the royal bath. Several rooms had cupboards with glass doors, which could be electronically operated by the Sultan, so that if anyone entered without his permission the doors would swing open and strategically positioned pistols inside would fire on the intruder.

On the very few occasions when he could be prevailed upon to leave his secure compound, Abdul Hamid rode in a bullet-proof coach, carrying one of his younger children on his lap. The child was not being taken on an outing. It was a kind of hostage or human shield. The Sultan believed assassins would have second thoughts about killing him if it meant killing a young child as well. The cowardly Turk was even afraid to look under his bed before retiring each night and forced one of his concubines to risk her life by peering into the cobwebs and chamber pots.

Such a nervous lifestyle was bound to affect the health of the sultan and he was frequently sick from real or, more often, imaginary ailments. If he needed to take any pills a curious rigmarole ensued. All the pills provided were taken from their bottles, boxes or wrappings and tipped into a large bag, which was thoroughly shaken. Abdul Hamid would then pick one from the bag. As with all 'creaking gates', Abdul Hamid died quietly in his bed – in 1918 – at the age of 77. He had presided over a corrupt and brutal regime that had committed atrocities in Bulgaria and Armenia, killing more than a million people in the worst act of genocide before Hitler's holocaust. Too delicate even to allow the Turkish population to know that the King and Queen of Serbia had been assassinated, he ordered editors to print that they had died of indigestion. When he was overthrown by the 'Young Turk' revolution of 1909, Abdul Hamid's wardrobes at the palace were found to be full of bullet-proof garments.

Frightened to death

Small children can be cruel without meaning to be, but the young Grand Duke Ivan of Muscovy, later to be known as Ivan 'the Terrible', was both cruel and fully aware of it. As a boy he liked throwing dogs and cats off the palace roof. He enjoyed torturing birds by tearing off their feathers, piercing their eyes and slitting open their bodies, but most of all he enjoyed pulling the legs off spiders and watching them spin round like rudderless boats. Even when he was Tsar he found relaxation in this early form of stress-management. In fact, from his early days there was every sign that Ivan would develop into a psychopathic killer. As he grew up he graduated from insects and birds to smaller mammals and then to human beings. Like a number of princes discussed in these pages he enjoyed roaming the streets with gangs of toughs, beating people and vandalizing their property as a means of exercising his divine right to do so. Yet – and this is an indictment of royalty throughout history – his behaviour was not so different from many of his peers in other states as to be particularly noteworthy. The event that really escalated Ivan's madness was a serious illness he suffered in 1553, when he was just 23 years old.

Like the illness that afflicted the Roman emperor Caligula, Ivan's attack may have been encephalitic in nature. In any case, the cruelty that already appeared to be a feature of his personality was now consolidated and accompanied by bursts of terrifying, maniacal brutality. From this stage onwards Ivan became 'the Terrible'. To list his atrocities would weaken them by repetition. In a history as brutal as Russia's it takes a very special kind of man to earn such a soubriquet. In Ivan evil and madness warred against each other for dominance and frequently settled for coalition. He often foamed at the mouth like a rabid dog as he uttered his terrible judgements. He tore his own hair out by the roots until his scalp was a mass of bald patches and bloody gashes. His eyes would light up as he heard the cries of the men he tortured to death and then he would beat his head against a wall in anguish at what he had done, calling on God to forgive him his sins and praying for his victims. Afterwards, he would call for wine and – drinking heavily – begin to utter threats all over again.

Ivan married eight times. Stated baldly it seems the most natural thing in the world. Yet one must spare a thought for the women who had to share the bed of this monster. His second wife died just two weeks after their marriage and his third wife expired as a result of his 'unbridled sexual passion'. The next girl, the fourth bride, who had married Ivan by 'proxy', died of fright on hearing that Ivan was coming to collect her. His fifth wife ran away, while his sixth wife was packed off to a convent after she unwisely took a lover and was forced to watch as he was impaled on a stake by her jealous husband. When Ivan discovered his seventh wife was not a virgin on their wedding day he had her drowned. Perhaps Ivan was just unlucky in love.

Paranoia dominated the latter years of his life. Many of his atrocities were reactions on his part to imagined threats. Prince Michael Vorotynski, accused of casting spells, was burned alive, while Ivan personally raked the coals under his tormented body. Archbishop Leonidas of Novgorod, accused of plotting against the Tsar, was sewn up in a bearskin and thrown to the dogs. Many other Novgoroders – 50,000 may be a conservative estimate – were drowned beneath the ice of the River Volkhov. Ivan Viskovatyi, Ivan's chancellor, was strung up upside down while the Tsar's soldiers hacked off pieces of his body until he resembled a butcher's carcass, and the state treasurer, Founikov, was alternately drenched in boiling and ice-cold water until his entire skin came off like an eel's. Ivan's sadism – and his imagination – found full expression in his last terrible days. Along with the sadism went a cruel sense of humour. It is said that he ordered the inhabitants of a town to present him with a cart full of fleas. This was plainly impossible but so earnest were the people in their endeavours to find the fleas that the fleas found them and they presented themselves in the cart, infested with vermin. It is said Ivan laughed and fined them instead of executing them. But mercy did not come easily to Ivan. He was far happier with cruelty, as when he ordered old peasant women to strip naked as targets for his bowmen, or when he tipped steaming soup over the head of his court jester and stabbed him to death because he cried out.

It is said that, in his quieter moments, Tsar Ivan enjoyed hearing a bedtime story. Apparently three elderly blind men were kept by him for this sole purpose. Ivan died in 1584, at the age of 53, worn out by a career as cruel as any man in history prior to the twentieth century. Having murdered his able son, Ivan (see p. 120), he was succeeded by the idiot Feodor I, the last of his dynasty. Russia went through a traumatic 'Time of Troubles' in the early seventeenth century before the election of Tsar Michael Romanov in 1613 restored a measure of stability.

Declaring war on common sense

Tsar Paul I of Russia got off to one of the worst starts of any ruler. On the death of his mother, Catherine the Great, in 1796, he looked through her private papers and found (a) that his father Peter III had not really been his father, (b) that his real father had been one of Catherine's lovers (named Serge Saltykov; see p. 82); and (c) that the father that he had always supposed to be his, i.e. Peter, had been murdered by his mother, in order to help her seize the throne. He ordered the secret papers to be filed away and sealed, and sat down to make some sense of his life. He failed, and when an emperor fails, one can expect trouble.

Two themes dominate the reign of Tsar Paul I. The first was his obsessive-paranoia: he saw revolutionaries everywhere. The second was his worship of the Prussia of Frederick the Great and his desire to remodel Russia along Prussian lines. Once in power he set about trying to regulate the lives of all Russians for twenty-four hours a day. Regulations were devised to cover every area of Russian life and Paul saw to it that they were implemented. Any opposition was ruthlessly crushed. What to wear, where to live, what to eat and how to travel – all these aspects of life came under his fanatical control. As his son – and future assassin – Alexander I wrote, 'My father has declared war on common sense.'

Paul believed that he could not trust anybody – not his wife, his son or his ministers. The progress of revolution in France after 1789 had profoundly shocked him and he was determined to stamp out even the tiniest threat of political upheaval in Russia. For Paul the most potent symbol of the French threat was the round hat that was worn by many Russians at this time. No sooner was he in power than hundreds of police and soldiers were sent into the streets to knock round hats off people's heads and beat them up for wearing them instead of Prussian-style tricorne hats. Innocent passers-by had their frock coats ripped by zealots bent on destroying 'unacceptable collars', while the wearing of a waistcoat was viewed as tantamount to treason. Within a matter of hours the news had spread throughout St Petersburg: the emperor does not like round hats; wear them at your peril. A passing Englishman wearing a round hat had it ripped from his head by a soldier. The Englishman knocked the soldier flat and was arrested and dragged off to prison. Only the intervention of the British ambassador saved him from execution. The Sardinian ambassador laughed when he heard of the ridiculous hat regulation and was ordered to leave the country within twenty-four hours. Exact regulations for all items of dress were soon made public and soldiers' uniforms were so tightly controlled that the precise length of material allowed from elbow to sleeve was laid down. Any deviation from official measurements meant banishment or worse. Civilians as well as soldiers were subject to the decrees, and women as much as men. Everything had its regulations, from baptisms to funerals, and concerts and entertainments were only allowed by permission of the local police chief.

Tsar Paul held a daily parade for the St Petersburg garrison, which took place without fail and without regard for the weather conditions. For three or four hours the Tsar took personal control of the assembled troops and drilled them and manoeuvred them as if they were his toys. Neither officer nor man was allowed to wear a coat, even in midwinter temperatures of minus forty degrees, and senior officers with rheumatism or bad chests had to make the best of it. Even the most minor errors were punished. One whole regiment was sent to Siberia as a result of a misheard order. Seven field-marshals were in the capital at the start of Paul's reign and all of them were called out on parade and put through their paces, from arms drill to marching, by one of Paul's favourite NCOs. When General Prince Volkonsky appeared on parade with a button undone he was called a 'blockhead' by the Tsar and threatened with exile. When a particular regiment displeased him, 231 officers were imprisoned in the Kremlin. A regiment of Siberian dragoons, which had just reached St Petersburg after serving on the Persian border, annoyed the Tsar by parading their tired and careworn appearance, so he ordered them to return whence they had come, a march of some 2,500 miles. Officers who were exiled for minor errors in drill were unable to return home, but had to leave for Siberia in the clothes they wore, and without being able to tell their families. As a result, officers always carried money with them on parade, knowing that they might be banished at any moment. When Paul began thrashing his officers with a cane, many retired from the army and went to live on their estates, as far from the capital as possible. It is estimated that 12,000 Russian officers were sent to Siberia for drilling errors during Paul's reign.

Under the reign of his mother, St Petersburg had become a fashionable city, rivalling London or Paris. But Paul was determined to put a stop to that. Clothing regulations of the most reactionary kind were introduced and all citizens were ordered to powder their hair and brush it tightly back from their forehead. Anyone travelling in a coach or on a horse who met a member of the royal family had to disembark and prostrate themselves on the ground regardless of the weather. Women in long skirts and even children had to lay flat in the snow as the Tsar rode past. Anyone who neglected to do so was severely beaten.

Strict censorship was introduced and letters in the public post were opened and read. Anyone who expressed even the gentlest criticism of the regime was sent to Siberia. The German Prince of Hessen-Rheinfels had his letters opened and was expelled from Russia, as was the British ambassador, Sir Charles Whitworth, for some inadvertent slight. In addition, the importation of all foreign books and musical compositions was banned. The speeches of Cicero were declared subversive as they were written when Rome was a republic. Overnight, it seemed, Russia had become a police state. The author Kotzebue was seized while travelling to see his wife in Estonia and sent to Siberia on the grounds that he was an author and therefore by definition a revolutionary agitator.

As the Tsar's madness increased his decrees became more bizarre. All cab-drivers were banished from the capital as one had been found carrying a pair of pistols. In matters of foreign policy Paul showed little more moderation. In 1801 he flabbergasted his fellow-European rulers with the startling suggestion that all future international disputes should be settled by single combat. Paul planned to take on England's prime minister, William Pitt, for a start. He also decided that he would send an expedition of Cossacks to drive the English out of India. He wrote the following instruction to General Orlov: 'Gather your forces then set off straight through Bokhara and Khiva to the Indus River on to the unsuspecting English. All the wealth of India will be ours. I am getting you some maps. God be with you.' Fortunately for Orlov, the new Tsar Alexander recalled the madcap adventurers after they had travelled but a few of the thousands of miles that the enterprise entailed.

Soon the whispers that the Tsar was mad had become a general outcry. On 11 March 1801, with the support of the Grand Duke Alexander, Paul's son, a group of officers forced the Tsar to abdicate and then murdered him. The crime was in the best interests of all the people. One can hardly imagine how a Russia ruled by Tsar Paul I could have resisted the overwhelming might of Napoleonic France as Alexander's Russia was to do in 1812.

The crazy gang

If one is to believe the ancient historians there was hardly a Roman emperor who was not touched by at least some form of dementia. Certainly in Caligula, Nero, Vitellius, Domitian, Commodus and Elagabalus (see p. 38), the Romans could field a strong team in any Olympiad for the deranged and criminally insane. Yet in considering the excesses of these men one has to ask how it was possible for them to maintain themselves in power for so long without the Senate overthrowing them? The blunders they perpetrated are, in a sense, less than the faults of those who allowed them to stay in power.

Caligula's antics as emperor are almost too well known to need quotation. Yet it must never be forgotten that he ruled by fear and was as arbitrary in his killings as any dictator in history. We may laugh to hear that he made his horse a consul or that, instead of invading Britain as he had claimed he would, he challenged Neptune to fight him and brought back the spoils of victory in the shape of huge piles of seashells. Yet after the death of his beloved sister/wife, Drusilla, his decrees became less whimsical and more deadly. During state mourning for his sister nobody was allowed to laugh, bathe or take meals with their parents, wife or children on pain of death. Drusilla, meanwhile, was deified. Caligula, of course, was already a god, and went about in a woman's gown and sporting a golden beard, carrying a trident, a lightning fork and a snake-entwined rod. Sometimes he was Hercules, sometimes Bacchus or Apollo. He was as confused a god as he was a man.

Caligula had been noted for his odd behaviour while still a young boy, but his madness became manifest after a severe illness he suffered in the year AD 37. It has been suggested that he suffered from encephalitis, as well as a form of epilepsy. Whatever the physical reason for what followed, Rome was not to see such insane policies from a ruler until

The Roman Emperor Nero was a brutal tyrant who had both his wife and mother murdered. Declared a public enemy by the Senate, he killed himsef rather than face the shame of public execution, his last words allegedly being, 'What a great artist the world loses in me.' (P)

the short reign of Elagabalus in the third century AD. Apparently Caligula found it almost impossible to sleep normally and rationalized this by claiming that gods needed less sleep than ordinary human beings. As Zeus, the Greek god from whom the Romans had taken their own chief deity, Jupiter, he ordered temples to be set up in which he, the emperor and god, could be worshipped. He staged ballets in which he played the leading part. But it was by terror that he kept himself in power. Nobody had the courage to denounce the madman for what he was. Surrounded by his German guards he was immune from popular discontent.

In the end it was Caligula's childish sense of humour rather than his madness that brought about his end. Cassius Chaerea was one of the bravest and most experienced soldiers in the Roman Army. He was an elderly officer of the old school, but as Praetorian Prefect he had to receive from Caligula the watchword of the day. The emperor used this occasion to tease the grizzled old warrior by giving him phrases of the 'Kiss me quick' or 'Chase me Charlie' variety. Cassius thus found himself in the humiliating position of having to reply to every enquiry from his fellow-officers with 'Bottoms up' or 'Hello sailor'. One night in AD 41 Cassius Chaerea and his fellow-conspirators waylaid Caligula as he left the theatre and stabbed him more than thirty times. Thus died the most insane and dangerous of all the Roman emperors, whose reign of just under four years was like an episode from a nightmare play acted by the inmates of an asylum.

The Emperor Nero (AD 54-68) had style. Of the lunatics who occupied the imperial throne in Rome he had the greatest claim to be considered talented – as a poet and a musician if not as an emperor. He sang and played at theatres throughout Italy and was desperately earnest in his efforts to succeed. In fact, his desire to be accepted as an artist was probably at the root of his insanity. Yet he achieved a notoriety that even Caligula was denied: being declared a public enemy by the Senate.

For sheer perversion, Nero ranks with Elagabalus. On the death of his beautiful wife Poppaea – Nero had kicked the pregnant woman in the belly – he found a male slave named Sporus, who was the very image of his late lamented wife. He had Sporus castrated and then married him instead.

As a builder Nero was a megalomaniac. He spent enormous sums of money on creating a new palace, outside which stood a huge statue of himself over a hundred feet high. To work on his lavish projects, Nero brought in slave labour from throughout the empire until Rome resembled the pyramid-building scenes from a Cecil B. de Mille spectacular. Yet the emperor was never at ease. Paranoia led him to kill most of his family and friends, whom he felt were plotting against him. Hundreds died at his whim because he did not like their expressions or thought they were laughing at him. Eventually, overwhelmed by the enormous task of turning Rome into the city he had dreamed of – Neropolis – he sent his servants into the streets to burn it down. Many of these arsonists were discovered at their work, but the Roman people were afraid to intervene for fear of incurring the emperor's wrath. Eventually, nearly two thirds of the city was destroyed after a week of burning. Whether Nero really played his lyre and sang as he watched the city burn is unlikely, but he certainly made little attempt to control the fire. In any case, Nero had already decided to blame the Christians. And the Senate, Nero decreed, who had allowed these interlopers to destroy the imperial city, must all die – by poison. The Senate responded to Nero's threats by declaring him a public enemy. He eventually took his own life to save himself the humiliation of capture and the execution by flogging that the Senate had decreed.

The year following Nero's death, AD 69, saw civil war in the Roman Empire and the 'year of the three Caesars' – Galba, Otho and Vitellius. Of these Vitellius, who ruled for just eight months, was undoubtedly the worst. Rarely has a nickname, in his case 'the Glutton', been so appropriate. Vitellius literally tried to eat as much of the empire as he possibly could before being murdered by the mob, who called for the death of the 'Guzzler' and the 'Glutton' and hung him up on a meat hook. It was cruel but appropriate.

Having gained power by force Vitellius felt he had earned a rest. He handed over the government to one of his freed slaves, Asiaticus, and settled down to some really serious eating. Asiaticus found the greatness thrust upon him unwelcome so he ran away and set up as a lemonade seller. Vitellius shrugged his shoulders and let the government go hang itself. He was too busy gorging himself and then tickling his throat with a feather and bringing it all up again. Vitellius made vomiting an art form.

The emperor's obsessive eating binges reflected a deep psychological insecurity. But to the Roman masses, for whom the price of their daily bread was a vital part in their struggle to survive, Vitellius was simply a 'fat cat', whose indulgences were paid for with poor men's taxes. Vitellius's most astonishing culinary creation – and one of the most amazing dishes in human history – was the one which he dedicated to the goddess Minerva, and which became known as 'Minerva's shield'. This vast creation was assembled on a silver platter the size of a large room. It consisted of vast quantities of the rarest delicacies from throughout the empire, including pike-livers, pheasant and peacock brains, flamingo-tongues and lamprey-milt, all mixed with the rarest and most piquant sauces. While it was being prepared normal commerce inside the empire virtually came to a halt. The Imperial Navy was given the task of scouring the entire Mediterranean and even the Black Sea for rare ingredients, while warships became fishing boats to satisfy the needs of the 'great dish'.

When Vitellius was not eating he was looking for food. During the night he wandered through the Imperial kitchens, ransacking cupboards and shelves for more and more delicacies, leaving behind him a trail of broken bottles and empty pots. As emperor it was his task to make burned offerings to the gods, but he could not resist the smell of cooking meat and often devoured the sacrifice before it could be offered up.

Had gluttony been his only crime, Vitellius might have earned the scorn of his people rather than their hatred. But the emperor was as fiendishly cruel as he was greedy. He took a delight in teasing, torturing and tormenting his enemies; he offered feverish men hot water or, if they wanted cold water, told them it was poisoned. He also reprieved men condemned by the courts so that he could have them executed in front of him. He is even accused of starving his mother to death. Eventually Vitellius was overthrown by the able general, Vespasian, who replaced him on the throne AD 69–79.

For a while – twelve years – Rome breathed a sigh of relief. But then, like gamblers never learning from their mistakes, the Senate appointed another monster as emperor. This time his name was Domitian, and he liked catching flies. In fact, apart from killing innocent people and ruining the Roman state, catching flies was what Domitian did best.

Roman historians tell us that the emperor's favourite colour was red, though whether because his face was so florid or because he loved the sight of blood we cannot tell. He wore a red toga at all times, added rouge to his cheeks and went everywhere accompanied by a scarlet-clad dwarf with a malformed head. He tried to model himself on Tiberius and Nero rather than such luminaries as Augustus and Titus, and staged fantastic spectacles in the Colosseum and the other amphitheatres. Chariot racing was a feature of his reign, while huge naval battles and gladiatorial games that included female participants were held in the arenas. As a demonstration that death never rests, gladiatorial games went on all night by torch-light. It was all enormously expensive but Domitian paid for it all by extorting ever higher taxes from unpopular groups like the Christians and the Jews and by confiscating property from his numerous enemies, whom he liked to invite to dinner and flatter for an evening before condemning them to death with the coffee and After Eights.

As well as being perverse and cruel, Domitian was also very superstitious. He consulted an astrologer only to be told that he would be murdered. Irritated, Domitian asked the astrologer how he himself would die. Torn to pieces by dogs, was the reply. Eager to prove the man a charlatan Domitian had him executed and quickly cremated, far from any dogs. Unfortunately for the emperor, the wind blew over the funeral pyre while the astrologer's body was only half-burned. As a result it was indeed torn to pieces by dogs, drawn thither by the smell of a barbecue. This convinced Domitian that he was doomed. He was finally murdered in AD 96 by one of his daughter's Christian servants.

Commodus (AD 180–192) was the son of one of Rome's greatest rulers, Marcus Aurelius, yet he was as unlike his father as it was possible to be. His philosopher father had taken the advice of wise men; his worthless son surrounded himself with degenerates, and tried to fritter the resources of the empire in one great debauch. Yet if at the start

Commodus was no more than a worthless son of a worthy father, it was not long before insanity became evident. He had the senate declare him divine and took on the persona of the demi-god Hercules. He often dressed in women's clothes and carried a massive club, with which he slew chained lions and pinioned prisoners. He forced cripples to dress as snakes and peppered them with arrows. Commodus took the greatest delight in humiliating men of rank and ability. He once threw the Prefect of the Praetorian Guards into a swimming pool and then forced him to dance naked in public.

But it was in the arena as a gladiator that Commodus made his most unusual contribution to the list of Rome's imperial peccadilloes. He often joined the gladiatorial battles, immune from injury as he was by the inviolable nature of his rank, and slew opponent after opponent. He even moved out of his palace and slept with the other gladiators at their barracks. Sometimes he stayed inside a protected area and used his bow to kill hundreds of wild animals of the most exotic kinds, including ostriches, elephants, rhinoceroses and giraffes. Rome's senators were so terrified by this psychopath they voted him the rather inappropriate titles of 'Pious' and 'Dutiful'. In return Commodus stalked round the benches where the senators sat to watch the games carrying the severed heads of men and animals, shaking them so that the blood spattered their togas and warning them what would be their fate if they opposed him.

Commodus was eventually poisoned by his mistress Marcia. When he took too long to die, she called in his wrestling partner, who strangled him. Thus ended an ugly and brutal period in Rome's history, during which a psychotic killer had enslaved a free people and Rome's senate had lacked the backbone to overthrow his tyranny.

Charles the Well-Beloved

Never has the phrase, 'Whom the gods wish to destroy they first make mad', been so apt as in the case of Charles VI of France. For a period of thirty years during the Hundred Years War, France was ruled by a madman, whose schizophrenic behaviour ranged from the irrationally violent to the pitifully grovelling. His feeble submission to the English king, Henry V, came close to losing for France her national identity.

Charles VI's mother, Jeanne de Bourbon, had suffered a complete nervous breakdown in 1373 and may have passed on to her son some mental abnormality, yet in the early years of his reign Charles showed no signs of the problems that were to come. In fact, he was generally a popular king who justified his soubriquet of the 'well-beloved'. At least that was true until he married Isabeau of Bavaria, a Wittelsbach princess with a fetish for slim waistlines. This daughter of Stephen the Fop had no sooner arrived in France than she had decreed that her ladies-in-waiting should reduce their waistlines to between ten and thirteen inches. While Isabeau was depopulating the court through starvation, Charles was struck down by a mysterious illness. His hair and nails fell out, possibly as a result of encephalitis, and although he appeared to make a full physical recovery, his mental condition was seriously undermined. This was clearly demonstrated when, a few months afterwards, Charles led an expedition against the rebellious Pierre de Craon, who had taken refuge with the Duke of Brittany.

Riding at the head of a column of knights on a sultry August day, Charles was suddenly accosted by a leper, who shouted to him that he must turn back or he would be doomed. Thoroughly disconcerted by this strange incident, Charles completely lost control of

CAROLI VI. regnum quo diuturnum, eo calamitosius
expertu est Gubernatore namq Duce Andegauenti (qui regium
Thesauru disperderat populumq super impositis grauaminibus pres-
serat) Gallia seditionib et cædibus obsessa ingeuit. Carolo uero regien
capessente ipse sibi binos natos ueneno præripi ambitiososq;
agnatus Principes statum ciuicis bellis cruminibusq commu
scere uidit. donec: malor. auge perculsus, phrenitideq; cor-
reptus ijsdem coactus est subyci infestis curatoribus, quibus
uicissim conflictantibus, Francicu Regnu præda
hostibus exponitur R. an. 42. m. 1. d. 5. mor. die. 21. octobr.
1422. ætat.   an. 55.

Despite his epithet of 'the well-beloved', the reign of Charles VI of France proved a disaster for his people.
His mental illness, which left France without government for long periods, encouraged the outbreak of a civil
war that culminated in English invasion and occupation north of the River Loire. (ME)

himself when the page carrying his lance accidentally clattered it against the armour of one of his knights. Shouting that he was surrounded by traitors, he drew his sword and attacked the knights riding closest to him, killing four or five of them before he was dragged from his horse and laid out upon the ground. His attendants found an ox-cart in which to carry him and the entire column returned to Paris. But the damage was done. The King had revealed himself to be afflicted in the mind and this was a signal to ambitious courtiers and nobles to exploit the weakness at the centre of government.

With the help of the physician, Guillaume de Harcigny, Charles made a partial recovery, but in the early days of 1393 he was plunged into even deeper mental disorder by an incident that occurred at the Queen's New Year masque. Isabeau had persuaded a number of young courtiers, including the King himself, to dress up as 'wild men'. They were kitted out in linen costumes soaked in resinous pitch 'so that they appeared shaggy and hairy from head to foot'. Naturally torches were banned. Unfortunately, the news had not reached the King's youngest brother, who marched into the great hall accompanied by attendants carrying torches. The result was predictable. A spark landed on one 'wild man' and he went up in flames, igniting the man next to him. Soon the 'wild men', including the King, were jumping and screaming in real earnest. Four of the seven wild men died from their burns and the King was only saved by the quick thinking of the Duchess of Berry, who engulfed him in her voluminous skirts. The shock was too much for Charles, however, and he plunged back into madness.

Charles now suffered from delusions, claiming that his name was Georges, refusing to believe that he was married or had any children and even denying that he was the King. He would run from room to room shrieking that his enemies were upon him, smashing the furniture and urinating on his clothes. He then went through a stage of believing that he was made of glass and insisted that iron rods should be inserted into his clothing to prevent him breaking. To humour him, all his clothes were thus reinforced. At their wits' end his physicians reached a remarkable conclusion: he would only recover if he received a sudden shock. They therefore arranged for ten of his courtiers to blacken their faces and then hide in his room. When the King entered they all jumped out, presumably shouting 'boo'. Strange to relate the cure appeared to have worked. For a few weeks Charles's behaviour became more reasonable but then he lapsed again into lunacy. After the 'short, sharp shock' therapy failed, one of the court physicians carried out a trepanning operation involving the drilling of holes in Charles's skull but again to no avail.

Charles reserved his most extreme reactions for his wife. Whenever she came near him, he made obscene gestures at her, saying 'Who is that woman, the sight of whom torments me? Find out what she wants.' Not surprisingly Isabeau refused to share his bed and hunted around until she found a pretty peasant girl named Odette who was willing to take her place. In the meantime she took a lover. Charles, in one of his saner moments, had the man drowned in the Seine.

While the King was powerless to govern France, factions led by the King's brother, Louis of Orléans, and Philip of Burgundy began to tear the country apart. By 1415 the chaos was so serious that King Henry V of England decided to reassert English claims to the crown of France. His invasion, followed soon after by the decisive victory at Agincourt, forced the feeble French King to agree to give him the hand of his daughter Catherine, and to agree that their children should succeed to the French throne. In 1422 both Charles VI and Henry V died, leaving Henry's baby son to be crowned king of both France and England in Rheims Cathedral. It looked as if the mad French King had surrendered his posterity to the English, but Charles VI had given the English more than just his throne. Through his daughter he had passed on a deadly legacy to the infant King: Henry VI would inherit his grandfather's mental instability and through the turmoil that this would cause in England, France would regain her independence.

In 1904 the Prince of Wales, later King George V, received a phone call from one of his friends, Sir Arthur Davidson, who asked him, 'Did you happen to see in the papers that some damned fool has given as much as £1,400 for one stamp?' There was a silence at the end of the phone. Then the King said, 'I was that damned fool.'

Eric the Viking

Gustavus Vasa, first king of newly independent Sweden in 1523, was a man of great gifts but of doubtful stability of mind. Liable to bouts of intense violence, during which he once pulled out his daughter's hair by the roots and on another occasion hacked to death a royal goldsmith who took a day off without permission, Gustav was probably the only king in history to have been fined for swearing. Admittedly Gustavus *was* foulmouthed, but then so were the Swedes in general. Nevertheless, Master Olaus Petri, one of Sweden's reformed clergy, gave a sermon entitled *On horrid oaths*, which was directed specifically at the King. Instead of pulling out the preacher's beard hair by hair, Gustav apologized and made a contribution to the church.

Mental derangement was a significant feature of the Vasa family make-up. Apart from King Gustavus himself, one of his sons, Magnus of Ostergotland, later became insane, while another son, John III, 'spoke softly and carried a big hammer', which he used on anyone who annoyed him. Even a later king like Charles XII, 'the Swedish Thunderbolt', was dangerously unbalanced on occasions. Still, Gustavus Vasa was renowned as a great king and was a difficult act to follow, even for a son as apparently talented as Eric XIV. Yet in spite of his Renaissance skills in learning, music and statecraft, Eric suffered from an immense inferiority complex, which revealed itself in both schizophrenia and paranoia. He desperately wanted to be a king in the great tradition of Swedish kings – in fact, there had been no such great tradition, but he was an imaginative lad and revelled in the idea of a semi-fictional Gothic golden-age not a little akin to Arthurian Britain. Yet his father had not been King Uther Pendragon but merely a parvenu when it came to the quarterings and family escutcheons of genuine royalty. Who were the Vasas when compared with the Habsburgs, the Valois, the Wittelsbachs and so on? Just another family of Swedish noblemen who had pulled themselves up by their bootstraps. And as they had risen so they could fall again and be toppled by another ambitious Swedish family. Such thinking fuelled Eric's paranoia and made him suspect that all men were against him and that every Swedish nobleman was plotting to replace him.

Eric sought to enhance his reputation as a great king not just in Sweden but among other European monarchs by making a grand marriage. Unfortunately for him his choice of wife was that most elusive of princesses, Elizabeth Tudor. Elizabeth was able to keep poor Eric dangling for years without any real intention of marrying him. Eric's frustration at this treatment was truly terrible, particularly when he learned through his envoy Nils Gyllenstierna that Robert Dudley, Earl of Leicester, was the Queen's favourite. He thereupon determined to challenge Dudley to a duel. Gyllenstierna was not keen on this idea. He could see that if such a duel were to take place he would be forced to stand proxy for the king and be skewered by Dudley's sword in the interests of Eric's frustrated love life. Aware that Eric was already showing signs of instability, Gyllenstierna managed to flatter him into dismissing Dudley's rivalry as that of a mere courtier.

Rejected in marriage by Queen Elizabeth and with a growing feeling that his every action was being foiled by Sweden's aristocracy, Eric's paranoia began to take control of him. With sword drawn he paced up and down the corridors of his palace looking for someone to find fault with. Pages and servants who were too smartly dressed were put to the sword as they were obviously intent on seducing the ladies of court, while coughing at inappropriate moments or whispering were obvious signs of subversive conversations. A sudden movement or an unfortunate gesture would bring Eric's latent violence into play.

On the rebound from Elizabeth of England, Eric decided to marry Karin Mansdotter, a waitress in a tavern and daughter of the city gaoler. It was not the grand match he had been seeking but he appears to have loved the girl. Nevertheless, Eric's inferiority complex led him to suspect that men were laughing at him for his choice of bride. In fact, the great families of Sweden were wondering why he had not chosen one of their daughters. For Eric, however, with his cockeyed reasoning, there was no alternative but to strike out at his enemies. Soon Sweden's prisons were groaning under the weight of noble prisoners and Karin's father was making a fortune taking bribes. Eric was so disturbed when he summoned a meeting of the national assembly at Uppsala that he lost the notes he had made and had to ad lib. He blamed his enemies for stealing his notes and trying to embarrass him.

Many of Sweden's leading aristocrats found themselves sentenced to death after show trials. Chief among Eric's enemies was Nils Sture, eldest son of one of Sweden's greatest families. Eric therefore had both Nils and his father imprisoned in Uppsala Castle, on vague and general charges of treason. On 24 May 1566 Eric announced that he was going to seek a reconciliation with the Stures. However, he went into the castle alone, ran over to the cell where Nils Sture was kept and, without saying a word, stabbed him to death. As the body slumped to the ground, Eric turned and ran out of the castle. When the guards asked him what was amiss he replied by telling them to kill all the prisoners except 'Herr Sten'. The guards were shocked at first but promptly obeyed his orders. But who was 'Herr Sten'? There were two 'Stens' in the castle. Unsure which to kill and which to spare the guards let both live. Meanwhile, Eric had mounted his horse and had ridden into the woods nearby, pursued by some of his servants. At the head of the pursuers was Eric's former tutor, Dionysius Beurreus, whom the King loved. As he overtook Eric he called on the King to come back. But Eric's mind was full of demons and he suddenly turned on his tutor and stabbed him to death also. Unhorsed, Eric wandered alone and in darkness through the woods, his mind prey to fears of pursuit by imagined enemies.

It was a moot point as to whether he was more afraid of his people than they were of him. So confused did Eric become that he believed he had been deposed by his brother John, who in turn feared that he had been sentenced to death by Eric. When the two met they both insisted on kneeling to each other and then grovelling at each other's feet begging for mercy.

The chaos into which Sweden was falling had to be arrested. Eventually John recovered his nerve enough to seize the throne, joining with his younger brother Karl to imprison Eric and eventually have him poisoned. It was a dismal end for so talented a man as Eric Vasa, yet in view of the disintegration of his mind it was by way of being a merciful end to his inner torment.

Papal indulgence

The visit of the Empress Carlotta of Mexico to meet Pope Pius IX at the Vatican in 1867 has a special place among royal visits. Probably for the first and certainly for the last time visiting royalty were provided with sleeping accommodation in the Papal Library. It was not the Pope's idea; he was instead a victim of *force majeure*. As he cried out in frustration, 'Nothing is spared me in this life – now a woman has to go mad in the Vatican.' What made matters worse was that the woman in question was a reigning empress, sister-in-law of his Catholic and Apostolic Majesty, Franz Josef of Austria, sister of the King of the Belgians and first cousin of Queen Victoria of Great Britain. And when she slept in the Vatican library she expected the best: bronze bedsteads with the finest lace coverlets, golden candelabras and a dressing-table set of vermeil: strictly five-star luxury with room service thrown in.

Princess Charlotte of Saxe-Coburg was the wife of the Archduke Ferdinand Maximilian of Austria. In 1865 the young couple had accepted the throne of Mexico and the leading role in the Emperor Napoleon III's ill-fated 'Mexican Adventure'. With the support of French arms, Maximilian and Carlotta, as they became known, attempted to establish a new Catholic Empire in the New World. Unfortunately the Mexican people were unwilling to accept the European invaders and in this they had the full backing of President Andrew Johnson of the United States, who invoked the 'Monroe Doctrine' of 1823, which warned against all future attempts at European colonization in the Western hemisphere. Already facing a threat in Europe from the growing power of Bismarck's Prussia, Napoleon III was unwilling to call America's bluff and so he withdrew French military support from Maximilian and Carlotta. Maximilian, unprepared to give up his throne and face a humiliating return to Europe, decided to send his wife to plead with the French Emperor – as well as the Pope – not to abandon him. Carlotta was a strong-minded woman, but the strain of the next few months was too severe even for her robust disposition. Maximilian's decision to send her to Europe soon proved to be a disaster.

Carlotta arrived in France in August 1866 and set out at once to 'beard' Napoleon III in his den by demanding that he continue to support her husband. But after a stormy meeting with both Napoleon and the Empress Eugénie, during which the latter staged a 'diplomatic faint' to distract the enraged Carlotta, it was obvious that there was no hope of the French changing their minds. During this meeting Carlotta's paranoia became clear to everyone. A servant had entered with refreshments for the royal visitor in the shape of a jug of orange juice on a silver tray. Carlotta had refused the drink, claiming that she was being poisoned and that she was surrounded by enemies.

Against the advice of her doctor, Carlotta next travelled to Rome to meet Pope Pius

IX, believing him to be her last hope. The train journey from Paris was a nightmare for her servants. Everyone who passed her carriage was regarded by the distraught Empress as a potential assassin, either in the pay of the Mexican rebels or of Napoleon III. A puzzled organ-grinder at a station was one of the many who felt the sharp edge of her tongue. Carlotta now began to reveal to her startled ladies that crowned heads throughout Europe were being regularly poisoned. In her fantasies her mother and father had died that way and she believed, as well, that Prince Albert, Queen Victoria's consort, had also died from poison.

Upon arriving in Rome Carlotta was met by the Pope's secretary-of-state, Cardinal Antonelli, who explained to her in no uncertain terms that she could expect no help from the Vatican. Naturally the Pope was prepared to grant her an audience, but not to discuss politics. By this stage Carlotta was desperate. She continued to talk obsessively about poison and her servants and friends now realized that their mistress was seriously deranged. In her hotel room she would eat nothing but oranges and nuts and studied each item closely for signs that the skin or the shell had been tampered with.

Carlotta's final mental collapse began on 30 September. Dressed in black and wearing a mourning veil, she summoned her carriage and drove to the Trevi Fountains. To the surprise of onlookers, the Empress alighted by the fountain, knelt and began scooping up handfuls of water to drink, saying 'Here, at least, I will not be poisoned.' She then returned to the coach and ordered the driver to go straight to the Vatican. She arrived just as the Pope was eating his breakfast, ran across the room towards him with tears coursing down her face and fell at his feet, clinging on to his legs. She begged him in a hysterical voice to save her from the assassins who were trying to kill her. The Pope could see that she was mentally disturbed and he acted gently, indulging her whims. Seeing the Pontiff's cup of hot cocoa steaming on the table, Carlotta stuck her fingers into the cup and sucked them greedily, telling him, 'I'm starving. Everything they give me is poisoned.' The Pope rang for another cup of cocoa for Carlotta, but when it arrived she refused to drink it and insisted on drinking his instead. They chatted quietly together, sometimes about Mexican affairs and sometimes about the best antidotes for poison. The Pope suggested trying 'the rosary and prayer', but Carlotta was not convinced. As their conversation dragged on the Pope desperately tried to think of how to escape from his predicament. He managed to send a message to his servants to fetch two doctors disguised as Papal chamberlains. It was one of these who persuaded Carlotta to return to her hotel, having told her that all those she suspected had already been arrested. But as she approached the door of her room she broke into hysterics, screaming that the room would be full of assassins. Nothing would calm her except a return to the Vatican and so, even though it was late in the evening, she was taken there, arriving in floods of tears and begging admittance. For the first time since the probably apocryphal Pope Joan slept in the Vatican, a woman – admittedly an empress – was demanding of the Pope a bed for the night. More cocoa, this time sedated, helped the poor tormented soul to find rest. How the Pope felt about his visitor comes under the heading of 'papal indulgence'.

Carlotta woke refreshed but was soon refusing all food unless it had been prepared for the Pope. Matters now took a turn for the worse as she began to claim that even her beloved husband Maximilian was trying to kill her because she had not provided him with an heir. News of her ramblings quickly spread around Rome and crowds gathered outside in the streets hoping to see the crazy Empress. Carlotta resolutely refused to leave the Vatican and the Pope went about stealthily, fearing to meet her in one of the corridors. It was only by a ruse that Cardinal Antonelli at last got rid of her. A message was sent to Carlotta from the Mother Superior of a nearby convent, inviting her to visit an orphanage. Carlotta agreed but as she passed through the kitchen there one of the nuns offered the Empress a sample of the stew she was cooking. Although she was half-starving Carlotta screamed that it was poisoned. But having just said this she suddenly thrust her hand into the simmering stew and tried to take a piece of meat. Her hand was badly scalded and she fainted with the pain. While she was unconscious her servants hurried her back to the hotel, but when she woke she began to lash out with her hands and feet and had to be restrained by two strong men. There was no alternative now but to commit the Empress Carlotta of Mexico to a strait-jacket. Her next temporary home was to be the Vienna Lunatic Asylum before her brother King Leopold ordered her to be brought home to Belgium.

Napoleon III's 'Mexican Adventure' ended in tragedy for the young couple who had been its dupes. Empress Carlotta lived out the next sixty years – she died in 1927 – in close confinement in a chateau in Belgium. Her husband, Maximilian, crushed by the news of her mental collapse and of his abandonment by France, surrendered to the Mexican rebels and was executed by firing squad.

Juana the Mad

The great theorists of history, the Karl Marxes and their like, would have recoiled in dismay as their waves of social and economic forces broke in vain on the walls of the fortress of Tordesillas in Castile. For within, during the first half of the sixteenth century, there lived a pitiful old woman, incontinent and insane, whose body gave the lie to their theories that historical progress was not affected by individuals. Her name was Juana of Castile and her people called her 'Loca' or 'the Mad'. For Juana was nothing less than a genetic time-bomb, trapped in a human chain of insanity that was centuries long. Revolutions might come and revolutions might go but the tainted genes of Juana seemed to go on for ever, condemning Spain to a series of mad rulers who oversaw their nation's spiralling decline in the seventeenth century.

When the wily Ferdinand of Aragon married off the children of his union with Isabella of Castile, he had an eye to the future. Yet nobody, not even he, could be sure which of the marriages would bear the most fruit. His third child Juana, for example, was married to the Archduke Philip, son of the Holy Roman Emperor, Maximilian I of Habsburg. The Habsburgs were just at the start of their plan to take over the world by using marriage as a weapon – a sixteenth-century diplomat described this policy as *Tu, felix Austria nube; alii gerant bella* – and when Ferdinand's two eldest children died, Juana found herself heiress not only of a united Spain, but also of Spain's new possessions in the New World. It was a glittering prospect. All the Emperor Maximilian had to do was to wait for Ferdinand to die so that the whole of his Spanish dominions would devolve on the house of Habsburg.

Juana was a jealous girl and marrying someone called Philip the Handsome cannot have been easy. Although she had five children by Philip, including two future Holy Roman emperors, two queens of Portugal and one of France, Juana never felt really confident of her husband's love. Philip was too easy-going for the pent-up Juana. When he left her behind in Spain and returned to his possessions in Flanders, she began to suffer from psychosomatic illnesses. Often she would sit for hours on end staring at the ground. When she wanted to sail to Flanders to join her husband, her mother, Queen Isabella, refused to let her go as the journey was too dangerous. This was too much for Juana to bear. She went out into the courtyard of the castle where she was staying and sat by the portcullis for a day and a night, staring vacantly into space and waiting for her husband to return. So pitiful was her behaviour that her mother eventually allowed her to risk the long voyage to Flanders. But once Juana got there she found her greatest fears confirmed. Philip flirted openly with the ladies of a glittering Flemish court that was a far cry from the rigid and formal courts of Spain to which she was accustomed.

When Juana learned that Philip had a mistress she completely lost her head. Seeing her rival reading a letter, she rushed at the woman and snatched it from her hand. The woman promptly snatched it back, screwed it up and swallowed it defiantly. In a blind rage, Juana took up a pair of scissors and began ripping at her rival's hair. When the woman fought back Juana stabbed her in the face with the blades of the scissors. She then ordered servants to cut the woman's hair off. When Philip heard of what had happened he was horrified at his wife's behaviour and criticized her openly. Juana promptly took to her bed, screaming hysterically. Philip locked the door of her room, which adjoined his, whereupon Juana banged on his wall throughout the night. The Flemish courtiers referred to Juana as the 'Terror'.

It was at this supremely inappropriate moment that Juana was told that her mother had died and that she was the new Queen of Castile. Isabella, doubtful of her daughter's capacity to rule, had added a codicil to her will which stated that in the event of Juana not wishing to rule, Castile should be governed by her father or her husband. Naturally, both Ferdinand of Aragon and Philip of Flanders were very interested in Juana's mental condition. Should it not improve it might be necessary for them to divide up her territory between them. This additional worry cannot have helped to settle Juana's mind. She now acted like Ophelia, wandering about the castle and mumbling incoherent thoughts to the courtiers. She constantly wove ornaments from flowers and put them in her hair.

In June 1506 Philip decided to go to Spain to uphold his claim to Castile. He had methodically listed all Juana's acts of mental instability since she came to Flanders and was going to use them to get her declared insane. On learning of this Juana was terrified that either her father or her husband would have her confined. On their journey home to Castile, Juana refused to enter one town, believing she would never be allowed to leave again. Instead she rode up and down on a donkey outside the city walls throughout the night. Philip would probably have had her declared insane there and then. However, he was suddenly taken ill himself and on 25 September 1506, he died at Burgos.

This was the final straw for Juana. Following royal tradition, Philip's heart was cut out and returned to Flanders for burial. In the meantime, Juana set off on a hideous torchlit pilgrimage across Spain to have the rest of his corpse buried in Granada. Each night of the journey she had his coffin opened so that she could look at him and talk to him. She even embraced the decaying cadaver. So jealous was she that she had soldiers with drawn swords accompany the coffin with orders to let no women near Philip except herself. Her father, Ferdinand of Aragon, now seized the opportunity to have Juana taken to the castle of Tordesillas, which she was never allowed to leave for the remaining 46 years of her life. Philip's body was buried nearby so that she could gaze from the castle roof at the place of his interment.

Incredible to relate, though Juana was at best vacant and childlike and at worst a wailing banshee, her father still had hopes for her. He negotiated with King Henry VII of England for a royal marriage. Henry, apparently keen on a healthy dowry, was unconcerned that his future wife might be mad. But Juana would have none of it. In her mind she was still married, what matter that it was to a corpse. She waited only for Philip to arise and renew their love.

Henceforth Juana ate virtually nothing and took no interest in her dress or appearance, frequently assaulting her maids and throwing objects about her room. As a result her windows were barred and even when her father died in 1516 she was not allowed to go free. Her son Charles ruled in Castile in her place. He visited his mother just once, and found her as mad as he suspected. Years later an extraordinary event occurred. The leaders of a Castilian rising against Charles decided to free her as the true and legal ruler of the kingdom. They broke into the castle, but when they entered her room they were so shocked at what they found that they abandoned the idea of letting her loose. The previously devout daughter of the Church had become hostile to religion, refused Communion and claimed that she lived surrounded by demons. She said that she had seen ghostly cats devouring the souls of her mother and her beloved Philip. She died in 1555 at the age of seventy-six, yet through the children of her body, notably through her son Charles, the curse of madness would be passed on to future generations of Spanish rulers.

Too much Turkish Delight

Since the end of the Crimean War in 1856, Britain and France had enjoyed close and friendly relations with the Ottoman Empire. When a new sultan, Abdul Aziz, came to the throne Queen Victoria and the Emperor Napoleon III went out of their way to maintain the alliance. In 1867 they invited Abdul Aziz to visit London and Paris on state visits. Intended as a genuine demonstration of friendship between allies, the visits instead had the most disastrous effect on both the Sultan and his people.

The problem was that even before he went to London Abdul Aziz was such a spendthrift that he had almost bankrupted the Turkish state. At 230 pounds Abdul Aziz was the largest if not the greatest of the world's rulers, using an eight-foot-wide bed for as many of his 900 concubines as he could cram on at one time, and eating a dozen fried eggs at a sitting when he was not pelting courtiers with his leftovers. An amiable brute of a man, peaceful and self-indulgent, but with living expenses more than the Ottoman state could bear, he was soon in debt to foreign bankers to the tune of £200 million. Just as serious was the growing threat from subversive groups inside Turkey who were aiming to achieve a constitutional monarchy. But Abdul Aziz was neither an accountant nor a bureaucrat, he was a sultan with a capital 'S'. His job was to behave as a sultan should: that meant spending everybody's else's money on having a good time and bedding everyone else's wives.

Abdul Aziz's visit to Europe disturbed his equilibrium. His eyes simply popped out of his head at the new ways he discovered to spend money and enjoy himself. In London he cut a dash by arriving for a banquet at the Guildhall mounted on a white charger, with a diamond-studded fez and a tunic covered in medals. Queen Victoria found him vulgar, recording her private hope that he would not come again. But even the dowdy little lady in black could not spoil his fun or disguise the staggering wealth that his eyes beheld in

A cartoon satirizing the excesses of Sultan Abdul Aziz, who went close to bankrupting the Ottoman Turkish state through the profligacy of his spending on Western luxuries. The Sultan's lavish expenditure heightened public discontent that eventually led to his deposition. (ME)

London. He wanted it and like a spoiled child he had to have it.

When Abdul Aziz returned to Constantinople his extravagance knew no limits. The annual expense of running just one of his palaces was soon more than £2 million. He kept a staff of 5,000 servants to cater for his nightly dinners for three or four hundred people. Four hundred musicians played to entertain his guests. Thrilled by the luxuries he had seen at Versailles, Abdul Aziz ordered a solid gold dinner-service, encrusted with rubies and other precious stones. The walls of one of the palace rooms were covered in mother-of-pearl. From the more functional British the Sultan bought locomotives and ironclad battleships, though there were no tracks in Turkey for the trains to run on and no seamen with the technical know-how to man the warships. Abdul Aziz ordered dozens of pianos from British music shops even though nobody in the palace had the skill to play them.

Abdul Aziz had taken some of his wives with him to Europe, as well as the Queen Mother, Pertevalé, and these ladies were encouraged to spend to their hearts' content. The Queen Mother bought fifty silk dresses each day she was in Paris and gave them away to her slaves in order to 'spread happiness around her'.

Exciting as the expedition had proved for all concerned, it had also served to confirm the fears of the Sultan's officials that their master was insane. He was not cruelly insane as so many of his Osmanli predecessors had been, but the effect he was having on the Ottoman state was no less damaging. He had new ideas on everything, notably education, and they were all absurd. To improve education and bring it up to a Western level Abdul Aziz decided to personally rewrite the school textbooks. From now on the history books, for example, would contain a greater degree of partiality than previously. All mention of Turkish defeats was erased, along with all references to Christianity. French history included a mysterious time-warp of twenty-five years, between 1789 and 1815, when nothing at all happened. It was as if Louis XVI had awoken from a long sleep like some royal Rip Van Winkle and found himself renumbered.

As his insanity took an even greater grip on him Abdul Aziz's range of eccentricities became increasingly surreal. At one stage he decreed that nobody but he should bear the name 'Aziz'. As a result, anyone in the palace named 'Aziz' was forced to change his name. Next he decided that he did not like documents written in black ink; everything must be in red ink. The Turkish bureaucracy was inefficient at the best of times and an order like this was bound to prove impossible to fulfil. But Abdul Aziz was relentless. The empire must by scoured for red ink and documents that had previously been written in black ink must be rewritten in red. Five hundred years of Ottoman records had to be recopied. A simple order to change the colour of ink used by the civil service could alone have brought the whole machinery of government to a halt, yet this was just one of hundreds of strange ideas that the Sultan tried to foist on his ministers.

For entertainment Abdul Aziz loved chasing chickens. He spent most evenings doing it. He chased them up and down the corridors of the palace and when he caught one he rewarded it with the Ottoman Empire's highest order of gallantry, which he hung round its neck. Each nightly chase began with a parade of chickens and each bird that had been honoured was required to wear its medal on a sash.

Abdul Aziz's eccentricities mirrored a profoundly disturbed mind. Afraid of being poisoned, he refused to eat anything but hard-boiled eggs cooked by the Queen Mother in person. And it took a lot of eggs to keep a growing boy of 230 pounds happy. His mummy cooked the eggs just the way that he liked them and wrapped each in a miniature black crêpe parcel sealed with her own personal seal.

As if the eccentricities of this ailing lunatic were not bad enough for the Turkish people to bear, he began spending even more money on his favourite Circassian slave girl, a beautiful sixteen-year-old who, he said, was the only person who understood him. Millions of pounds were squandered on this girl until in 1876 Abdul Aziz was suddenly deposed by a palace revolution in favour of his nephew, Abdul Hamid II (see p. 16). While the massive sultan, dressed in a pink nightshirt, clung to his Circassian slave girl and sobbed on her shoulder, the Queen Mother did not take deposition lightly. Having been a bath attendant before she became queen, she was a powerful woman. Confronted by the group of ministers who were staging the coup she laid the War Minister out with a hefty kick in the groin and then poleaxed another minister with a clubbing blow from her hefty fist. But it was too late. Abdul Aziz was already yesterday's man. Within a few days he had committed suicide by slashing his wrists.

During a tour of China in 1986 Prince Philip was introduced by his Chinese guides to a British student, Simon Kirby, who was studying in Beijing. The Prince's advice to Simon was succinct: 'Don't stay here too long or you'll go back with slitty eyes.'

The black knight

The Maharajah Jai Singh of Alwar has a claim to being the worst of all Indian princes. In spite of having adopted many English ways and having been rewarded in turn with an honorary knighthood and an honorary colonelcy in the British Army, Jai Singh never quite came to terms with the Englishman's love of animals or even young children.

Surprisingly his rule was tolerated until 1933, when the collapse of his mind forced the British authorities to depose him. By that time he imagined that he was the god Rama and was devoting all his time to calculating the size of Rama's head-dress so that he could replicate it. Had this been the extent of his misrule nobody could have complained, but this charming eccentricity was but a pale reflection of the Maharajah in his prime.

Jai Singh's treatment of his polo pony first alerted the British to the problems ahead. Disappointed at the poor beast's performance in an important polo match, he doused the animal in petrol and burned it alive. British upper lips were seen to weaken and quaver; strong men cried. But even worse was to follow. Jai Singh took to selecting babies from local villages to act as tiger-bait. He tried to reassure the mothers of the said offspring that he was a remarkably good shot and that, should he miss the tiger, the baby would hardly feel a thing. The final straw was when he began taking pot-shots at passing poodles and cocker spaniels. This assault on Man's Best Friend was not only a blunder, it was a mistake. In 1933 he received his marching orders from the British – Paris or bust. He chose Paris and died just four years later.

Perverse and Foolish

Until recent times it was necessary for a monarch not only to rule but to be seen to rule. A king's physical appearance was a vital part of the strength of his kingdom. An ailing monarch, weak, sick or effeminate, frequently mirrored a kingdom in decline and fatally decadent. And weakness at the centre of power was a formula for social unrest and civil war.

The flower fairy

It is open to serious doubt if a more grotesque and perverted individual has ever ruled a state in human history than Varius Avitus Antoninus, popularly known as Elagabalus (or Heliogabalus). He became emperor of Rome in 218, after a period of civil war, and it was hoped that he would restore to the empire the peace and prosperity that it had enjoyed under the great emperor Antoninus, whose name Varius bore. As a result his reign began in a flush of brilliant expectation. But Varius was just a boy of fourteen and very much under the malign influence of his grandmother, Julia Maesa, and his mother, Soaemias. They were prepared to leave the lad to indulge his perverse fantasies while they ruled the empire.

At the time of his elevation Varius lived in Syria and was high priest of the sun god Elagabalus, whose name he later took. He supervised a large temple at Emesa, where a black stone – possibly meteoric in origin – was the centre of the worship of the sun. When he went to Rome Elagabalus took the holy stone with him and built a new temple for it. His entry into the city came as quite a shock to the Romans, who must have thought they had seen just about everything – but Elagabalus was different. He lived in a world of flowers and faeces. As the procession wound through the streets flower petals rained down from the balconies to welcome him and his priests, who carried golden bowls filled with wine and the intestines of the children slaughtered in sacrifice to the sun god.

During his four-year reign, Elagabalus turned Rome into a kind of film set that only Fellini in modern times could have imagined. Unfortunately, the dreamy images were constantly interrupted by outbursts from Ken Russell's neighbouring studio. Thus Elagabalus's beautiful summer-banquets – which were staged daily in different colours, with blue days and green days and iridescent ones – were accompanied by lewd episodes and scenes of unspeakable brutality. Senators in pink togas drinking delicate rosé wine might wander through arbours of pink roses and carnations while clowns with giant phalluses chased naked, screaming girls down to the edge of the lake, where a ritual sacrifice of a child was taking place, and Elagabalus himself was probing the victim's steaming intestines for signs propitious to his god.

The soldiers who had cheered Varius's election to emperor clearly had not examined this strange hermaphroditic individual very closely, or they might have reconsidered their decision. Elagabalus never seemed certain whether he was a man or a woman, usually preferring to dress as the latter, particularly when he was plying for trade as a prostitute. It is said that he would sometimes stand naked in shop doorways, gently shaking the curtains and calling to passers-by.

The reign of Elagabalus was a time for feasting. The range and rarity of the food available surpassed anything in recorded history. Elagabalus liked to astound his guests by eating camel-heels and cocks-combs taken from living birds. These, he was assured, would make him immortal. In addition, he sampled flamingo-brains and the brains of partridges and thrushes, as well as the heads of parrots, pheasants and peacocks. He fed his dogs on goose-livers, his horses with out-of-season grapes and his pet lions and panthers on delicacies from his table, such as sows' udders. On some days he ate nothing but peas mixed with gold pieces, lentils with onyx, rice with pearls and fish sprinkled with powdered rubies. At one feast he had his guests served with six hundred ostrich heads, of which they ate just the brains, which were scooped out with golden spoons.

Elagabalus would sometimes challenge his guests to devise special sauces, made up of the most remarkable ingredients. When they were complete he would sample them and if he enjoyed the sauce he would reward the creator with silken garments. On the other hand, if he did not like what they had made he would order them to continue eating the sauce hour after hour until they had thought of something better. Nor were his feasts all that they seemed. As a practical joke he sometimes served particular guests with replicas of the food everyone else was eating made of wax, wood, ivory, pottery and even marble or stone. They had to act as if nothing had happened and pretend to eat along with the others. If they spoiled his joke he was liable to react petulantly.

Elagabalus had a childish sense of humour, but with it went a streak of cruelty. His pranks often had the direst possible consequences for the victims. Guests who became drunk at his banquets were sometimes placed in the cages where the wild animals were kept. When and if they awoke the next morning it was to find Elagabalus feeding them through the bars. Others who spent the night in a guest room found that while they were asleep bears and wild cats were put in alongside them. Some of the wild animals had had their teeth and claws drawn – others had not. No guest ever knew if he was facing certain death or just one of the emperor's pranks. Elagabalus loved games of chance and introduced the notion of 'trick or treat' to Roman society. At his parties some guests won ten pounds of gold, while others got just ten lettuces. Some won boxes full of precious stones, others boxes full of scorpions. The dancing girls who performed for him and his guests were always rewarded at the end of the evening. However, while one might carry off a hundred pieces of silver, another might have a dead dog tied around her neck. Each had to smile just the same. His slaves were no more fortunate. One was set the impossible task of collecting a thousand pounds' weight of spiders' webs.

Elagabalus also devised an early form of aromatherapy. The only problem was that its effects were fatal. But at least the process of death was sweet and soft. He had a special dining-room equipped with a reversible ceiling. When he had wined and dined some special guests he would retire from the room and reverse the ceiling, which would then release a seemingly endless rain of violet and rose petals, drifting down at first pleasurably, then chokingly and finally suffocatingly on those beneath.

Once Elagabalus staged a great naval spectacle in the arena, with boats sailing not on water but on wine. As night fell and the arena was illuminated with the lights of burning ships, he ordered slaves to scatter poisonous snakes around the feet of the spectators who were watching the battle. In the confusion that followed hundreds of people died from snake-bites or were trampled to death.

Elagabalus indulged in human sacrifice, outdoing even Gilles de Rais, the notorious fifteenth-century child-killer, in the numbers of girls and boys whom he slaughtered to propitiate his god. Sometimes he danced in worship of the deities Caelestis and the

Magna Mater along with celebrants who had opted for ritual castration. At other times he joined the orgiastic worship of Salambo, a Syrian cult. All these gods, he claimed, were just parts of the one great god Baal or Elagabalus, whose name he bore.

It was in the area of sexual perversity that Elagabalus excelled. Describing the Emperor's own sexual orientation is impossible. He was certainly bisexual and at times transsexual. He made up his face to resemble a woman's, and wore women's dresses and exotic wigs. He depilated his entire body and loved to take the role of Venus, arising naked from a huge sea shell and standing with one arm across his chest and the other covering his private parts. He surrounded himself with men he had selected for one reason only: the size of their sexual organs. In order to find these individuals, the emperor would visit the public baths hoping to procure some well-endowed specimens. Elagabalus gave orders for the whole city to be scoured for men whom he hoped would meet his requirements. Penis size was an unusual qualification for service in the Roman state but a number of 'studs' earned promotion purely on the basis of the magnificence of their genitals. One such was an athlete from Smyrna, named Aurelius Zoticus, who was specially brought to Rome on the Emperor's orders as a result of his sexual reputation. In a grotesque ceremony Elagabalus actually 'married' Zoticus and consummated the arrangement in full view of his wedding guests.

Elagabalus appointed a handsome male dancer to be the prefect of the Praetorian Guard, while a charioteer and a barber became ministers of state – all simply because of the size of their private parts. Mule-drivers, cooks and locksmiths soon ousted the traditional Roman bureaucrats, who failed to measure up to the emperor's expectations. Yet at other times Elagabalus showed heterosexual inclinations. He once ravished and 'married' a Vestal Virgin, a sect who were sworn to chastity. For this crime alone he was damned in the eyes of most traditional Romans. But Elagabalus never knew when to stop. This was a man who would deliberately waste quantities of food and then make it known how sorry he was that people were starving. Elagabalus never seemed aware of the consequences of his actions. His frenetic pursuit of sensual gratification blinded him to the real world closing in on him from outside.

Eventually the soldiers who had elevated him to the purple tore him down again, slaughtering his friends and trapping Elagabalus and his mother, who were hiding in a latrine. They dragged his body through the streets and threw it into a sewer. It found its final resting-place, weighted down, at the bottom of the River Tiber. For Rome and its empire the reign of Elagabalus had been like some drug-induced nightmare. The foolish boy – just eighteen when he died – had squandered so much money in just four years that he had taken Rome to the brink of bankruptcy.

The rule of the hermaphrodites

Between 1574 and 1589 France was ruled by the last of her Valois kings, Henry III, one of the most corrupt and certainly the most degenerate rulers in French history. Coming to the throne at the height of France's Wars of Religion, Henry took the country to the very brink of disaster through the excesses of his personal life and the effect that they had on his policies.

On his accession Henry still retained some semblance of normality, but on the death of his mistress, the Princess of Condé, in 1575, he appeared to suffer a breakdown.

Henry III, last Valois king of France, portrayed in characteristically foppish attire. With his pampered favourites, 'les mignons', Henry indulged in excesses of a dubious nature and spent so extravagantly that he nearly bankrupted his kingdom. (PN)

Eccentricities that had appeared harmless, like carrying a basket full of puppies round his neck everywhere he went, now assumed a darker and more disturbing complexion. In mourning for his lost love, he dressed in black and attached silver and ivory skulls to his clothing. He became the first king of France – indeed probably of any state – to join the flagellants. This fanatical sect – in France called the *Blancs Battus* – were a hangover from the time of the Black Death in the fourteenth century. Their aim was to purge their sins by travelling in long columns from town to town, barefoot and stripped to the waist, flogging each other's backs and buttocks with steel-tipped whips until the blood flowed. Eccentric as was the King's decision to join the *Blancs Battus*, many of his courtiers felt it expedient to join with him. Even the Cardinal of Lorraine, the head of the church in France, joined the King's procession. Although the cardinal managed to avoid the whipping, travelling stripped and barefoot in the wet and chilly weather eventually cost him his life from exposure.

Henry's experiences on the road worsened rather than relieved his mental problems. On returning to court he began to dress in the most fantastic costumes, with his faltering masculinity now finding refuge in the most outrageous exhibitionism. He was often seen in magnificent ladies' gowns, with billowing sleeves. Surrounded by sycophantic courtiers willing to indulge his every whim, the King's latent transvestism became more prominent. He painted his face and wore his hair piled up on top of his head, as well as sleeping each night in a face mask. And increasingly his followers, known as *mignons*, egged him on to even wilder excesses. The *mignons* were well-bred young men who combined the curious qualities of effeminacy with masculine swagger. They wore their hair long, so that it could be curled up in piles on their heads, and topped by a tiny bonnet, aping what was the current fashion for whores in brothels. Around their necks they wore ruffs of astonishing size which made it look as though they carried their heads on platters. Like any gang of young men they gambled and whored, but uniquely they postured, muttering threats like 'Scratch your eyes out', and then fell to fighting amongst themselves or with passers-by.

Supported by this anarchic caste, Henry metamorphosed into a queen bee, served and serviced by her followers. Sodomy was the chief pleasure of the bisexual *mignons* and the king was first among equals when it came to the arts of love. Prominent among his lovers was Louis de Guast, for whom Henry dressed himself in dainty women's shoes, with silk stockings, gloves, rings and all forms of jewellery as well as carrying a fan. He plucked his eyebrows, powdered his face, painted his lips and wore false teeth as an affectation.

The *mignons* were bitterly resented by more conventional courtiers and by the public at large. As well as being degenerate they were also violent and fanatically loyal to the King. They frequently indulged in duels to the death and the streets were not safe when they were about. But as time passed the influence wielded by the *mignons* on the King strengthened and they threw up political leaders, like the Duc d'Épernon and the Duc de Joyeuse, who helped to determine policy. And that policy was disastrous for Henry and France. They planned to create a third force in the Wars of Religion, standing between the Huguenots of Henry of Navarre and the Catholics led by the Duc de Guise. To ensure their success they advised the King to begin by assassinating Guise, who was in alliance with Philip II of Spain. Henry took their advice, armed ten of his bodyguards with daggers and invited the Duc to visit him in his bedchamber. When Guise entered the King's room, he was attacked and stabbed to death.

But Henry had blundered. Guise had been the leader of France's Catholics and as his murderer the King was excommunicated by the Pope and declared 'an assassin, a heretic and an infidel'. It was not long before Henry paid the full price for his treachery, being stabbed to death by a Dominican friar named Jacques Clément. Henry III's murder of the Duc de Guise was a political blunder that further inflamed the bitter factional struggle in France – a struggle that was not to be resolved until the triumph of Henry of Navarre as Henry IV, the first Bourbon king, in 1598.

Broken Rulers

In the Middle Ages reigning meant ruling, and that took more than an interest in the church or education, or chasing pretty French boys about the court, or even wearing long-toed shoes that had to be tied at the knee. It meant being able to overawe a bunch of thugs masquerading under titles like duke, earl and baron, and knocking their heads together from time to time, or even cutting them off when things got bad. Three English kings of the Middle Ages suffered deposition or martyrdom because they were too weak to govern the country. One was insane, though admittedly in a gentle, understated English way; one was depraved, at least in the eyes of his contemporaries; and the third was too interested in women's clothes and comparing colour schemes for the good of the country.

Behind every great man

Following a father like Edward I was always going to be difficult, particularly for a lad who enjoyed bricklaying, fencing and thatching. Admittedly his father was known for his use of the hammer, but that was not for repairing horseshoes but for crushing, maiming and slaying the Scots. Edward II preferred more homely pastimes. In fact, he was good at swimming and rowing – but that only made him a 'wet bob' to his contemporaries, who took their sport seriously and practised killing in as many different ways as possible. Contemporaries describe Edward as keeping company with 'buffoons, singers, actors, carters, ditchers, oarsmen, sailors and others who practised mechanical arts'. But this was seen as merely idling for a man of his rank and if he had devoted as much time to arms as he gave to 'rustic arts', England would have prospered and his reputation as a warrior-prince would have been secure.

Edward II had a lonely childhood, his mother having died when he was just fifteen months old, and his father being too busy campaigning to concern himself about his son. And what the King had already heard about the boy, and of his relationship with his French friend Piers Gaveston, a young squire at court, gave him no reason to want to know him. When the prince asked his father to make Gaveston Count of Ponthieu, all the frustrations that had been building up between father and son came to a head. Furiously the King accused Edward of being a 'base-born whoreson'. He then tore out some hair from his son's head, sent him from court and banished Gaveston from England. Presumably he had heard rumours, or even had direct evidence, of his son's homosexual relationship with the handsome French squire. But within months the old King was dead and Edward II reversed the banishment, welcoming Gaveston back to England and creating him Earl of Cornwall. Both Edward and Gaveston now married, but this was merely a cloak for their own forbidden love. The new King had four children by his wife, Isabella of France, but his true affections were kept for Gaveston. As a chronicler of the time wrote, they 'fell so much in love that the King entered upon an unbreakable bond of affection with him, before all other mortals'. This understandably infuriated the Queen, particularly when Edward gave Gaveston the best of her jewels and wedding presents. Gaveston, meanwhile, lorded it over the English nobles 'like a second king'.

In 1308 the English nobles demanded that the King banish Gaveston again. Edward was forced to accede to their wishes to avoid civil war, but instead of banishing Gaveston he appointed him Lord Lieutenant of Ireland. Edward soon recalled his lover and this drove the nobles, led by the Earl of Lancaster, to take up arms against him. Gaveston was trapped in Scarborough Castle and murdered, his headless corpse being left for the dogs to eat.

Edward learned nothing from his disastrous affair with Gaveston. Instead, he plotted to avenge himself on Lancaster and his allies. He began a new relationship with Hugh Despenser, son of the Earl of Winchester. When he felt strong enough Edward captured Lancaster and executed him after a mockery of a trial. But in this game of roundabouts, Lancaster's son, Roger Mortimer, found an ally in Queen Isabella, who was thoroughly disgusted with her husband and took young Roger to her bed. Mortimer and Isabella now openly flaunted their relationship, and soon captured Hugh Despenser, who was killed after suffering barbaric mutilations, involving castration and disembowelment, because 'he was a heretic and a sodomite'. Soon afterwards Edward himself was taken prisoner by the Queen and her paramour and imprisoned in Berkeley Castle, where he was later murdered (see p. 149). The story of Edward's overthrow by his wife and her lover was an important one for medieval writers. Though the murder of a King could never be condoned, Edward's love for Gaveston violated the 'natural order' and, in a sense, justified the 'wronged' Queen Isabella in taking her terrible revenge.

During the period 1272 to 1399 only four kings occupied the throne of England. In a curious way it was a case of 'odds and evens', with Edward I and Edward III sharing conventional manly traits, such as physical strength, and a martial disposition, and Edward II and Richard II sharing gentler natures, latent or actual homosexuality, and a dislike of war. In fact, Richard felt so strongly for his tragic great-grandfather, Edward II, that he pressed the Pope to have him canonized, but without success.

King Henry II of England was a red-haired firebrand of a man, with a ferocious temper. It is said that sometimes he would become so angry that he fell to the ground and chewed the very straw. In 1170, while at Caen, in Normandy, he heard news from England that Archbishop Thomas Becket was still opposing his will, and he angrily broke out with words that he was later to regret: 'Who will rob me of this turbulent priest?' It was a rhetorical question but four of his knights took him at his word, travelled to England and murdered Becket in Canterbury Cathedral.

Costume drama

In the aftermath of the first glittering English successes of the Hundred Years War, the noble warriors who followed Edward III and the Black Prince to France and won renown at Crécy and Poitiers, saw the late fourteenth century as a golden age, and the accession to the throne of Richard, son of the Black Prince, seemed to promise even greater glory for England. But what England got was not a warrior-king, a true 'Garter-knight' and a paladin, but a vain, foppish, narcissistic boy, who was aesthetic rather than militaristic. Richard loved his mother, the beautiful and gentle Joan 'the Fair Maid of Kent', and was frankly fed up with all the stories of how great and good his father was and how he was not fit to clean his trophy cabinet. It was the same burden as Edward II had been forced to bear, and its consequences were similar.

Richard was a tall, handsome young man, with thick, golden hair which he was careful to keep immaculately coiffured. It is said that he bathed often – a most suspicious sign of effeminacy in the eyes of his lords – and even invented the pocket handkerchief. He kept a well-filled library, and was a patron of artists, musicians and poets. He was, one might suggest, an early manifestation of a Renaissance ruler, but he was to find that the England he ruled was just not ready for him. Furthermore, the early death of both his parents brought him to the throne at too early an age and imposed burdens which were too much for any child. He had shown courage during the Peasants' Revolt of 1381, but for much of his youth he was dominated by his uncles, the powerful sons of Edward III – John of Gaunt, Edmund of Langley and Thomas of Woodstock. They were a band of seasoned warriors, enough to overawe any boy. Richard found that he needed to find his own friends and political allies and he turned to Robert de Vere, Earl of Oxford, with whom he conducted a homosexual affair. On Robert's death, he ordered his coffin to be left open so that he could look on the dead man's face and kiss his hand.

Richard's reign coincided with military setbacks in France, and the English nobles equated this military decline with the effeminacy of the royal court. It was a period of fantastic excesses. Money was lavished on entertainments that had never before been seen in England. Self-glorification replaced duty and loyalty as the watchwords of the age. Freaks of all kinds were brought to court to entertain the hundreds of hangers-on who filled the palace every night with their carousing and debauchery. The 'Sumptuary laws' which ruled what materials could be worn by the different social ranks were brushed aside. People wore what they wanted and could afford. Sleeves became so lengthy that they brushed the ground, women's head-dresses so tall that they brushed the sky, toes so long that they had to be tied by gold chains at the knee or even the waist. One day a royal carriage carrying maids of honour became so top-heavy that the wind blew it over on London Bridge, and the ladies all fell upside down in the mud on their pointed or horned head-dresses. Richard himself was said to have owned a dress, covered in gemstones, that was valued at more than a thousand pounds. It was at this time that codpieces first made their appearance.

But Richard seemed to lose everyone that he loved best and after the death of Robert de Vere he became profoundly depressed, so much so that he sometimes sat on his throne looking vacantly ahead and saying nothing. Yet it was action rather than inaction that cost him his throne and his life. Following a dispute between Henry Bolingbroke, son of John of Gaunt, and the Earl of Norfolk, Richard banished the former. With Bolingbroke out of the country, Richard then tried to seize the valuable estates of his

Officers of the court of Richard II of England, late 14th century. Their long sleeves and even longer stocking-toes reflect the sartorial eccentricities of the period. The gold chains used to tie recalcitrant stocking-toes to the knee are clearly visible in the picture. (ME)

father, who had just died. Bolingbroke returned to claim his rightful inheritance and, finding the majority of Englishmen content to see him depose the King and tend his ailing kingdom, he forced the King to abdicate in 1399 and imprisoned him in Pontefract Castle. How Richard died we cannot be certain. Some reports state that he starved himself, others that he was murdered. Whichever is true there was none of the drama that had accompanied Edward II's overthrow and death. In his last days Richard II was clearly unfit to rule and his death was perhaps a cruel necessity in the sense that a deposed king has lost all purpose and thus all claim to live.

Vaulting ambition

Of the three Plantagenet kings to be murdered in the fourteenth and fifteenth centuries, Henry VI's case evinces the most pity. He shared none of Edward II's vices or Richard II's extravagance, and was more a priest than a king. He inherited mental illness through his mother, the daughter of Charles VI of France, and was also unfortunate in succeeding one of England's great warrior-kings, Henry V.

Coming to the throne as a baby, and being crowned both King of France and King of England, was a burden for anyone to bear, let alone a weakling who had more of the saint than the soldier about him. And when one considers that he was married to Margaret of Anjou, the 'She-wolf of France' and the fiercest queen ever to sit on the throne of England, one can easily appreciate the problems young Henry VI was going to face. Furthermore, like Richard II, he was surrounded by uncles who had won glorious victories in France under his father and expected more of the same. While Henry established schools and churches throughout the realm, the warrior-nobility fretted at the lack of opportunities for making war. Medieval noblemen were trained to kill and were not impressed by the glories of Eton College, established in 1440, or King's College, Cambridge, begun the following year. Fan vaulting was all right for a ceiling but where was the profit in it for real men?

Henry VI was also unlucky in that the early part of his reign coincided with the rise in France of a phenomenon known as Joan the Maid. In 1429 she inspired a French revival that recaptured the initiative from the English in the Hundred Years War. The English were finally evicted from France in 1453, leaving England a prey to hundreds of nobles and thousands of soldiers who had come home from France knowing nothing but warfare. Such men were not content to beat their swords into ploughshares, and regarded the feeble administration of a weak king as an opportunity to practise what they had learned in France on England's green and pleasant land.

The civil war known as the 'Wars of the Roses' was also a direct consequence of King Henry VI's declining mental health. From 1455 until 1471, Henry was a mere pawn, in a struggle for control of the realm between the Lancastrians, led by the Beaufort dukes of Somerset and Richard, Duke of York, and his sons. The disastrous Lancastrian defeat at the battle of Tewkesbury in 1471 confirmed Edward of York as King Edward IV (he had been ruling *de facto* since 1461) and acted as a death sentence on Henry himself. He was duly murdered, probably on the orders of Richard of Gloucester, later Richard III. If the fate of the 'royal saint', as he was called, was tragic it was yet more confirmation, if it was needed, that holding the throne of England during the Middle Ages was a man's job.

The effects of intermarriage within the Habsburg family can be clearly seen in this engraving of the Holy Roman Emperor Charles V (above). His hugely enlarged jaw made eating difficult and closing the mouth completely impossible. (PN)

Charles VIII of France (right) was a most unfortunate physical specimen. His dwarfish body and spindly legs supported an enormous head and a huge 'parrot nose', here flatteringly understated in the interests of royal dignity. (ME)

Ugly Customers

Inbreeding has been one of the great blunders of royal history. Not only has it resulted in the transmission of mental illness, and diseases such as porphyria and haemophilia, it has also handed down to future generations a legacy of physical deficiency and facial ugliness that has condemned many rulers to lives of humiliation and shame. One has only to think of the parrot-nosed Charles VIII of France and the elephant-nosed Ferdinand of Coburg, not to mention the Habsburg emperors Maximilian I, Charles V or Leopold I, all of whom were afflicted by the notorious 'Habsburg Jaw'. It is said that the genes carrying the exaggerated jaw of the Habsburgs originated with a Polish princess named Cymburga who married Ernest the Iron Duke in the fourteenth century. Cymburga apparently was strong enough to hammer nails into wood with her bare hands, but her legacy to the Habsburgs was more than merely physical strength. Nevertheless, the problem of Cymburga's faulty genes would not have been so serious had it not been for the Habsburg tendency to marry their own cousins.

In 1477 Maximilian of Habsburg, son of the Emperor Frederick III, married Mary of Burgundy, daughter of Duke Charles the Bold. Territorially the alliance was a triumph for the Habsburgs, who thereby acquired the Burgundian Low Countries. Aesthetically and genetically, however, it was a disaster. Maximilian was a remarkably ugly man, with a large hooked nose, a protruding jaw and very thick lips. Pictures of his wife show that she also had a thick lower lip and a heavy jaw. The result was that the already pronounced Habsburg jaw became so accentuated in their descendants that Maximilian and Mary's grandson, the Emperor Charles V, had a jaw so malformed that he found it almost impossible to close his mouth. A possibly apocryphal story goes that a Spanish peasant on seeing the emperor for the first time remarked, 'Your Majesty, close your mouth at once, for the flies of this country are very insolent.'

Tragically, this malformation of the jaw was often accompanied by other inherited aspects of endocrine malfunction, including mental problems, epilepsy, nervous disabilities and sexual inadequacy. All of these features were present in both the Spanish and Austrian branches of the Habsburgs and were exacerbated by the tendency of the family to intermarry.

Probably the most extreme example of the Habsburg jaw was seen in the person of the Emperor Leopold I (Holy Roman Emperor 1658–1705). His parents were cousins and he thereby inherited a double dose of Habsburg genes, leaving him with an appallingly distorted face. His chin was so extended and his lower lip protruded so far that he too was nearly incapable of closing his mouth. When it rained the drops kept falling into his mouth. Contemporary representations, though presumably attempting to minimize his defects, serve only to convince us of his great misfortune. On top of his physical ugliness, his speech defects made him appear half-witted. To add insult to injury he was also small in stature and near-sighted.

The family of King Christian IX of Denmark were responsible for spreading 'giraffe necks' around the royal houses of Europe. Even the beautiful Princess Alexandra, who married Edward the Prince of Wales (see p. 65), had a long neck which she concealed on state occasions with multi-stranded necklaces of pearls. Her eldest son, the Duke of Clarence, concealed his long neck with very high collars, earning him the nickname 'Collars and Cuffs'. King George I of the Hellenes, grandfather of Prince Philip, the present Duke of Edinburgh, also had a most pronounced neck, as did his brother Waldemar of Denmark.

A PANTOMIME DANE: CHRISTIAN VII OF DENMARK

Christian VII of Denmark set new standards in the field of royal insanity. His behaviour made Hamlet's 'antic disposition' appear a very model of sanity. Yet whatever sympathy we may feel for Christian is suspended when one reads of his antics, which more resemble those of a character from the *Beano* than a prince of royal blood. Which other king, for example, ever let himself be beaten up in a fist-fight by one of his courtiers? Or played leapfrog over the backs of visiting dignitaries as they bowed to him? Or ran around the corridors of his palace at night banging doors to keep people awake? Which royal personage threw a bowlful of sugar over the head of the Dowager Queen at a royal reception, or stuck pins in the seat of the throne to see the same lady jump? On a state visit he made to England, Lady Stuart summed him up perfectly as the 'Northern Scamp'. In fact he was a thoroughly foolish person who almost plunged Denmark into a ruinous war with England.

Christian may have inherited some of his mental instability from his father, Frederick V, though there were also doubts about the stability of his delightful English mother, Louisa, daughter of George II, whose Hanoverian background was a fertile breeding-ground for mental problems. What is certain, however, is that Christian's childhood years were so traumatic that they might have blighted anyone's development. The early death of his mother, when he was just two, the collapse of his father into alcoholism and *delirium tremens*, and the brutality of his tutor all inflicted damage on a young and physically frail prince. Starved of affection and subjected to a regime of training more appropriate to a prison inmate than to a future king, Christian developed an obsession with physical toughness which was quite at odds with his scrawny physique. Beaten (sometimes senseless) by the tutor Reventlow, who referred to the tiny prince as his 'doll', Christian soon learned that nobody would listen to his tears. He therefore cultivated an image of spurious manliness that took the most bizarre forms. With a gang of fellow-minded boys he stalked the streets of Copenhagen, armed with a spiked medieval club, which he used to vicious effect on passers-by. He masturbated so obsessively that his doctors feared for his health and felt that there was no alternative but for him to marry early. His pranks were beginning to take on a darker hue when in 1766, at the age of just seventeen, he ascended the throne.

His marriage to Caroline Mathilda, daughter of 'Poor Fred' the Prince of Wales and sister of King George III of Great Britain, was just another of the disastrous misalliances that pepper royal history. Frankly Caroline Mathilda was too delicate and refined for so rustic a court as that of Denmark. When Christian saw a painting of his new wife he had it hung in the royal privy. No sooner had Caroline Mathilda arrived at the Danish court, deprived of all her English ladies-in-waiting, than both the King and his courtiers expressed the view that she was far too good-looking. Christian made it publicly known that he could not love her as it was unfashionable to love your wife. Caroline Mathilda would have done well to pack her bags straight-away. However, she tried to love her husband and, remarkably in view of Christian's known predilection for whores or boys, she eventually became pregnant.

Fatherhood did not help Christian settle down, however. He was neither mature enough to marry nor indeed even to be let out alone. He was suffering from severe schizophrenia. Diplomats complained of his extraordinary tendency to be discussing affairs of state at one moment and then without warning to slap them violently round the face. On one occasion he rose from the dining table and addressed one of his courtiers, Count Enevold Brandt, with the words, 'I am going to thrash you, Count, do you hear me?' An astonished Brandt later challenged the King to a duel, whereupon Christian agreed to a fist-fight. The much heavier Brandt promptly knocked the King down, 'battered him without pity, wrestled with him and reduced him to asking for quarter'. The Queen, when she heard, thoroughly approved of what had happened.

Free of the restraining influence of his tutors Christian decided either to 'paint the town red' or demolish it in the process. With a gang of friends including Count Conrad Holcke and a whore named Anna Catherine Benthagen, better known as 'Catherine-of-the gaiters' – whom he made a baroness and who went around in the uniform of a naval officer – Christian rampaged round the streets of Copenhagen, smashing up shops and destroying brothels. He frequently returned to the palace with black eyes and cuts and bruises. One night two watchmen caught the King jumping out of a downstairs window of a brothel and creating a disturbance. Feigning ignorance of his identity they gave him a thrashing. Shrieking that he was their King, Christian was told, 'How dare you tell us you are the King, you lying, mean-looking lout.' Public anger reached such a pitch that Christian was plainly told either to dismiss 'Catherine-of-the-gaiters' or face being overthrown. A coward at heart, he exiled Catherine to Hamburg, where she ended her days in a common gaol.

Christian had a strong streak of sado-masochism. He enjoyed public executions and often took on the persona of those he had seen die. He staged mock executions of his courtiers and built his own rack. Holcke was ordered to stretch him on it or flog him until his back was bleeding. On other occasions, to demonstrate his manliness, he would charge at walls

King Christian VII of Denmark and Norway, known as the 'northern scamp'. His mental disturbance – which destabilized his kingdom and nearly led to a ruinous war with England – may have had its roots in the brutal treatment he received at the hands of his tutor. (P)

and butt them with his head, or burn his flesh with firewood and rub salt into his wounds. Sometimes he went out bare-chested into the snow and rubbed it on to his skin to demonstrate his imperviousness to pain.

Bored with his English wife and having stirred up a hornets' nest in his own backyard, in 1768 he decided – uninvited – to visit England. He refused to take Caroline with him, however, and took some of his fellow-roisterers instead. On being welcomed as he entered the city of Canterbury he boastfully replied, 'The last king of Denmark who entered Canterbury laid that city in ashes and massacred its inhabitants.' Diplomatic laughter from his followers covered their King's gaffe. King George III was singularly unimpressed when he met him, regarding him as the sort of gnome or goblin one read of in Scandinavian folktales. Londoners seemed to love the mad Dane, cheering him wherever he went, but in courtly circles his behaviour was viewed as quite appalling. Lady Coke observed him picking his nose at the opera, 'which you know is neither graceful nor royal'. It is as well that the good lady was well tucked up in her bed later that evening, for after midnight Christian and his fellows went on the prowl. Disguised as sailors, the randy Danes explored London low-life, taking a prostitute back with them to their apartments in St James's Palace. Not content with that, they smashed up the furniture and threw it out of the windows. Despite Christian's success with the British public, King George was only too pleased to see the back of him.

On his return to Copenhagen he found that Queen Caroline had undergone a metamorphosis. The pretty, powdered doll whom Christian had found so unstimulating had transformed herself into a horsey 'point-to-pointer', who rode astride, dressed in breeches and aped men's behaviour. It was Caroline Mathilda's last attempt to win her husband's love and for a while Christian enjoyed it. When he and Caroline Mathilda were seen walking together, the current joke in Copenhagen was that she was the better man of the two. But it could not last and Christian soon returned to his previous ways. Frustrated and lonely, the Queen looked for consolation, and found it with one Count Struensee.

The visit to England had been the making of the king's physician, Johann Friedrich Struensee, as tall and handsome as the king was short and weedy. Struensee was unconventional – he read by the light of two candles held in the hands of a skeleton – and egotistical. Christian's decision to appoint him his chief minister was a fateful decision for all concerned. The ambitious Struensee saw the chance to take from the King not only his control of the country but his wife as well. Caroline Mathilda, trapped in a loveless marriage, was only too willing to accept his advances.

Christian's madness, meanwhile, was getting worse. His schizophrenia became so extreme that he often lost contact with reality. One day he would claim to be the son of Catherine the Great, next the son of his own wife or the King of Sardinia or a number of French or English noblemen. To reassure himself of his masculinity he would pinch his skin and pummel his body until he was numb, then order his friends to beat him with whips. Sometimes he would run from room to room in the palace destroying all the furniture or throwing it through the windows. Then he would detach whole window frames and send them spinning into space.

On one occasion at dinner, Christian decided to announce a new appointment to his council. His favourite dog, Gourmand, was lying at the King's

feet quietly dreaming of canine paradise when suddenly he felt the king's boot in his ribs. He let out a startled yelp. 'Can you bark, Gourmand?' asked the King, kicking him again. Gourmand duly obliged with some more yelps. Christian was delighted. 'My dear Gourmand,' he said to the dog, 'you have shown me you can bark, so you shall be made one of my councillors.' He then turned to his fellow diners, who included Queen Caroline Mathilda and Count Struensee, and proposed a toast to 'Mr Councillor Gourmand', ordering Struensee to arrange for the dog's salary to be paid from the Treasury.

The next day Christian was presented with a document for the appointment of a new chamberlain. He knew the man being proposed and disliked him, but he felt obliged to approve the appointment. Suddenly he noticed one of his servants, a filthy menial, cleaning his stove. 'Would you like to be chamberlain?' he asked the man. Shocked, the stove cleaner mumbled that it was the king's decision. 'Quite right,' said Christian, 'you shall be my new royal chamberlain.' He led the man, sooty as he was from his work in the chimney, into the great hall of the Christiansborg Palace, where he introduced him to all his courtiers and to the foreign ambassadors. Although it raised a few titters at the time, this arbitrary appointment marked a turning point in Christian's relations with his people. They had been prepared to tolerate a 'scamp' – even an outrageous one – but they could not countenance the idea of being governed by a raving lunatic. Struensee, unknown to the King, visited the sooty chamberlain and bought back the title in return for a cash sum and a small estate outside Copenhagen.

Caroline Mathilda was by now involved in an affair with Struensee. Everyone in Denmark seemed to know about it except the King. When the Queen gave birth to a daughter in July 1771 Christian was in a minority of one in believing that he was the father. At court there was a strong feeling that Denmark could not continue to be ruled by a parvenu like Struensee who was openly cuckolding the King. In January 1772 a group of rebels led by the Dowager Queen presented Christian with a document authorizing the arrest of Struensee and the indictment of the Queen on a charge of treason and adultery. Christian signed it, though how willing he was or even how aware he was of what he was doing is open to doubt. Struensee was imprisoned and later executed by disembowelment and decapitation, while Caroline Mathilda and her new daughter were confined in some discomfort in the castle of Kronborg. Many Danes wanted the Queen to follow her lover to the block, but the Danish court eventually satisfied itself with formally terminating the royal marriage and sentencing Caroline Mathilda to life imprisonment.

At this stage Christian was suddenly confronted with the consequences of his grossly irresponsible actions. By divorcing and dishonouring his wife, a British princess and the sister of King George III, he had plunged his country into a dangerous diplomatic dispute with the greatest seapower in the world. Shocked as many Britons had been at news of Caroline Mathilda's adultery with Struensee, everyone knew how much she had suffered at the hands of the unbalanced Danish King. George III had no wish for his sister to return to England, but he could not stand by and watch her ill-treated by foreigners. The British ambassador, Sir Robert Keith, pre-empted his government by formally warning the Danes that if the ex-Queen, as a British subject, should have 'a hair of her head touched' then the Royal Navy would lay waste to Copenhagen. Keith knew he was taking a big risk if he was not backed up by London. Nevertheless, his dramatic declaration frightened the Danes, who moved

Caroline Mathilda to more comfortable quarters. A whole month passed before Keith got a reply from George III. It was in the shape of a small parcel. As he opened it with some trepidation, the Order of the Bath fell at his feet. Triumphantly Keith donned the decoration and demanded to see the king. Christian was nowhere to be found, but the Danish courtiers soon learned of the British response. In the letter King George had sent was a chilling message. Either Caroline was released immediately into Keith's hands or else the ambassador was to declare war on Denmark forthwith. Ten ships of the Royal Navy were already heading for the Baltic.

Caroline got her freedom but she did not live long to enjoy it. She died in May 1775 – at the age of just twenty-four – in the castle of Celle in Hanover. Although Christian lived for another thirty years, he ruled in name only. He lived in seclusion, his mind completely unhinged. He was treated as an idiot and servants were instructed not to obey his orders. Sometimes he could be seen at windows making faces at passers-by or marching up and down like a clockwork soldier. But for most of the time he was sunk in the confusion of multi-identity. Ironically the son that Caroline Mathilda had borne him lived to become Frederick VI, one of Denmark's better kings.

BUILDING CASTLES IN THE AIR: LUDWIG II OF BAVARIA

Like some great movement in the arts, European royal insanity, which had produced such horrors as Ivan the Terrible and Don Carlos of Spain, reached its splendid apogee in the person of Ludwig II of Bavaria, the 'Swan King', known to composer Richard Wagner as Parsifal, the 'pure knight', and to his fellow-spirit, Elizabeth of Austria, as 'Cloud climber'. Ludwig made madness into an art form, from which like Prospero he conjured spirits in the air. These spirits were castles of such miniature perfection that it was as if they had been built by a younger, purer race than man. Prussian ogres like Bismarck and Moltke may have shaken the world about them but they never quite found the key to Ludwig's secret world.

As a Wittelsbach, Ludwig was surrounded by

relations who were either mad or deeply disturbed. Even his mother, Queen Marie, herself a Prussian and not directly tainted, probably suffered from porphyria and was odd enough to suggest that the poetry books of the world should be reprinted with the word 'love' replaced by 'friendship'. Ludwig's father, King Maximilian, was also apparently free of madness – that is if starving, beating and humiliating one's sons is construed as normal parental behaviour. Maximilian, whose sister was profoundly insane, felt that both his sons, Ludwig and the younger Otto, were too soft. When they told him that they both heard 'voices', he believed that a piece of black bread and a swim in the icy lake would soon cure them of that sort of thing. Maximilian liked beating his boys, taking over from their tutors when they

Schloss Neuschwanstein in Bavaria, King Ludwig II's fairy-tale castle made real. Ludwig's mania for building fantastic castles may have exhausted the coffers of the Bavarian state, but it has bequeathed a happy legacy of unforgettable tourist attractions. (PN)

got tired. He believed in Spartan values – which may account for Ludwig's latent homosexuality – and made them both rise early, eat frugally, exercise hard, and take cold showers. When Ludwig became affectionately attached to a tortoise the animal was removed from the boy's presence. The boys were kept so short of rations that they sometimes begged for scraps from the servants. Ludwig once tried to sell one of his teeth to a Munich dentist so that he could buy something to eat.

When Ludwig ascended the throne, at the age of eighteen, after the premature death of his father in 1864, everything changed. He was a young man of extraordinary beauty – tall, athletic and with hair and complexion that matched that of his cousin, Elizabeth of Austria. They were regarded as the two most beautiful people of their time. But Ludwig, aware though he was of his physical qualities, was not as narcissistic as Elizabeth. If there was one love in his life it was the world conjured up by the romantic and nationalist operas of Richard Wagner. They drove him to a frenzy in which he empathized totally with the mythical heroes of old, like Lohengrin and Tannhäuser.

However, during the 1860s German nationalism was on the move. The *Zollverein* (customs union) now bound the separate German states together in its economic web and Otto von Bismarck was striving for a political unification. However, Ludwig was comically out of step with militant German nationalism. While Bavarian peasants tilled the soil as they had for generations, and paid their taxes, and while his ministers viewed their borders fearfully as the storm of battle broke over neighbouring Austria in 1866, Ludwig dressed in silver armour and paddled round a lake in a boat shaped like a swan. While the Bavarian state treasury was raided so frequently that it suffered withdrawal symptoms, Ludwig sat on a peacock throne and planned to turn his kingdom into a theme park. Euro Disney had come to Bavaria a hundred years early.

Ludwig seemed to understand nothing but excess. Yet, in spite of the essentially *kitsch* nature of many of his designs, the imagination that went into the creation of his numerous castles and palaces was truly astounding. The west wing of his residence in Munich exhausts Roget's Thesaurus in its Amazonian variety. There were trees of all kinds, and plants and flowers in profusion, watered by little waterfalls and hanging in bowers under a glass roof that stretched the length of the entire garden. Ludwig's artificial forest teemed with wildlife; gazelles and peacocks passed each other in little glades, while from a golden trapeze a parrot swung, calling 'Guten Abend' to passers-by. At one end of the garden there was a Turkish kiosk in blue and a perfect, miniature Indian village. The wall of the palace nearest the garden was covered in painted views of the Himalayas, with snow-tipped mountains rising into an azure sky. Ludwig had forgotten nothing. Above the snow were clouds tipped with gold and an artificial rainbow.

Beyond this amazing garden stood the lake, its waters stained the deepest blue. It was Ludwig's imposition of art on life. At night the whole area was hung with lanterns, and the little wooden bridges that linked the separate parts of the lake were drenched with the scent of violets. It was here that Ludwig loved to play the Wagnerian role of Lohengrin, with mechanical swans swimming by him as he stood by the lakeside in his silver armour, while minstrels in medieval costume serenaded him.

Ludwig shared his world with just one man – Richard Wagner – the only man who could really appreciate his bizarre genius and for whom Ludwig had an admiration akin to worship. A genius but a poor one, Wagner could not afford to set himself above the world of ordinary people. He needed money and Ludwig had it. This created an even stronger bond than their kinship of spirit. Ludwig's patronage enabled Wagner's music to reach a wider audience and thus the world's debt to the crazy King is a great one. In return for his money Wagner gave Ludwig the chance to join with him in the act of creation. Childless he might have been but Ludwig saw each Wagner opera as his own foster-child. He learned all Wagner's librettos by heart.

Ludwig's highly aesthetic and spiritual world was occasionally disturbed by intrusions from the real world outside. One such ended in fiasco, though it is doubtful if the severe young king found it funny. Dressed in his silver armour, Ludwig was walking by the lakeside with Wagner when one of the composer's prima donnas, Josephine Scheffzky,

began singing from a nearby clump of bushes. Ludwig was about to set sail in his 'swan boat' and he invited Josephine to join him and Wagner on the trip. The boat was operated by foot paddles and they were making good progress when suddenly Josephine made an unfortunate error. Unaware that Ludwig was not amenable to the physical attentions of young women, she ran her fingers through the King's curls only to be pushed away with such force that the swan took a dive and the boat tipped over, throwing all three of them into the water. In spite of the weight of his armour Ludwig stood up in the lake and waded towards the bank without looking back, leaving it to Wagner to fish out his 'mermaid', who was spluttering about in the mud and screeching imprecations of an unregal kind.

Besides his obsession with Wagner's music, Ludwig loved to design and build castles in the antique style. In 1869 he began work on the fairyland castle to top the lot – Neuschwanstein. If the exterior appears to owe its inspiration to a combination of the Grimm brothers and Walt Disney, the interior – with its walls of marble and gold leaf and wood carvings, which had kept seventeen carvers busy for four years – was genuine Ludwig. Nor could the physical setting have been improved. Whatever blunders the 'Swan King' may have perpetrated in his reign, millions of modern Bavarians live better lives for the tourist income that floods in yearly as a result of Ludwig's miraculous follies.

Ludwig's creations were a *pot-pourri* of architectural styles. If Neuschwanstein was nineteenth-century Gothic, with a Romanesque interior, particularly the astonishing throne room with its vast gilded candelabra, Linderhof was closer to rococo, and was constructed as an act of homage to the king he admired most – Louis XIV, *le Roi Soleil*. Inside the dining-room there was an astonishing dining-table which was lowered through the floor and then raised again at the beginning of the next course. Tragically, Ludwig never put it to any use as he never invited anybody to dinner. This fantastic palace was unique in that it possessed just one bedroom. The architect-king was little better than a recluse and grew more so as each year passed. The grounds of the palace were truly bizarre, as they were filled not with the wonders of the animal world but of science: mechanical automatons of birds and beasts, made of bronze and glass, wandered about the lawns. Beyond the lawn was Ludwig's

Ludwig II as Lohengrin, the legendary knight of the Holy Grail immortalized by Wagner's opera of the same name. Ludwig was a generous patron to the composer, his enthusiasm for Wagner's music being such that his castles in Bavaria included interiors based on images from Lohengrin. *(ME)*

secret grotto, which could only be entered by uttering the secret password. Ludwig has sometimes been called the 'Moon King' in contrast with Louis XIV. At the castle of Hohenschwangau he ordered his architect Pfistermeister to install an artificial moon and rainbow in his bedroom, in place of conventional lights. The ceiling of his room was painted with orange trees against a blue sky and a fountain played within the room to provide hazy lighting effects as of moonlight and starlight. Unfortunately, wondrous as this all sounds, the fountain once malfunctioned, causing rain to fall on to the head of an elderly guest in a room directly below the King's.

Ludwig behaved as if he were the man who had everything or at least could have everything, but the fantastic costs of all these buildings were, in fact, borne by the Bavarian taxpayers, who began to enquire as to the use to which their taxes were being put. But Bavaria was no democracy and Ludwig continued to rule the kingdom as if it was his personal property.

Far more ominous, however, was the extent to which Ludwig was collapsing into severe mental illness. His eccentricities, amusing at the outset,

became more worrying. He rarely left his palace and was hardly ever seen by his people. Instead, he took on the form of some legendary character who lived high up in a castle and only appeared at night to terrify anyone unwise enough to be out late. His nocturnal sleighrides became the stuff of fairy tales. With a huge fur coat wrapped around him, Ludwig would ride out into the countryside in a huge golden sleigh, with a gilt mast capped by a crown, all wrapped around by climbing gilt cherubs, and pulled by four horses. Illuminated by its great lanterns, the sleigh was an astounding sight, and must have confirmed to the more superstitious villagers the existence of troll kings. The grooms and outriders who accompanied him were all dressed in the costumes of Louis XIV's time. Indeed, as his mind weakened, Ludwig frequently behaved as if he was dining with the French kings of the *ancien régime*, and addressed his servants as if they were Louis XIV or Louis XV.

Rather than travel far from home Ludwig preferred to make nocturnal rides which, to his disturbed mind, represented actual journeys to his chosen destination. Thus, for instance, instead of travelling the actual distance to Innsbruck in Austria, he would calculate it and then work out how many laps of his riding stable he would have to complete before he could claim to have reached journey's end. He would order his grooms to provide fresh horses and then mount his steed, riding round and round and round, until, sometime in the middle of the night he arrived. He would then dismount and retire to bed.

On rare occasions he was forced to hold state receptions for visiting dignitaries and for these he took the fairly conventional precaution of becoming so drunk beforehand – drinking at least ten glasses of champagne – that he knew nothing of what occurred either during the evening or afterwards. Once he ordered a gigantic spread of flowers to be displayed and then spent part of the evening hiding inside it, while on another occasion he ordered his band to play so loud that all conversation was drowned out.

Ludwig rarely entertained anyone to dinner. In fact, his most famous dinner guest was his horse named Cosa Rava, who enjoyed the various courses offered up rather less than breaking the dinner service with her hooves. Ludwig was not annoyed at her behaviour, observing that at least horses could be trusted not to tell lies.

Ludwig was squandering the resources of his kingdom and dragging Bavaria to the brink of bankruptcy. The rulers of other German states saw him simply as a lunatic, who should be deposed and put under restraint. By 1880 Bavaria was facing debts of close to ten million marks, but Ludwig was still demanding more – at least twenty million marks to build a new castle with jewel-encrusted walls. But his ministers were proving obstructionist. They believed that he had played with his toys long enough and it was time for him to stop. Ludwig was first hurt at this treachery and then infuriated. He threatened to leave Bavaria for ever and take his skills elsewhere. When this failed to elicit the right response he began trying to raise loans to pay off his debts and fund new projects. He tried to raise loans with his fellow-sovereigns in Europe, but they all cited 'cash-flow problems' at the crucial moment and had to decline. Neither the Emperor of Brazil nor the Sultan of Turkey would oblige and so Ludwig now devised a daring – and crazy – scheme to rob banks throughout Germany, leading a team of Italian bandits and desperadoes. They also planned to kidnap the Crown Prince of Prussia, keep him in chains and hold him to ransom.

His nocturnal rides became ever more fantastic. Innsbruck was no longer adequate and his servants scoured the world for suitable destinations, both real – like Samothrace or Afghanistan – and imaginary, like Shangri-la. Once he had completed these epic rides he would dismount and spend some time in contemplation.

Ludwig's mind was in hyperdrive by the time his ministers decided that His Majesty was barking mad and had better be stopped. They appointed a commission to inquire into the King's state of mind, intending to depose him if the evidence showed that he was insane. Unfortunately, there was no possibility of offering the throne to his brother Otto, who was already confined in the royal castle of Furstenreid, where he lived until his death in 1916. Even Ludwig found Otto's state pitiful, saying: 'In some respects he is more excitable and nervous than Aunt Alexandra, and that is saying a great deal. He often does not go to bed for forty-eight hours. He did not take off his boots for eight weeks, behaves like a madman, makes terrible faces, barks like a dog, and at times says the most indecorous things.'

The overthrow of the 'Swan King' contained elements of both tragedy and farce. By 1884 the King whose stunning good looks had caused by-standers to liken him to a Greek god wore an increasingly ravaged look. Paranoia gripped him and he was plainly insane. Servants heard him talking to imaginary guests at his dining table, laughing uproariously. In snowy weather Ludwig would insist that he wished to dine *al fresco*, complaining to the servants of the heat of the sun. He often related his dreams, one of which was that he had cracked his mother on the head with a water-jug and then stamped on her, and another that he had pulled his father out of his coffin and boxed his ears. In his extremity the root of much of his madness became clear. He also ordered the stage machinist from the Bayreuth Opera House to build him a flying-machine so that he could travel over the Alps, and he sent a man to Capri on three separate occasions to check if the water of the Blue Grotto was still blue.

What Ludwig felt to be mere eccentricity others interpreted as terminal insanity, as when he ordered Munich to be burned to the ground, or told one of his guards to establish absolute rule in Bavaria, or when he took to crawling on all fours with his head on the ground in the style of a Chinese *kiao tow*.

But his financial extravagances were seen as his most serious crime, and for these he was condemned. The Head of the Commission to inquire into his mental health, Dr Bernard von Gudden, now announced that the King was insane and should be forced to abdicate. The Bavarian Minister President sent troops to Neuschwanstein, but when the news broke a group of loyal peasants drove off the commissioners and saved the King. But the next attempt to capture Ludwig was more determined and he was taken a prisoner to the castle of Schloss Berg, at the head of the Starnbergersee. On the evening of 12 June 1866 Dr von Gudden walked with King Ludwig around the shores of the lake. They were never seen alive again. What happened remains a mystery, but the two men's bodies were fished out of shallow water the next day. The doctor had been a slight man and Ludwig, though he had put on much weight, was still powerful and muscular. Only two interpretations are possible. Either the King murdered von Gudden and then drowned himself or the two men drowned after a struggle. In either case it is clear that Ludwig wished to end his own life. Whether he saw his 'swan boat' coming to bear him away and drowned reaching out for it we cannot know, but it would have been a fitting end for this beautiful but tormented man.

CHAPTER 2: POMP AND CEREMONY

Coronations

A coronation represents a moment of the greatest significance for the monarch and the nation. In the great cathedral or church, surrounded by their peers, and with masses of people cheering in the streets outside, the moment that the crown, often centuries old and of immeasurable value, is placed upon the new sovereign's head by the senior religious figure of the realm is an emotional, even a spiritual one, when the monarch can truly believe that he or she has been chosen to rule by God's will. Yet, as with other royal events, coronations have sometimes been the source of unintentional farce.

The best-laid schemes of mice and men, and Earl Marshals, can go wrong. At the coronation of King George I, for example, the Deputy Earl Marshal, Lord Effingham, responsible for the planning of the great event, had to admit that not everything had gone as expected. He apologized to the new King: 'It is true, Sir, that there has been some neglect; but I have taken care that the next coronation shall be regulated in the exactest manner possible.' It is doubtful if King George I was amused. In the first place he hardly spoke a word of English and in the second place he was a military martinet, who would have preferred to stand Effingham against a wall and blow his head off.

A challenging situation

The role of the King's Champion in England was held as a hereditary right by the Dymoke family, to whom it had been given by William the Conqueror. At the banquet that followed each coronation it was the task of the champion to challenge anyone present to contest the right of the new sovereign to wear the crown. It was unheard of for the challenge to be taken up, but, oddly, as late as William III and Mary's coronation in 1689, the champion's gauge or gauntlet was picked up by an old lady on crutches. Champion Dymoke assumed that it was a hoax and refused to accept battle to the death against the wizened old crone. Strictly speaking, therefore, the two monarchs were successfully challenged and should have forfeited their crowns. All in all, it was a thoroughly bad day for William. According to tradition, he was supposed to make an offering to the people of a pound of gold. As he felt for his purse he discovered that it had been stolen, and he had to borrow twenty guineas from Lord Danby.

Following the coronation of Charles I in 1625, the Champion suffered a mishap, possibly occasioned by too much drink. He rode into the great hall, bellowed his challenge, threw down his gauntlet and promptly fell off his horse. At the coronation of King George III in 1760, the King's Champion rode the horse that George II had ridden at the battle of Dettingen in 1743. This hardly reflected well on either the late king or his mount as the animal had a predilection for retreating rather than advancing and insisted on entering the banqueting hall backwards.

Horse play

The festivities accompanying the coronation of Edward I in 1272 lasted for a fortnight. The consumption of food was truly astronomical, involving 380 head of cattle, 430 sheep, 450 pigs, 18 wild boar and twenty thousand fowl. Hearing that a 'good feed' was on offer, King Alexander of Scotland rode to the coronation with a hundred of his knights. As the knights dismounted to pay homage to King Edward I, their horses were stolen by people in the crowd. In case it is assumed that coronation mishaps occur only in England, one has only to turn to Denmark to find other examples. At the crowning of Frederick IV in 1699, the King's favourite hound, fearing that the bishop was mistreating his master, broke loose and attacked him and would not let him approach the King with the crown.

William Hickey's column

The best seats at coronations in Hanoverian times cost some fifty guineas to hire. At the crowning of George III in 1760, the diarist William Hickey had forked out for a seat at the top of one of the great columns, overlooking the assembled multitude. Hickey, having paid out so much, felt that his family should enjoy themselves, and had brought a picnic into Westminster Abbey with him. Without further ado Hickey and his wife and children set to work demolishing cold veal, ham, tongue, meat pies, wines and liqueurs, served up by two servants. As the archbishop embarked on his sermon, Hickey's horde tucked into their desserts. The noise of people eating, with the clattering of knives and forks, plates and glasses, interrupted the service below. As the worthy divine looked up to see the cause of the noise the diners burst into laughter and waved their wine glasses at him.

Food riots

Coronations in Russia had a markedly more serious character. The day following the coronation of Tsar Nicholas II and his Tsarina, Alexandra, was by tradition set aside for a great public event – a huge, open-air feast held in fields outside St Petersburg, which the new sovereigns attended. However, by daybreak over half a million citizens had assembled in the fields, many of them already drunk. When the wagons bearing food and drink arrived from the city and set up behind a thin wooden palisade, a rumour suddenly spread about that there were many fewer wagons than expected and that there would not be enough food or drink for everyone. The single squadron of Cossacks in place to control the crowds was swept aside as the masses began to charge towards the wagons, afraid to miss out on a feed. First hundreds and then thousands of people tripped and fell and were crushed by the relentless horde behind them. By the time police and more soldiers arrived, multitudes of bodies were being passed overhead to the back of the crowd. Nobody knows how many thousands of people died in the catastrophe, but the Tsar and Tsarina spent all that day visiting hospitals and talking to the wounded.

The Tsar's first instinct was to cancel that evening's grand reception at the French embassy, but his uncles intervened, advising him that the French had gone to enormous expense to stage the event, bringing priceless tapestries and treasures from Paris to honour the Tsar's coronation, as well as a hundred thousand roses from the south of France. Tsar Nicholas took the advice of his uncles and attended the ball. This aroused the anger of the people who believed the Tsar cared little for their suffering. It was a royal blunder that did much to turn the Russian people against their new Tsar and his German wife (see also pp. 4–11).

The Emperor's new clothes

Central Africa was hardly the venue one would have expected to host the social event of the year in 1977. Thousands of guests from all parts of the world came to Bangui, capital of the Central African Empire (aka the Central African Republic) to pay their respects to the Emperor Bokassa I on the occasion of his coronation. Anyone present with a sense of history would have noted similarities between the event and the coronation of the French Emperor Napoleon I in 1804.

Like Napoleon the Emperor Bokassa was a short man, but there the similarities ended. Certainly he was as grandly dressed as his distinguished model, wearing an ankle-length velvet tunic and shoes of pearl. His mantle was embroidered with gold bees in exactly the style that had been prepared for Napoleon. Behind him trailed a 30-foot, crimson velvet, ermine-trimmed mantle weighing over 70 pounds. The cost of this single garment had been astronomical. By his side he wore a jewel-encrusted, golden-hilted sword and he carried an ebony staff of office. His crown was an exact replica of that worn by Napoleon, which was fronted by a French Imperial Eagle. The throne upon which he placed his stately posterior was trimmed with gold and over it hung a vast golden eagle, shading himself and the Empress Catherine (lately of a peasant village somewhere near the Zaire River). The Emperor's progress to the church – renamed Notre Dame de Bangui for the occasion – had been by a golden coach drawn by eight imported Normandy horses, all of the purest white. (Six other horses perished in the unbearable heat.)

Every European political leader and monarch had been invited as well as rulers from throughout Africa. Bokassa had spent hours studying a video of Queen Elizabeth II's coronation to see how things were done. Many of those invited had diplomatically discovered prior engagements. The British, however, refused to attend the coronation of the self-proclaimed 'Emperor' and the Americans replied by cutting off all aid to Bokassa's country. Nevertheless, many dignitaries had attended, particularly from France, which had seen fit to indulge the dictator with a further grant of $2.5 million to buy powdered wigs for his flunkies.

Once the magnificent ceremony was concluded, Bokassa addressed his people, promising to continue the democratic evolution of his 'empire'. Then it was time to tuck in. While starvation and malnutrition ravaged the people of the Central African Empire 4,000 guests enjoyed a French-style banquet, while bands of liveried players offered up renderings of French classical music. In all a third of the entire national income of the country was frittered away on this single event. As a gesture of goodwill for his coronation Bokassa had 'fattened up' a number of political prisoners who, it has been claimed, were themselves served up at the banquet in the 'Boeuf Bourguignonne'.

When, little more than twelve months later, the blood-crazed maniac who had occupied centre stage at this coronation was overthrown, he was sentenced to death in

The emperor Jean Bedel Bokassa on his coronation day, 12 April 1977. Behind the splendour of his two-ton gilded throne and coronation robes Bokassa was a blood-crazed maniac who visited unspeakable atrocities on the people of the Central African Republic. (P)

his absence for uncounted murders. But in one way he was unique. As far as history records he is the only ruler to have been tried and convicted of cannibalism.

Royal Weddings

Throughout history most royal marriages have been 'arranged' ones – often when the young couple were very young and sometimes even before they had been born – and usually they served a diplomatic purpose, in helping to cement alliances between states. The celebration of the nuptials was therefore of far greater importance than the mere marriage of two individuals. As a result, royal weddings were not only the pre-eminent social events of their time but also of surpassing diplomatic importance. So much was riding on the success of these occasions that it is hardly surprising that so many royal weddings were accompanied by mishaps ranging from minor slips of the tongue – as when Princess Diana at her wedding in 1981 promised to obey Prince Philip as her husband rather than Prince Charles, her intended, or when Charles, in return, promised to share Diana's worldly goods with her, instead of his own – to full-scale assassination attempts as during the 'blood wedding', described below.

A wedding and more funerals

The wedding of Prince Henry and the Infanta Blanca of Navarre – mere children at fifteen – at Valladolid in Castile in 1440, was one of history's most unfortunate. What should have been the happiest day of their young lives was turned into a fiasco by the antics of their relatives.

Blanca and her mother were welcomed to Valladolid with a great tournament, which was supposed to set an appropriately festive note. However, it only added to the air of gloom which descended on the young couple. Staged by the major-domo Ruy Diaz de Mendoza, the tournament for some obscure reason was fought with combat lances, and the jousts took on a ferocity that was quite inappropriate to the occasion. As Blanca sat down in the place of honour reserved for her, she witnessed instead of a riot of coloured pennants and heraldic devices an orgy of death and mutilation. One knight from Toro had his skull split open with a lance through the visor and expired in a welter of blood. Another knight had his arm torn off, while the Count of Castro was carried screaming from the field with a lance head through his pelvis. By the time the Admiral's brother had his arm snapped in two, Blanca was feeling distinctly queasy and Henry's father, King Juan II of Castile, had to cancel the rest of the event.

While this was happening, one Sancho de Reynoso decided to settle old scores by kidnapping his stepfather from the wedding party and holding him to ransom. The King, temporarily forgetting the reason for the general assembly in his capital, ordered the bridegroom to ride after Sancho and demand the release of his captive. Removing his festive garb and donning his armour, Henry set out on his mission. He reached the castle and demanded entry but the gate was slammed in his face. Next he shouted, not very effectively, that he was on the King's business. Sancho briefly appeared on the battlements, poured a torrent of vile abuse on the young bridegroom, and then retired.

Henry was left waiting at the gate and eventually returned, humiliated, to the King. His father next sent a more formidable negotiator, who carried with him an assurance that the King would pardon Sancho if he returned his prisoner. Sancho duly released the captive, whereupon the King ordered his execution. While the final wedding preparations were being made, Sancho was beheaded in the main square of Valladolid. It was turning out to be a more interesting wedding than usual for the local undertaker.

By this stage Blanca must have been wondering what she had let herself in for. And now on top of a tournament more akin to some bloody spectacular from *El Cid*, a kidnapping and a public execution, the guests began to drop like flies. Nobles, courtiers and churchmen mysteriously died as if they had all been poisoned. Soon the joy of wedding festivities had been replaced by formal court mourning. The wedding banquets were cancelled and the guests decked themselves out in black. But the wedding still went ahead. The ceremonies were reduced to the bare essentials, though we are reliably informed that for his wedding Henry had consented to bathe himself – a practice with which he was apparently 'unfamiliar'.

After the church ceremony, a dismal affair akin to a funeral, the guests held a discreet family dinner. But even this turned out badly. Prince Henry never drank wine and sat gloomily drinking cups of water, the very picture of melancholy. The roasted meats left King Juan singularly unimpressed as he was a vegetarian. There was also a 'ghost at the feast' in the person of the aged Infanta Beatriz of Portugal who had turned up unexpectedly and whom nobody knew.

Finally it was time for the young couple to be bedded. In medieval and indeed later weddings this was the central point of the day's activities. Outside the bridal chamber stood a pair of heralds armed with trumpets. The moment the bloodstained bedsheets – proof that the marriage had been consummated – were passed out, they blew a fanfare. Inside the room stood three notaries who were required by law to witness – either visually or aurally – the moment that the prince penetrated his bride, thereby confirming her virginity. Blanca was undressed and brought to the marriage bed by her ladies, who then retired, leaving her to await her husband. Henry duly entered the bridal chamber, climbed into bed and nervously pulled the curtains around the four-poster. The notaries sharpened their nibs and everyone began to concentrate.

Moments passed, then minutes, then hours. The notaries strained their ears and their necks, and their backs. They sat down upon a hard wooden seat. It was cold and gloomy and very, very quiet. Nothing seemed to be happening within Blanca's virginal fortress. Outside the bridal chamber Henry's father paced up and down, eagerly awaiting the signal to let the trumpets sound. Had he been able to see what was happening behind the curtains he would have screamed and torn his beard out by the roots. The young couple were asleep. As the notaries later reported, 'The Princess remained exactly as she had been born.' Henry had failed in his prime function: there would be no stained sheets – the prince had earned his soubriquet of Henry 'the Impotent' (see also p. 75).

'Poor Fred' takes the plunge

The wedding of 'Poor Fred' – Frederick Louis, Prince of Wales – in 1736, was in keeping with much of his life: farcical. It might have been supposed that a father would have taken his son's wedding a little more seriously. However, even a slight acquaintance with Fred's father, George II, would have been enough to put paid to such a thought. Hanoverians, either by nature or tradition, felt an intense loathing for their children, notably their eldest sons. George, for instance, had tried to foist on Fred the Danish princess Charlotte Amelia, a sadly deformed and mentally deficient creature, who would never have been able to bear children. Fortunately Fred stood up to his father and refused. But when it was next suggested that his eldest son should marry Augusta, daughter of the Duke of Saxe-Gotha, George II refused to take 'no' for an answer. He even agreed to make a swift detour from visiting one of his German mistresses in order to inspect the young lady. What he first saw was a tall woman in a voluminous dress, which left almost everything to the imagination. He later saw Augusta in her night clothes, but even these were sufficient to hold at bay all but the most inquiring eyes. He did not insist on investigating the young lady in a more scanty outfit. She was clearly too skinny for his taste, which ran to women of ampler proportions. He concluded that the girl would do for his son, being tall and 'ill made', 'crooked, with a pocky complexion', long arms and an awkward gait. Still, she was presumably made as other women were and would serve to people a palace with 'mewling and puking' brats. Neither George nor his wife, Queen Caroline, had a good word to say for their eldest son. Caroline once observed of Fred, 'The villain! I wish the ground would open up and sink the monster to the lowest level of hell.'

Having inspected the property, King George was eager to see it occupied. The subject of the Prince's marriage was keeping him away from really important matters, like returning to the arms of Madame Walmoden, his current paramour. He told Augusta's father that the marriage must take place before the end of April 1736, or else they should not expect him to attend. The Duke of Saxe-Gotha took George at his word and got his daughter to England by 26 April, carrying a doll and ready for marriage to a man she had never even seen. She landed at Greenwich but none of the royal family bothered to meet her there. King George liked to put his future in-laws in their places right from the start. Augusta spoke not a word of English but had been told by her mother that this would present no problem. The Hanoverians had been on the throne of England for twenty years and she supposed everyone would speak German by now.

The wedding ceremony was due to take place on the evening of 27 April in the Palace Chapel at St James's. It was preceded by a wedding dinner. To humiliate his son, King George decreed that the bride and groom must eat in the nursery with the royal children. Fred took the insult in his stride and ordered his servants to provide armchairs for himself and Augusta and stools for his brothers and sisters. The princesses, seeing what their brother had done, now ordered their servants to remove the stools and bring chairs instead. A minor fracas now ensued, involving the throwing of food by the royal children.

The wedding ceremony passed off without incident, but when the guests and the young couple returned to the royal apartments all the pressures of the day caught up with poor Augusta. As the King gave the newlyweds his blessing she was violently sick. At the wedding supper afterwards, Fred began to behave in an eccentric fashion, gobbling down great quantities of jelly, which he believed to be an aphrodisiac, until his mother felt quite sick to watch him. His ogling of his new wife and his winking at and nudging of the servants was regarded as the height of bad manners. After they had all eaten, the bedding ceremony took place. King George faced what he described as 'the odious task' of preparing his son for bed, while the princesses prepared Augusta. The Queen, convinced that her son was impotent, remarked later that Augusta had looked tired when she went to bed and remarkably refreshed in the morning, which indicated that she had had a good sleep. When the royal couple were ensconced in their bed, the wedding guests were brought in to see them. Fred's nightcap, which was taller than a busby, was a cause of general mirth. And so it was with ribald hoots of laughter in his ears that Fred settled down with his new wife.

Ironically, after such a bad start Fred and Augusta lived happily not quite 'ever after' – for one could not be happy for long at the court of King George II – but for some few months at least. However, when Fred dared to tell his mother that Augusta was pregnant she reacted as if he had told her that she had run off to the Sultan's harem in Constantinople. Queen Caroline simply would not believe it, or at least would not believe that Fred could be the father, and she roundly told him so. And so the wheels were set in motion that were to lead to the 'scandalous' birth of Fred's first child at St James's Palace (see p. 115).

Bertie's big day

The wedding of Edward, Prince of Wales, and Princess Alexandra of Denmark in 1863, took place under the shadow of the recent death of Prince Albert, the groom's father. His mother, Queen Victoria, still in deep mourning and unwilling to show herself to the public, insisted that the wedding should take place in Windsor rather than London and it was solemnized in St George's Chapel. Prior to this, the last royal wedding in Windsor had been held in 1121. One can only hope that it was better organized then than was the case in 1863.

It was always likely to be a difficult occasion. Queen Victoria did not approve of King Frederick VII of Denmark and did not invite him to the wedding. Furthermore, most of Alexandra's other relations were also not invited as the Queen was unwilling to appear pro-Danish at a time when the Schleswig-Holstein dispute threatened to bring about war between Denmark and Prussia, home of her beloved daughter 'Vicky' and son-in-law 'Fritz'.

Although Britain's reputation for staging royal events has been second to none since the First World War, in mid-Victorian times this was not the case. This royal wedding was a botched affair, with much evidence of 'penny-pinching' and lack of royal style and dignity. The arrival in London of the bride and her parents, Prince Christian and his wife, was rendered unimpressive by the shoddy and moth-eaten coaches that were brought out to drive them through the city to Buckingham Palace. The horses that drew the vehicles seemed little better than escapees from the knacker's yard, kitted out for the occasion in tattered and stained trappings, but with no rosettes and no outriders. *The Times* noted sharply that the procession was made up of the 'very dregs' from the Royal Mews at Pimlico. As one observer noted the coaches containing London's aldermen and civic worthies took precedence over the Danes and so many of these vehicles were there that it seemed that they would go on for ever. Sir William Hardman began to believe he was doomed 'to see Common Councilmen for the rest of our days as a punishment for our folly in being among the spectators. It seemed as if an endless ring of these distinguished tradesmen were going round and round St Paul's to jeer and mock our misery.'

But when everyone went down by train to Windsor matters got far worse. The main culprit was the Queen herself, who was intent on reminding everyone that her dear Albert had not been dead long – in fact little more than fifteen months. Before the wedding took place she insisted that Bertie and Alix, as the young couple were popularly known, should go with her to the newly completed mausoleum at Frogmore. The Queen 'opened the shrine and took them in. Alix was much moved.' Victoria held their hands and told them, 'He gives you his blessing!' For her this was a holier moment than the ceremony to come. Whom Albert had joined together let no man put asunder. She later had herself photographed with the young couple and the bust of Albert. It is one of history's most horrible and mawkish wedding photographs, with Victoria and Alix looking longingly at a lump of plaster.

At a party later that day the usually impeccably behaved Crown Princess Vicky made a *faux pas*, drawing everyone's attention to the marriage the previous year of her sister Alice to the Grand Duke of Hesse-Darmstadt. There was an embarrassed silence and the Queen observed, 'That poor unhappy marriage was more like a funeral than a wedding.' Undeterred, Vicky went on to say how much better things were this year and how happy she was to see her brother Bertie getting married. The Queen froze her with a gorgon look, adding that her happiness on this occasion was incomprehensible. 'Will you be able to rejoice,' she said, 'when at every step you will miss the blessed guardian angel, that one calm great being that led all?' Vicky was told by her mother that she must ensure that the wedding festivities were not too festive, that laughter was kept to a minimum and that noise was checked in her presence. The Queen would eat alone and not join the wedding guests, either in the church or at the reception.

Once the guests had assembled in the Chapel the processions began. The numerous participants were obviously under-rehearsed. The Garter knights, instead of processing two by two, scuttled up the aisle like little boys trying to get the best seats. They were followed by a mass of royalty in the shape of Princess Mary of Cambridge. As Lord Granville observed, 'Morally as well as physically the place was not big enough to hold her.' The much-loved Princess Mary contrasted sharply with the unpopular little lady in black who had surreptitiously taken up her position in Catherine of Aragon's closet, overlooking the rest of the guests. Queen Victoria had come to observe but not to be observed. But the truth was that everyone, dare one even suggest her own children as well, was getting a little tired of her obsessive mourning for the lost Albert.

Down below Vicky's darling, the three-year-old Prince William of Prussia – later to be nobody's darling as Kaiser Wilhelm II – was attending his first royal event. He had already blotted his copybook by addressing his grandmother, Queen Victoria, as 'Duck'. Next he had thrown his aunt's muff out of the carriage window on the way to the Chapel and now, sitting between two of his younger uncles, Prince Alfred and Prince Leopold, he was planning to take over the world, at least that small part of it that you can see when you are only three feet tall. He began by biting the legs of the two Englishmen, who had tried to 'encircle' him and keep him from 'his place in the sun'. Next he pulled the Cairngorm (a gemstone) from his tiny dirk and threw it across the stone floor of the Chapel. It made only a tiny sound but one day he would be heard.

According to Lord Clarendon the bridegroom, dressed as a general and wearing the robes of the Garter, looked better than usual, 'more considerable' he thought, with a semi-humorous allusion to Bertie's swelling 'tum-tum'. The bride was late; no more than ten minutes which, in view of her later record for poor timekeeping, constituted a triumphantly early arrival. She looked splendid. But Lord Granville thought the

The marriage of Edward, Prince of Wales and Alexandra of Denmark in St George's Chapel, Windsor, 10 March 1863. Shoddily organized, the event was overshadowed by Queen Victoria's continuing gloom over the recent death of the Prince Consort. (P)

bridesmaids were hideous and much better viewed from the rear. The Archbishop of Canterbury droned on and on about the sanctity of marriage, while Bertie reflected on his already lengthy list of conquests and warmed to the thought of all those still to come. The musicians, tired of the Archbishop's preaching, began tuning up their instruments and drowned him out. To the sounds of the Hallelujah Chorus the newly-weds emerged from the Chapel and set off for their honeymoon at Osborne, on the Isle of Wight. Then it was every man for himself and pandemonium broke out. The planning, if planning there had been, now experienced some hiccups.

As the carriage carrying the young couple drove away the seething crowds in the Windsor streets broke through the police cordon. Dozens of Eton schoolboys, released from their studies for the day, raced after the honeymooners. One of the boys involved was the young Randolph Churchill, father of Winston, who recalled the event as 'a second Balaclava'. The police tried to stop the boys but were knocked down. When some genteel ladies told them they should know better, Churchill snapped his fingers in their faces and shouted 'What larks!'

The royal train got away safely, but the 'special' brought up to take the wedding guests back to London was not so lucky. It was literally overrun by the rabble and the 'good and the great' of the realm found themselves rubbing shoulders with the *hoi polloi* for perhaps the only time in their lives. The Duchess of Westminster, with half a million pounds in diamonds round her neck, was lifted off her feet in the crush and then swept away by a gang of roughs. But the mood was good-humoured and she was returned, safe and still bedecked like a Christmas tree, to the train, though she was forced to travel third class back to Paddington. Lord Palmerston, the Prime Minister, had to travel third class as well, while Benjamin Disraeli could find no seat and was forced to sit on his wife's lap. Ministers of state and church either stood or sat next to those they regarded as the 'great unwashed'. It was a thoroughly democratic experience – unfortunately one that was never to be repeated. The Archbishop of Canterbury could find no transport at all and only caught the train by hanging on to the back of a carriage that was heading towards the station.

A clockwork wedding

In contrast with the wedding arrangements for the marriage of Bertie and Alix, the preparations for the wedding of Elizabeth of Bavaria and Emperor Franz Josef of Austria nine years earlier had been impeccable. Literally everything had been considered – except the small matter of the happiness of the bride. The beautiful Bavarian girl, nervous and highly strung as a fawn, was to be exposed to the full rigour of a bureaucratic monarchical system that had evolved over half a millennium. She was made to feel that she was merely a cog, and a very small one at that, in a machine no longer designed to serve but to be served by the expendable royal lives that comprised the Habsburg monarchy.

Behind the scenes all was not well. The bride just could not comes to terms with her situation. She loved Franz Josef as a man but hated him for being an emperor. She wanted to be married, but did not want to lose her freedom. Most of all, she feared her mother-in-law to be, the Archduchess Sophia, who was to make her life a misery. Although Sophia was a Wittelsbach like Elizabeth, she had learned to accept the rigid life of a Habsburg princess and expected Elizabeth to do the same.

On her arrival at the royal palace of Schönbrunn outside Vienna, Elizabeth was introduced to her chief lady-in-waiting, Countess Catherine Esterhazy-Liechtenstein, an elderly and sour-faced woman of such flawless aristocratic pedigree that she made the young girl feel like a 'Bavarian provincial'. The Countess handed Elizabeth an enormous tome, entitled 'Order for the Ceremonial Procedure of the Public Entry into Vienna of Her Royal Highness, the Most Gracious Princess Elizabeth', telling her to learn it by the next day – just two days before the wedding took place. It contained precise instructions for a Habsburg bride on how to behave and how to welcome guests according to their precedence. Already she was part of the royal machine. The wistful Elizabeth wrote the following lines at this time:

> Farewell, you quiet rooms,
> Farewell, you ancient castle.
> Those first dreams of love –
> They rest beneath the waters of the lake.

The next day was an overwhelming experience for a young girl who had grown up in a Bavarian farmhouse rather than a palace and had danced barefoot in the grass while her father Duke Maximilian, disguised as a wandering minstrel, had played at peasant weddings and feasts. She made her official entry into Vienna in a state carriage made of glass, with panels painted by Rubens, and the wheels encrusted with gold, pulled by eight magnificent Lippizaner horses. As she travelled through streets filled with thousands of cheering people, she mumbled, 'On show like a freak in a circus'. The occasion proved

The wedding procession in Vienna of the Emperor Franz Josef of Austria and Elizabeth of Bavaria 24 April 1854. Elizabeth, unprepared by her simple and unaffected upbringing for the rigours of Habsburg etiquette, was deeply traumatized by the occasion. (AR/IS)

too much for her and she dissolved in tears. Afterwards, Archduchess Sophia brought her two more documents to learn: 'Most Humble Reminders', which paraphrased the earlier book and emphasized key points on how she should behave at the wedding, and a booklet nineteen pages long which she would need to know by heart, as it contained details on the precise ranks and honours of all the guests at her wedding.

The wedding took place on 24 April 1854 in St Augustin's Church, not far from the Hofburg Palace in Vienna. In her wedding clothes Elizabeth was so beautiful that she elicited a general gasp of admiration as she entered the church. The rest was a cross between Hollywood and an operetta by Franz Lehar. Once the key had been turned the machine worked like clockwork. What was going through the minds of the young couple as they stood at the altar, surrounded by a thousand stuffed shirts and padded bodices, all wearing tiaras or hung with tinsel decorations like a thousand separate Christmas trees, was unimportant. All that mattered was that it had been another triumph for the toy soldiers, the clock makers and the painted dolls that comprised the Habsburg state, and all accompanied by lashings of fresh cream and dark chocolate.

But now the wrappings came off, the ribbons were discarded and the coloured paper smoothed flat and put aside for next time. It was the wedding night. Elizabeth was taken by her mother, Ludovica, down the long corridor to the bridal chamber, lit at every stage by powdered pages holding golden candelabra. It all seemed unreal to her. Once she was prepared for bed by her mother and her ladies-in-waiting, Franz Josef was led into the room by his mother, the Archduchess Sophia. Elizabeth was so frightened of her mother-in-law that she pretended to be asleep to escape any further instructions. Angrily Sophia announced in a loud voice that the family would expect to see Elizabeth at breakfast. She then withdrew, closing the door.

The next morning Elizabeth duly appeared at breakfast, but was tired and tearful. The Archduchess had already been informed that the marriage had been consummated but that was not enough for the inquisitive mother. She now began to question Elizabeth about how successful their lovemaking had been and how well she thought Franz Josef had performed the sexual act. Elizabeth was shocked at this prurient interest in what she considered a private matter and burst into tears, fleeing from the room. Elizabeth was later told that it was only recently that royal consummations had stopped being witnessed by notaries and officials. This was the start of a deep-seated antipathy between the two women, which was to do much to break up Elizabeth's marriage with Franz Josef. The gentle romanticism of Elizabeth could not cope for long with the down-to-earth realism of her mother-in-law. Soon Elizabeth was writing the following lines:

> What are the delights of Spring to me
> Here in this far and foreign land?
> I long for the sun of my home.

The blood wedding

The wedding of King Alfonso XIII of Spain and Princess Victoria Eugenie of Battenburg, granddaughter of Queen Victoria, on 31 May 1906, was sensational but not in the sense that the young couple might have hoped. Ever afterwards their happiest day became known as the 'blood wedding'.

It was a hot summer's day in Madrid and the forty state coaches, drawn by teams of six or eight horses, all sporting orange and pink ostrich feathers, made up a cavalcade of brilliant colours passing through streets lined by cheering crowds and bedecked in flags and bunting. It was a day of flowers, with blooms of every hue filling every window and balcony. The English princess, known to everyone as Ena, was beautiful, blonde-haired, blue-eyed and with a complexion of 'milk and roses' that prompted the Spaniards to call her 'La Reine hermosa'.

After the ceremony at the Church of San Jeronimo, the newly-weds returned to the royal coach and joined the lengthy procession back to the royal palace. Progress was slow and as they passed through the old quarter of the city the coach was forced to draw to a halt momentarily. This was the signal for a bouquet of flowers to be thrown from an upstairs window of one of the buildings they were passing. The bouquet landed in front of the coach and exploded with a tremendous roar, tipping the vehicle backwards and filling it with thick black smoke. The air was filled with the screams of injured men and horses. For a moment Alfonso thought Ena was dead as she was thrown across the coach and lay like a rag-doll, her magnificent wedding dress torn and blackened. When Alfonso was sure that Ena was all right he leant out of the window and called for the reserve coach to be brought up. He and Ena then stepped out into the carnage. One of their horses had been killed and the others were screaming with the pain of their wounds. Mutilated bodies of onlookers lay everywhere, and the road was awash with blood. Ena lost one of her shoes and found herself paddling in blood, while the train of her dress was already soaked and reddened. Leaving bloody footprints Ena climbed into the reserve coach and the young couple were driven through the side streets to the palace. Behind them on the road lay twelve dead and over a hundred injured people.

The royal couple were luckier than they can have realized. Horrific as their experience had been things could have been much worse. The young anarchist responsible for the outrage, Mateo Morales, had arrived too late to find a place in the Church of San Jeronimo, where he had originally planned to throw his bomb, and had been forced instead to find a new position along the route of the procession.

In spite of their experiences the young royals obeyed the standard showman's phrase, 'The show must go on.' Reaching the palace, with Ena muttering to herself in horror, 'I saw a man without any legs!', they went upstairs to change and were down promptly for the wedding reception. The foreign royals present reacted with typical aplomb. Edward, the Prince of Wales, kept a 'stiff upper lip' and sought a solution in champagne. 'I proposed their healths,' he said. The eccentric Russian princess, Maria, Duchess of Edinburgh, poured scorn on this trifling incident. Just twelve dead? She had seen worse. After all, she was accustomed to this sort of thing. Both her father and her brother had been blown to bits by terrorists in Russia.

With the entertainment over the young couple had to present themselves on the palace balcony to wave to the crowds. Eventually, after a seventeen-hour day of ceremonies and celebrations – not to mention a short break for slaughter and mayhem – the royal couple retired to bed.

Wedding Nights

In theory the wedding night should be the most enjoyable and most important occasion in a royal bride's life. But this has not always proved to be so, as the following unfortunate examples demonstrate.

The wrong motions

On 12 May 1499, Cesare Borgia, the son of Pope Alexander VI, married the French princess Charlotte d'Albret, daughter of the Duc de Guyenne. Their marriage night proved to be an eventful one in more ways than one. Although Cesare later reported to the Pope, his father, that the marriage had been consummated and that he had 'broken two lances before supper, and six by night' he may have been boasting. The truth was that Cesare had approached an apothecary for an aphrodisiac so that he might maximize his bride's pleasure. But some of his friends played a practical joke on Cesare, substituting laxatives for the love philtres that he had hoped would improve his performance. Charlotte's ladies, spying through the keyhole, later reported that Cesare had spent as much time in the privy as he had with his bride. Nevertheless, Charlotte later wrote to her father-in-law that she was very satisfied with her husband.

Sick of each other already

It is certain that the same could not have been said for the Archduchess Maria Sophia of Bavaria, sister of the Empress Elizabeth of Austria, on the occasion of her marriage in 1861 to the Duke of Calabria, heir to the throne of Naples. Tradition dictated that the newly-weds should be locked in the bridal suite and the doors were not opened until the morning. Unfortunately, the young Duke had eaten something at the wedding banquet that violently disagreed with him and he spent the whole night vomiting. Maria Sophia got little sleep between her husband's bouts of sickness and spent most of her time on her knees praying. The marriage was not consummated and the Archduchess gained what little comfort she could from her pet canary, Hansi.

Cruel necessity

The wedding night of the Habsburg Emperor Ferdinand I stands as an example of the the cruelty that political necessity can impose on human beings. Ferdinand of Habsburg was one of the most unfortunate of men, incredibly ugly and a moron into the bargain. He came to the throne in 1835 but was quite incapable of ruling the country, a task that was taken up by Count Metternich.

The common people referred to him as Ferdinand the 'good-natured'. In fact, he was epileptic and hydrocephalitic, and could hardly string two words together. His favourite activity was climbing into waste-paper baskets and rolling about the floor in them, or catching flies with his hands. His most coherent recorded utterance was 'I'm the Emperor and I want dumplings.' Ferdinand had a grossly enlarged head and could not lift a glass to his lips or open a door with one hand. He reigned for thirteen years during which Metternich assumed almost vice-regal powers, referring to his emperor as 'a lump of putty'.

Cruel necessity – or Metternich's greed for power – dictated that Ferdinand should marry and try to father an heir. Incredibly, Ferdinand's physicians allowed him to marry a 28-year-old princess, Maria Anna of Sardinia. There was never any real chance that the marriage would be consummated but such was the pressure for him to play the part of the royal stud that on his wedding night Ferdinand had five epileptic fits. Maria Anna thereafter lived the life of a saint, which was probably just as well.

Taking precautions

The wedding night of Catherine the Great was one of the most extraordinary ever recorded. Catherine, one of Russia's greatest rulers, was in fact a German princess named Sophia Frederica Augusta who was brought to Russia in 1745 by the Empress Elizabeth to marry her nephew, the Grand Duke Peter. The problem was that Peter was an idiot who was obsessed with things military.

On her wedding night Catherine waited in bed for the appearance of her prince but hours passed and a servant brought her the news that her husband was drinking and gambling with his friends. When at last Peter came to bed he was drunk and he immediately got out his toy soldiers and began to play with them on the bed. Next he told Catherine that he was going to sleep and ordered her to stand guard at the door while he did so. She was forced to get out of bed and stand at attention like a guardsman, then to march up and down. In this way she spent her first night with her husband (see p. 81).

A WEDDING AT THE ICE PALACE

You don't have to be mad to be the ruler of Russia but it helps. Since the time of Ivan the Terrible in the sixteenth century, rather more than half of the Tsars and Tsarinas have either been certifiably insane or so eccentric and cruel in the treatment of their subjects that they have either been deposed or assassinated. Perhaps it has something to do with the sheer ungovernable size of the country and the opportunities this affords for evil on an unprecedented scale. Even the Empress Anna, niece of Peter the Great and something of a practical joker – she once ordered fire-bells to be rung throughout St Petersburg just to watch everyone panic – was also a cruel and perverted woman, who took pleasure in the suffering and humiliation of her courtiers. Prince Nikita Volkonski, for example, was appointed keeper of her favourite dog with orders to feed the bloated creature with jugs of cream throughout the day, while his wife tended Anna's pet rabbit and fed it tasty morsels of lettuce with her teeth. But her special vitriol was reserved for Prince Michael Golitsyn.

Golitsyn had once been one of the favourites of her predecessor, the Empress Catherine I, but by 1739 he was out of favour. He had married an Italian woman without the permission of the new Empress and so Anna decided to relegate him to the rank of court buffoon. Once she ordered Golitsyn to 'marry' Prince Volkonski and both had to dress as birds and sit in a straw basket outside her room, flapping their arms like wings and cackling like hens. It sent the Empress into fits of laughter. But as Golitsyn was now a widower, she decided to humiliate him in the most extraordinary way ever devised. We may laugh when we read of her 'Ice Palace', or even admire her ingenuity in devising the charade, but we should never forget that she ruled through terror and that her black sense of humour ill-suited her role as guardian of her people. She was not all smiles. When her dwarf was too ill to perform one day she had him flogged almost to death.

During the winter of 1739–40, one of the coldest on record, Anna decided that it was time for Golitsyn to take a new wife. In fact, she told him that she had found the partner of his dreams: Avdotaya Ivanovna, who was nicknamed 'Bujenina' after the Empress's favourite dish of roast pork and onions, which she was said to resemble. Avdotaya was so ugly that milk turned sour in the jug as she peered into it. Nevertheless, the lady was looking for a husband and she could hardly hope to do better than a court buffoon who had been a prince. In addition, the Empress told the prospective bridegroom that she was prepared to provide accommodation for his wedding night. Golitsyn knew Anna too well to find much pleasure in this offer.

For the next few weeks, the whole of the city was alive with rumour. Something odd was going on down by the bank of the frozen River Neva. There were hundreds of workmen toiling away behind serried ranks of soldiers, with bayonets fixed. Whatever it was going to be, it would be enormous.

At the beginning of January 1740 everything was ready and Golitsyn was summoned to attend the court early one morning. There he found that a great procession was forming up, at the head of which was a menagerie of animals, goats, pigs, cows, camels, dogs and reindeer, all harnessed to carriages and carts in which sat representatives of all the races in Russia, from Lapps to Tartars, dressed in their national costumes. Behind them came an elephant with a large cage on its back. Golitsyn now discovered that this was the bridal car and that he and the blushing Avdotaya must climb up inside it. To the sound of musical instruments of every kind producing a horrible cacophony, the 'blessed' bridal pair were taken to the palace's covered riding school where they enjoyed a hearty if bizarre banquet. But this was just the start for, when everyone was replete, the bride and groom were taken to the splendid palace that had been set aside for their night of love. And Golitsyn cannot have been the only one of those present that day whose eyes refused to believe what they saw, for the accommodation the Empress had provided for them was a palace made entirely of ice.

The Ice Palace contained no other materials to support it and was, in its way, a masterpiece of

The Empress Anna Ivanovna, niece of Tsar Peter the Great, became Empress on the death of Peter II. Coarse and cruel, her bizarre sense of humour found expression in the building of the 'Ice Palace' as a deadly wedding present for the out-of-favour Prince Golitsyn. (ME)

While bride and groom had eyes for naught else but each other, the rest of the guests gasped in wonder at the palace. It was eighty feet long, over thirty feet high and some twenty-three feet in depth. It had steps leading up to the entrance, baroque-style balustrades, cornices, columns and decorative figurines all made of ice. Even the window panes were made from ice, cut so thinly that they were translucent. Inside the palace all the furniture was made of ice, including a four-poster bed, complete with ice mattresses, pillows and blankets, dining chairs, dining tables, commodes, an ice clock and a statue of Cupid, looking rather blue in places. To while away the evening, the young couple could even play with a perfectly made pack of cards, with the suits coloured in appropriately. In the gardens, ice sculptures of trees and plants had been made, with birds perched in their branches. Other wonders included an ice cannon which actually fired charges, ice dolphins breathing fire and smoke – in fact, naphtha – and a full-size ice elephant, which could squirt a fountain of water from its trunk hundreds of feet in the air.

But if it was a wonderland it was a deadly one. Golitsyn and his bride were escorted to their ice bed by soldiers, who ensured that the couple got in and under their covers. Drunken jeers from well-wishers completed a scene of surreal horror and a guard was placed on the door, to prevent any peeping-toms disturbing the lovers. Content that Golitsyn had gone to his death, Anna withdrew to her own palace, and sat by a roaring fire reminding herself of what the circulation of the blood feels like.

But the laugh was on the Empress. She had spent thirty thousand rubles to stage this bizarre spectacle and yet, the next morning – and readers will have to suspend their disbelief at this point – the newly-weds emerged unscathed, arm-in-arm, with Avdotaya already well on the way to presenting her husband with twin boys. Ironically Golitsyn out-lived the vicious and corrupt Empress, who died later in the year, to everyone's great relief.

human ingenuity. Unfortunately, its purpose was both ridiculous and cruel, for Anna was not expecting the bride and groom to emerge alive the next morning. Although a stove had been installed in the ice bedroom, it was not thought that humans could possibly survive a night in the palace, in temperatures of many degrees below zero. Nevertheless, Golitsyn had no alternative but to give it a try and Avdotaya had no intention of missing her wedding night.

During a visit to the Tate Gallery, King George V was heard to call to his wife, Queen Mary: 'Come here quick. There's something that will make you laugh.' It was an exhibition of French Impressionist paintings.

CHAPTER 3: UNHAPPILY EVER AFTER

A Lack of Breeding

Breeding is the prerequisite for membership of the 'Royals' club. No prince or princess can lay claim to their own bodies; they are the property of the state. In their capacity to guarantee each new generation lies the security of the state and so the ability of royal persons to breed is of paramount political and dynastic importance. Intelligence and good looks count for nothing in the histories of dynasties. For every wise and wonderful king or emperor there have been hundreds of dullards who have served their states with their loins. This has been a fundamental fact of royal marriages throughout history and great events – one thinks of the Henrician Reformation in England – have sometimes resulted from the inability of a king or queen to produce an heir to the throne.

Many royal marriages have foundered on the rock of male impotence or female sterility. And yet until modern times a barren royal union was assumed to be the fault of the woman, as impotence among men was rarely understood and was often assumed to be a sign that the man had been bewitched. Yet there is clear evidence that impotence on the part of the prince was frequently a problem and a particularly humiliating one as the prime function of any royal male was to breed and produce a healthy progeny.

Just not up to it

As we have seen elsewhere the young Prince Henry of Castile, later to be known as Henry the Impotent, and his wife, Blanca of Navarre, endured a frightful wedding day and an even worse night (see p. 62). Henry's failure to consummate his marriage was later blamed on Blanca and she was eventually divorced for non-consummation. But, in fact, the problem was entirely Henry's. A German physician, Hieronymous Münzer of the University of Padua, who had reason to examine Henry at the Spanish court, reported that a structural deficiency in his sexual organ made it most unlikely that he would enjoy normal sexual relations. But no royal prince could allow such a report to become public. Instead, the news was circulated that Henry was, in fact, impotent only with his wife, while with his mistresses he was as successful as any man. The reason for this lie was that his father was in the process of arranging a new marriage for him, with Princess Juana of Portugal, who would hardly consent to the union believing that her future husband would be unable to father children. In the event, Juana was trapped into a loveless and fruitless marriage. Henry was no more capable of consummating his relationship with Juana than he had been with Blanca. Ingenious attempts were made by Henry's physicians to bring the newly-weds together. Münzer devised a tube, made of solid gold, through which to transfer sperm from Henry to his new wife. But successful artificial insemination was still centuries away and such attempts were doomed to failure. There could be no heir to the throne. Ironically, Juana did eventually bear a child, but nobody was fooled as to the identity of the father and the girl was nicknamed 'La Beltraneja', after her 'secret' father, Beltran, Count of Ledesma.

Staff training

However important perpetuating a dynasty may be to a king, teaching a small child to worship the royal penis is too heavy a psychological burden to impose. Yet this is precisely what King Henry IV did to the tiny Dauphin, the future Louis XIII of France. Henry IV was a renowned stallion when it came to sex and had mistresses numberless, yet the obsessively sexual upbringing of his son Louis damaged the young Dauphin's development to such an extent that when he married, at the tender age of fourteen, he proved to be not only impotent but seriously disturbed in sexual orientation. At just three years of age the future Louis XIII was shown his father's penis and was told that it was this noble tree from whence he sprung that ruled the kingdom and ensured its future. The nurses and ladies at court frequently manipulated the young child's genitals and urged him to demand that the courtiers kiss him there instead of on his hand. His father's latest mistress frequently made him giggle not with tickles but by putting her hand under his skirts. His nurses teased him by telling him what would be his duty when he grew older and how he must marry the Spanish Infanta and make babies. This terrified the child and he screamed that he did not want to. But he was told by both his father and Marie de Medicis, his mother, that he must make a little Dauphin just like himself. To add to his anxiety his nurses told him that if he let anyone touch his penis they would cut it off. Even the royal doctor joined this assault on his infant mentality by warning him of the dangers that surrounded him of people chopping off his penis. What passed for child-rearing in seventeenth-century France could have provided material for a whole psychiatric conference on infant trauma and personality disorders.

The assassination of Henry IV in 1610 brought Louis XIII to the throne at the age of just nine years, and by 1614 his prearranged marriage with the Spanish princess, Anne of Austria, was solemnized. In view of the age of the young couple, both just fourteen, and the extraordinary upbringing of the Dauphin, it was no wonder that the wedding night proved to be a disaster. Matters were not helped by the intense pressure imposed on the boy by his mother.

After a day of ceremony, coupled with extensive feasting, both of the royal children were exhausted and longed rather for sleep than for a sexual performance designed to satisfy their parents rather than themselves. In fact, Louis had already retired to his own bed when a group of courtiers came into his room and began to try to rouse his sexual passions by telling him provocative tales. When they had roused him to a pitch of anxiety rather than lust, his mother then came in and told him his duties as a king. 'My son,' she told the cringing boy, 'it is not all done in getting married; you have to come to see the queen, your wife, who awaits you.' Realizing there was no escape, Louis replied, 'Madame, I was only waiting for your command. I am happy to set out with you to find her.' Mother and son now went to the bride's bedroom where the equally frightened young girl was waiting. She had been undressed by her ladies, who had giggled inanely and suggestively before retiring. Marie de Medicis brought the bashful bridegroom into the room saying, 'My daughter, here is your husband whom I bring to you; receive him into your bosom and love him well, I beseech you.' And that was it. They were on their own. Two hours later Louis officially informed the two waiting nurses that he had done his duty twice and the bedsheets were removed for the Queen and the Spanish ambassador to inspect. They were apparently satisfied that the royal marriage had been consummated and the alliance of the two realms, France and Spain, had been consolidated.

But what had really happened behind the curtains of the four-poster bed? Certainly the marriage had not been consummated in any normal way. Louis had apparently tried to penetrate his wife but nothing substantial had been achieved and the nurses later reported his horrified words as, 'Look out! I'm going to piss into her body.' Far from ejaculating as the law required for a proper consummation, Louis' doctor reported that he produced only urine. Louis was so shocked by the experience of this one night that he refused to sleep with his wife for the next four years. This nightmarish coupling had completely broken his nerve.

As months and finally years passed without the slightest sign of Anne of Austria becoming pregnant it became a matter of concern to both French and Spanish courts that King Louis was not sleeping with his wife. He occasionally flirted with court ladies, notably the ravishing Duchesse de Luynes, but he remained a stranger to his wife. Even the royal confessor tried to force him to sleep with his wife, invoking all the power of the Church, but to no avail. The King's ministers suggested that if he were to take a mistress first that might help him overcome his problems, but he remained steadfastly chaste.

It is doubtful if Louis would ever have overcome his childhood inhibitions had his step-sister, Mademoiselle de Vendôme, not married the Duc d'Elbeuf in January 1619. Louis had stood alongside the bed and, with curtains opened, witnessed the consummation of his sister's marriage. Unembarrassed, she had turned to him and said, 'Sire! You do the same thing with the queen and you will do well.' What prayers and maternal exhortation could not achieve, voyeurism did. A week later the Duc de Luynes dragged a sobbing Louis to the queen's bedroom, threw him in and locked the door. The next day the happy couple emerged as true man and wife.

But the King's problems were not entirely over, for he had reckoned without the foolish antics of the Queen's lady-in-waiting, the beautiful Duchesse de Luynes. This high-spirited young woman, as renowned for her affairs of the heart as for her pranks, had a bad influence on the young queen. Four years later, as the Duchesse de Chevreuse, and one of Princess Henrietta Maria's party in England, she was to astonish the good people of Richmond by throwing off her clothes and swimming naked across the Thames and back, just two weeks after giving birth. By 1622 Anne of Austria was at last pregnant and Louis counted the days to the birth of the child that meant so much to him and to the French kingdom. But on 14 March the Queen and a friend were racing along the corridors of the Louvre pursued by the Duchesse de Luynes, a ridiculous and irresponsible thing to be doing in the Queen's delicate state of health. The Queen tripped and fell and suffered a miscarriage. Louis was furious and immediately banished the Queen's companions. The Duchesse de Luynes had recently been widowed and the Queen was heartbroken to see her friend punished. Eventually Louis relented but only after the Duc de Chevreuse had undertaken the responsibility of marrying the over-exuberant young woman and curbing her behaviour. He never succeeded in this but that is another story. Eventually Anne of Austria did produce a child – the future Louis XIV, the 'Sun King'.

Bewitched, bothered and bewildered

Spain in the late seventeenth century had declined from its position as a great power a hundred years before and when its last Habsburg king, Charles II or Carlos 'the Bewitched' as he was known, came to the throne in 1665 the country was facing bankruptcy. What was needed was a strong king who would restore the national credit and secure the throne by fathering a healthy brood of children. What Spain got instead was a four-year-old child, a direct descendant of Juana the Mad (see p. 32), and as such a physically and mentally retarded warning of the dangers of inbreeding. In appearance Carlos was grotesque. He had been breast-fed by fourteen different wet-nurses until the age of four, could hardly walk because his legs were too weak, was slow-witted and was unable to read or write until he was at least nine. As king he was almost entirely under his mother's thumb and it was she who wanted him married as soon as possible. But her candidate was a five-year-old Austrian princess and eventually it was decided not to wait for this toddler to grow up but instead to go for a beauty who was entirely wasted on Carlos. Marie Louise was the daughter of the Duc d'Orleans and was reputedly the prettiest princess in Europe, possessed of all the courtly graces, as well as riding well and having a lively personality. But the Spanish court valued none of these qualities. All it was concerned with was her fertility. Could she and their crippled king produce an heir to continue the line of Habsburg monarchs in Spain?

Marie Louise must be one of history's truly tragic brides. At seventeen she had much to offer a husband and yet in 1680 she was forced to marry a man whose jaw was so deformed that he could not chew his food and instead had to swallow it in lumps. Carlos was thin and feeble and constantly ill with one ailment after another. If Marie Louise had a calling to be a nurse she could hardly have found better material on which to practise her skills, but if she was looking for a husband and a lover she was doomed to disappointment.

The hopes of the kingdom rested on the King's ability to beget a child but Carlos was sexually inept and almost certainly impotent. Yet the nature of his impotence has long confused historians. In the first place Carlos seemed to have a strong sexual drive. One of the reasons he was rushed into marriage by his mother was because of his obsessive masturbation, which was believed to be endangering his health. It is known that he found his new wife attractive and, after their wedding night, she told the French ambassador that she was no longer technically a virgin. But what exactly did she mean? Had Carlos performed the sexual act to the satisfaction of the law? Had he achieved both penetration and ejaculation? The answer, it would appear, was 'No'. Carlos apparently suffered from so severe a case of premature ejaculation that penetration was impossible.

When the news of the young couple's sexual problems became public knowledge – this rarely took long as the mating of royal personages was a matter of national importance – the blame was laid on the young princess. Marie Louise had been chosen to breed and if she failed – even if the fault was her husband's – then she would be dismissed as a barren, sterile wife. But in France, Louis XIV was convinced that Marie Louise was guiltless. He had long suspected that the feeble Spanish king would have trouble begetting an heir. So he sent a young diplomat named Rébenac to the Spanish court, with specific instructions to find out what was really going wrong in the royal bed. Rébenac took incredible liberties in his investigations, even going so far as to steal a pair of Carlos's drawers, so that surgeons could examine them for signs of semen. Rébenac also questioned Marie Louise, who shyly told him that her relationship with the king made it unlikely that she would ever have children. From this Rébenac concluded that the young couple were practising a form of non-penetrative sex, known at the time as 'la petite oie'. This may have satisfied Carlos and may even have sufficed for the Queen, but it was of no use as a means of producing an heir. Since it involved the spilling of semen outside the body, it was also contrary to every moral tenet of the Catholic Church. It is doubtful if Carlos and Marie Louise indulged in this practice from choice. Carlos had been chaste before marriage and knew little of the mechanics of sex, nor would his wife have presumed to offer advice to him, even had she known what to do. Carlos was virtually a mental defective and it was surprising that he could even enjoy 'la petite oie'. It was expecting too much of him to make the imaginative leap to 'la grande oie' – or full intercourse – and his wife was too shy to take the initiative.

Rébenac, and many officials at the Spanish court, reached the absurd conclusion that the King was bewitched. Only spells could explain a man's impotence towards his wife. And so a witch hunt was started to find the guilty parties. Members of the queen's entourage were questioned under torture, but the source of the harmful 'spells' was never found. After eight years of a fruitless and loveless marriage Marie Louise died. Deprived of the satisfaction of motherhood she had turned increasingly to the delights of the table, eating far too many sweet things and becoming enormously stout. The Spanish people pointed to her figure as conclusive evidence of why she was unable to stimulate her husband.

Ten days after the death of his wife, in 1690, preparations were made for Carlos to marry again. This time Carlos's mother chose Maria Anna of Neuberg, the formidable sister of the Empress of Austria. Maria Anna was no beauty but she came from a good line of breeders and after the marriage there were continual rumours of the new queen's pregnancy. But the 'bewitched' king was no more capable of impregnating Maria Anna than he had been his first wife. Carlos was not bewitched, he was simply impotent.

Carlos's inability to produce an heir meant the end of the line for the Spanish Habsburgs. But the ensuing uncertainty over who should inherit the throne also had serious and long-term political implications for the rest of Europe. Carlos's death in 1700 plunged Europe into a bloody 'War of the Spanish Succession' between the France of Louis XIV – who supported the claims to the Spanish throne of his grandson, the Bourbon Philip of Anjou – and an English-dominated alliance of states which – alarmed at the prospect of French domination of the continent – supported the claims of the Austrian Habsburg Archduke Charles. Rarely can impotence have had such far-reaching consequences.

Madame deficit

The important dynastic marriage between the Habsburg princess Marie Antoinette and the French Dauphin, later Louis XVI, in 1770, was not consummated for eight years as a result of a deformity of the prince's penis. Much was expected of the union, which marked a transformation of traditional Habsburg-Bourbon rivalry, but it could only be cemented by the birth of a future heir to the French throne. In a sense, everyone in Paris and Vienna was present, at least in thought, in the royal bedroom at Versailles, when the young couple were put to bed on their wedding night. It was an enormous responsibility

Marie Antoinette, daughter of Maria Theresa of Austria, had to wait eight years before her marriage to the French dauphin – later Louis XVI – was properly consummated. Disillusionment with her marriage drove her to embrace a profligate lifestyle that earned her the hatred of the French people. (ME)

for the pretty young Austrian princess, but she had been schooled by her mother, the Empress Maria Theresa, and she knew exactly what was expected of her. Unfortunately, nobody seemed to have taken the trouble to tell Louis what to do. He fell asleep without touching her. The next morning there was consternation throughout the palace. The chamberwomen had found no sign that the marriage had been consummated. The news spread like wildfire. The Austrian ambassador immediately wrote to Vienna to tell the dreadful news. Maria Theresa was thunderstruck. Was there something she had forgotten? That was unlikely, after all she had borne her own husband sixteen children. Day followed day and still the princess remained a virgin.

King Louis XV and the Empress Maria Theresa were in almost daily communication. What was the matter with their children? Naturally the king blamed the princess, who was obviously failing in her duty to arouse his son. Maria Theresa was more realistic. Could the fault lie with young Louis? Some people had described him as having the appearance of a eunuch. Could this possibly be the case? The Austrians were notably disappointed. They had great hopes of seeing a prince on the throne of France who was half Habsburg. They knew that if she failed to produce a prince, Marie Antoinette might even be set aside. Something had to be done.

When King Louis XV consulted the royal doctors he was told – rather implausibly – that his son was as yet too immature at sixteen to consummate the marriage. The doctors went on to say that with the right food and appropriate exercise the Dauphin would eventually succeed. But they were wrong. They had failed to get to the root of the matter, which was that the Dauphin suffered from phimosis, the same complaint that afflicted Peter III of Russia (see p. 82) involving an overtight foreskin. In fact, Louis was not so much impotent as afraid of the pain of intercourse. A simple operation could have put the matter right, but he was afraid of this as well. Instead, he sublimated his sexual urges by eating so much that he frequently made himself sick. In the meantime, Marie Antoinette just had to wait. The young princess did not understand the nature of her husband's problem and believed him when he told her that he had decided to postpone intimacy with her until his sixteenth birthday. In the meantime, well-wishers or interfering busybodies offered suggestions: that Louis was bewitched, that he should take a mistress, use aphrodisiacs or eat mandrake root. Unfortunately, his birthday came and went with no great reason for celebrations. In fact, seven more birthdays came and went before the matter was fully put right.

Instrumental in the change for the better was Marie Antoinette's brother, the Emperor Joseph II, who made a special journey from Vienna to try to save his sister's marriage. He came disguised as a Count Falkenstein and had the most candid discussions with his sister and her husband. He learned from each separately that Louis only indulged in sexual relations from a sense of duty and never achieved penetration or ejaculation. Joseph was incensed at what he called 'these two complete blunderers'. Nevertheless, he had a tactful heart-to-heart discussion with Louis and persuaded him to have the operation which would save his marriage. He had a similar talk with his sister, instructing her how to entice her husband to her bed before rather than after dinner and how to arouse his passions. He told her in no uncertain terms that time was running out for her and unless she produced an heir quickly she would be divorced or else the marriage would be annulled on the grounds of non-consummation.

The eccentric Austrian emperor – marriage-guidance counsellor extraordinaire – returned to Vienna hardly aware of the dramatic success of his mission. Soon Marie Antoinette was writing to her mother that Louis had had the operation and that their marriage was now consummated. Within a matter of months she was pregnant and all seemed well. But was it? The eight barren years of Marie Antoinette's marriage had made her seek satisfaction in other ways, not only in the arms of a lover but – far more damagingly for France – through indulging her frivolous nature in a spending-spree of catastrophic proportions. When she should have been guaranteeing the future of the French monarchy with her belly she was in fact digging its grave with her purse. The pretty Austrian Princess Marie Antoinette's extravagant lifestyle had, in eight years, made her the hated Austrian intruder, 'Madame Deficit'.

Safe sex

The Empress Catherine the Great of Russia, born Sophie of Anhalt-Zerbst, endured an unusual wedding night in 1745. And the political consequences for Russia and the personal consequences for Catherine of the Grand Duke Peter's failure to consummate his marriage were profound. The Empress Elizabeth blamed Catherine at first for failing to stimulate the young man, but had she seen him as Catherine saw him she would not have been so sure. Instead of coming to bed with her Peter spent all his time with his footmen, playing military games or drilling them in the corridor outside the bedroom. His servants were made to change uniform sometimes twenty times each night and Catherine wisely pretended to be asleep lest she be put on parade as well, with a soldier's uniform over her nightclothes and boots on her bare feet. For hours Peter instructed

Catherine in the military manual and how to go through military arms drill.

Peter, like Louis XVI, suffered from phimosis – an abnormal tightening of the foreskin which means that it cannot be retracted over the tip of the penis and makes erection painful – but refused to acknowledge the problem. Instead, he boasted to Catherine of his numerous 'conquests' and he tried to frighten her with his vulgarity and coarseness. In reality, his mentality was that of a young child and he really only took pleasure in playing with wooden soldiers, miniature cannons and toy fortresses. Catherine remembered that she and Peter spent many nights manoeuvring the soldiers over the bed cover, imitating the sounds of battles as they did so. Catherine was particularly good at sounding cannon fire with her tongue. But the young woman grew generally tired of such games by two in the morning and grew frustrated at not being able to lie flat for all the toys and dolls.

Peter later took to keeping ten pet spaniels in the royal bedroom. Many of them slept on the bed, making an awful stench and restricting the chances for royal lovemaking. The royal bedroom became a sort of torture chamber for animals as Peter cruelly tried to parade the dogs before his wife, shouting guttural orders at them and whipping them when they did not obey. Catherine once found Peter beating a dog as he held it up by its tail. It had disobeyed an order and was receiving the flogging that any of his soldiers would have got. On another occasion, Catherine entered the room to find a large rat hanging from the ceiling by its neck, with all the signs of having been tortured. Peter stood by it with gleaming eyes. Catherine asked what offence it had committed and Peter told her that it had gnawed two of his soldiers and had been consequently sentenced to death. It would remain hanging for three days as an example to other rats. When Catherine burst out laughing he was furious, saying that if she could not obey orders what use was she as a wife?

Later Peter told her that he planned to build a palace in the shape of a convent. He intended to dress his courtiers as monks and give them all donkeys to ride. Catherine spent many nights with him drawing hundreds of complex architectural plans. But when he grew bored with this he took up his violin and scratched and scraped at the strings for hours on end. According to Catherine, 'He did not know a single note but he had a strong ear and made the beauty of the music depend on the violence with which he drew the sound from the instrument.' When he finally left the room, she said, silence was the purest bliss and 'the most boring book delightfully amusing'.

Catherine had long since got over the disappointment of the wedding night. She soon learned to hate the repulsive and feeble-minded Peter and was glad that he was impotent towards her. At the age of 23, after eight years of virgin marriage with Peter, she finally took a lover, Serge Saltykov. She was soon pregnant with the future Tsar Paul I. Ironically, the famous Romanov dynasty in fact reached no further than Peter III (as the Grand Duke Peter became in 1763). The tsars who succeeded Catherine the Great should have carried the name Saltykov, for there is no doubt that he rather than Peter was the father of Catherine's son. But once pregnant Catherine knew that she must at last consummate her marriage with Peter to protect herself. The wretched Peter was forced to submit to the surgery that cured his phimosis and afterwards, at the suggestion of the cunning Saltykov, the Grand Duke sent to the Empress Elizabeth the bed linen, suitably bloodied, to reveal that Catherine was no longer a virgin. Many courtiers laughed behind their hands at the news, but the Empress was apparently convinced. Catherine and Saltykov sighed with relief and returned to their lovemaking.

A new angle on sex

Our examples show that procreation – the most natural thing in the world for most married partners – has presented significant problems for some royal couples. Almost certainly we have only glimpsed the tip of an enormous iceberg of human suffering. It is therefore reassuring to record a case where a solution for a royal sexual problem was found through ingenuity. It may surprise some to find that this case of sexual incompatibility originated in the land that gave the world the *Kama Sutra*, and whose carvings of gymnastic couplings have suggested that there are no amatory difficulties that cannot be overcome by suppleness and imagination. However, in the case of the Maharajah Jagatkit Singh of Kapathurla the problem that bedevilled his relations with his bride was a weighty one. Although only nineteen years of age, he weighed in at more than 300 pounds, and most of this excessive weight was concentrated in his enormous belly. In spite of the fact that he had been offered the services of the most beautiful, energetic and supple young ladies to teach him the arts of love prior to his wedding, he found it impossible to overcome his tendency to crush his partner virtually to the point of suffocation – that is when he could even reach her. The sexual manuals of the sub-continent were scoured for a solution but none could provide one. Something was coming between the groom and his hopes of perpetuating his family name. And then a wise woman, greatly experienced in the amatory arts, suggested that so 'large' a prince should take his example from the bull elephants. How did such mighty beasts mate? The Maharajah's family consulted an expert on elephants who told them a fantastic tale of how ramps were built in the woods against which the female elephants could rest their backs while the bulls did their work. This provided the germ of an idea and a carpenter was immediately set to work to construct an upright bed equipped with a mattress on which the Maharajah's new wife could rest while she enjoyed the attentions of her husband. It was a triumph of imagination and the Maharajah took the bed with him on his honeymoon. How successful it proved to be we cannot be sure. Significantly, after his wedding, the Maharajah lost a lot of weight and in later life was known for his relatively slender frame.

Marriages that Failed

Marriages may be made in heaven but the participants, *aka* 'the happy couple', frequently spend their time in hell. And royal marriages – arranged as they have been throughout history – are no more blessed with good fortune than any other.

The Habsburg chore

It is difficult not to sympathize with the Emperor Joseph II of Austria, whose success as a marriage counsellor to his sister and her husband (see p. 81) did not enable him to overcome the tribulations of his own unfortunate marriages. His first marriage to Isabel of Parma was tainted by the fact that, though he loved her, she was in love with the idea of death as a result of being told by a gypsy that she would die early. In addition, the formality of the Habsburg court made her depressed and suicidal, as the following letter home suggests:

> A princess cannot, like the poorest woman in a hut, relax in the midst of her family. In the high society in which she is forced to live, she has neither acquaintances nor friends. It is for this that she has to leave her family, her home. And why? To belong to a man whose character she does not know, to enter into a family where she is received with jealousy.

For Isabel life was a misery and she welcomed the idea of death as a way of finding 'her heavenly home'. After three years of marriage she was still obsessed with dying, admitting that if her religion allowed it she would have killed herself already. An outbreak of smallpox finally gave Isabel her wish and she died 'willingly'. Joseph was never really aware of his wife's true feelings and was overwhelmed by the blow. But at the age of just twenty-two, his duty as the heir to the Imperial throne required him to remarry and his mother, Maria Theresa, began searching for a new wife for her son. Political expediency was the real matchmaker, and his choice of brides was narrowed to just two German princesses, a Saxon and a Bavarian.

Like a prospective buyer at a horse fair, Joseph went to 'look over' the girls. He was not impressed. He thought that Princess Cunigunde of Saxony would be the better of the two, as she was reported to be less ugly. But when he met her he soon changed his opinion. Although she possessed virtues and graces, she was, in his words, 'hideous and bulky'. Even so, he would have sacrificed himself for his country had a Saxon alliance been politically desirable. But Maria Theresa's ministers stressed the need to incline towards Bavaria, and so Joseph's mind was made up for him: he must marry Princess Josepha of Bavaria, whose attractions included 'a small, squat figure, pimples and red spots on the face and repulsive teeth'. The Empress had already asked one of her courtiers which of the girls he would have chosen. His reply made her laugh. He admitted that he would run away from either but, with a knife at his throat, he would take the Bavarian as she, at least, had a bosom. Maria Theresa, a martyr to duty herself, commiserated with her son. As she complained in a letter to one of her daughters, 'The most bitter thing of all is that we have to pretend that we are happy and delighted.'

Joseph married Josepha in 1765 but, far from being the happy bridegroom, he confessed to a friend that he found his wife loathsome, and that her appalling skin complaint disgusted him. His duty, however, required him to breed and ensure the succession. Far from this, he partitioned off the balcony which connected his room with his wife's. So much did he allow his anger to dominate him that he even criticized Josepha to other ladies at the court, saying on one occasion when pressed about his failure to secure an heir, 'My wife has become insupportable to me. They want me to have children. How can I have them? If I could put the tip of my finger on the tiniest part of her body that is not covered with boils, I would try to have children.' His cruelty towards Josepha earned her the sympathy of his sister, Marie Christine, who observed, 'I believe that if I were his wife and so mistreated, I would escape and hang myself on a tree.' Josepha had no need for suicide. The smallpox that killed her after just thirty months of marriage came as a relief. Joseph did not remarry.

The Duke of Norfolk's broads

Catherine Howard is almost certainly the least known of King Henry VIII's wives and the failure of his alliance with her, Henry's fifth marriage, is usually explained away as a mismatch between an ailing monarch and a promiscuous young woman. Even if this is fundamentally true it gives only part of the picture. Henry's marriage to Catherine Howard was as much a blunder as his previous match with Anne of Cleves had been. At least Anne kept her head and lived to a comfortable old age. Poor, foolish Catherine died on the block, unmourned and misunderstood.

Catherine Howard is usually dismissed as a pawn sacrificed by the artful Thomas Howard, Third Duke of Norfolk, in his struggle to advance his family's fortune. But who exactly was this pawn? Was she just the frivolous young woman who cuckolded the king? Or was she a victim of political chicanery?

Catherine's mother had died when she was just a few years old and her father, an impecunious member of the powerful Howard clan, was unable to raise the girl himself. Instead he placed her in the household of Agnes, Dowager Duchess of Norfolk, and Catherine spent her childhood in the Howard estates in Horsham and Lambeth.

She had a fairly conventional upbringing for a Tudor girl of the upper classes, but lacking any kind of parental guidance she mixed with women much older and more experienced than herself. As a result she matured early, notably in sexual matters. She was taught to play the virginal and the lute by a musician named Henry Manox, but music was not all that she learned from him. Manox, we are told, 'was in the habit of indulging in unspeakably lewd and frightful conduct' with the young Catherine in the dark places under the chapel stairs. Yet later Manox was to defend himself stoutly against the charge that he 'ever carnally knew her', and we must assume that he never went further than 'heavy petting'.

At the age of fifteen Catherine was apparently 'raped' by one Francis Dereham, a cousin of hers and a pensioner of the Duke of Norfolk. Perhaps the word 'rape' gives the wrong impression, for Catherine may well have been compliant in the matter. She certainly did not rebuff Dereham's advances and the young man became a regular visitor to Catherine's chamber. Once the Dowager Duchess caught the two of them kissing and cuddling and boxed Catherine's ears and sent Dereham packing. Dereham was one of the few people who seemed genuinely to like Catherine at this time, and he gave her little presents and referred to her as his 'wife'.

With privacy almost unknown in Tudor houses, Catherine's affair with Dereham was no secret. So regularly did the young man climb into Catherine's bed and pull the curtains that the women would often laugh to hear him panting, saying, 'Hark to Dereham broken winded.' Moreover, in spite of her young age Catherine knew precisely what she was doing. She had no intention of becoming pregnant, boasting 'a woman might meddle with a man and yet conceive no child unless she would herself'. While Catherine remained a relatively insignificant member of the Howard family the relations she enjoyed with Dereham could not pose a threat to her safety. After all, Dereham was a gentleman and, though beneath Catherine in rank, he was not so mean in standing that marriage between them would have been unthinkable.

However, when, in 1539, Thomas Howard found a way of placing Catherine at court, as a lady-in-waiting to Anne of Cleves, there was an immediate danger that Catherine's past might catch up with her. The ambitious Howard had already placed one of his nieces

– Mary Norris – at court, and now a third of the Queen's ladies were Howards. Catherine's elevation in status ended Dereham's hopes of marrying her at a stroke, for she was now the target for men of noble rank.

The marriage of Henry to Anne of Cleves was a disaster from the start. In the tumultuous repercussions that followed the wedding Thomas Cromwell was over-thrown and executed, while the Bishop of Winchester and Thomas Howard gained supremacy on the royal council. Yet even this was not enough for the ambitious Duke of Norfolk, who believed he could see a way of replacing Anne of Cleves on the throne with one of his own relations. Without a thought for what was already known about Catherine's past, Thomas Howard now pushed Catherine more and more into Henry's company, buying her dresses and praising her for 'her purity and honesty'. In this process Catherine was merely a pawn in a game of whose rules she was entirely ignorant.

While divorce proceedings were undertaken against Anne of Cleves, she was removed from court to Richmond, where, according to the excuse employed, she would be safe from the plague that was rife in London. Henry, however, stayed and 'risked death' to get better acquainted with the new Howard girl. At the age of fifty Henry could not afford to dally. No sooner had Queen Anne been divorced and become his 'sister' rather than his 'wife', than he married Catherine Howard, on 28 July 1540.

Catherine's first physical experience of the king was probably the last. She was a beautiful young woman of just twenty, who believed that she was marrying a lusty husband, a proven 'stud', who had bedded four wives already. But this was all romantic nonsense. Henry, at fifty, was a bloated monster of a man, very probably impotent and more likely to use the young woman as a piece of human jewellery to admire than as a wife. Furthermore, his health was bad and the ulceration of his leg was intensely painful, making him liable to violent mood swings. Yet for a while the King was delighted with his new acquisition. The saying 'there's no fool like an old fool' was never truer than at this time, with the King lavishing jewels and beautiful dresses on the giddy young Queen, while with saucy looks she eyed up the gallants at court and planned to cuckold him.

Catherine had rocketed from 'poor relation' to 'royal consort' so quickly that her wits were scattered and she could scarcely think clearly. She enjoyed her first few months as queen, dancing, partying and even flirting. But her promiscuous nature could not be so easily satisfied for long. Soon she grew bored as she realized that she had married an ugly old man, who could not satisfy her sexually. She had not asked to become Queen; it had been her grandfather's doing. It was not fair at her age to be surrounded by so many young and attractive people, and to have to spend your days tending your husband's repulsive ulcers.

As queen, Catherine was expected to use her powers of patronage to reward her family and friends. But Catherine's use of patronage was so indiscreet that one can only gasp at her brazenness. Remembering her relationship with Francis Dereham, she invited him to court and made him her private secretary. One can but wonder why a man as shrewd as Thomas Howard did not intervene to stop her. Perhaps the Dowager Duchess had not been honest with him about the girl's flirtations.

Meanwhile, Catherine had foolishly fallen head-over-heels in love with the dashing Sir Thomas Culpeper, one of the King's grooms. Culpeper believed that he had already established an understanding with Catherine while she was one of Queen Anne's ladies, but now that she herself was Queen, he felt embittered, as he had hoped to make her his wife. Neither of the two young people was prepared to put an end to the relationship

*Catherine Howard, fifth wife of Henry VIII of England, during her trial for adultery. The marriage of the
ailing monarch and the 19-year-old Catherine was born of the political ambitions of her Catholic relative,
the Duke of Norfolk. Protestant enemies of the Howard family instigated the accusations that would lead to
her beheading. (PN)*

and so, with the help of Lady Rochford, Culpeper and Catherine met often in the palace
in secret and pursued their affair. The risk that Catherine was taking should have been
imprinted on her mind. Adultery – though unproven – had been used to condemn the
first Howard queen, Anne Boleyn, and now Catherine was risking everything for her
'sweet little fool' Culpeper.

So many people knew of Catherine's affair in the Dowager Duchess's household that
it was only a matter of time before greed or jealousy or some other unsatisfied passion
drove someone to tell what they knew to one of Thomas Howard's enemies on the
council. Then the whole edifice would crash down on the head of poor, foolish
Catherine. Eventually one of the ladies who had known her and Dereham at Horsham
blurted out a whole string of accusations against the young Queen. The story was soon
passed to Thomas Cranmer, Archbishop of Canterbury, who, alone, dared tell the King.

Catherine must have been living in a fool's paradise if she thought she could cuckold
Henry in his own palace. But she was a girl who acted on instinct and took her pleasures
without a thought for the consequences. At first Henry hoped that the scandal would
stretch no further than to Dereham, who had courageously come forward and
proclaimed himself to be Catherine's 'betrothed', arguing that his relationship with her
took place years before her marriage to the King and was entirely innocent. At first Henry
seemed content. But Catherine foolishly denied that she was ever betrothed to Dereham.
Furthermore, at this moment the Culpeper affair broke and, under torture, the groom
confessed that he had slept with the Queen – an admission of high treason. When Lady
Rochford was threatened with torture, she confirmed 'that Culpeper hath known the
queen carnally considering all things that she hath heard and seen between them'.

Catherine was stripped of her jewels and sent first to Syon House and then to the
Tower. Further investigations implicated others. Manox was accused of 'feeling the

secret and other parts of the Queen's body'. This was true, but it had been seven years before, when she was just thirteen, and this saved him. But for Dereham and Culpeper there was no such escape. Catherine confessed that Dereham had 'used me in such sort as man doth his wife many and sundry times'. Both Dereham and Culpeper were found guilty of high treason. As a gentleman, Culpeper – whose crime, as an adulterer, was surely the greater – escaped the agony that Dereham was to suffer, and died by decapitation. Dereham, however, suffered the full extremity of the law for treason: hanging, dismembering, disembowelment and quartering. Catherine herself died by the axe on 13 February 1542, though the King had many times cursed her and wished to 'let her die through torture'. Lady Rochford, who had acted as go-between to the lovers, lost her reason under interrogation but shared the Queen's fate on the block.

If there was a villain in this sorry episode it was Thomas Howard. He had used Catherine for political advantage and had readily abandoned her to her fate once he realized that he could gain nothing more from her. But King Henry cannot altogether escape blame. For a man of his age and physical condition to marry a beautiful and healthy young woman was in itself unnatural. He could not be a true husband to her and yet he expected her to remain faithful to him, to endure his violent moods and to tend his repulsive ailments. The marriage was a blunder, but it was also a tragedy.

Messalina's hobby

Thanks to the work of Robert Graves, the disastrous marriage of the Emperor Claudius and his third wife, Messalina, has become more widely known than any other in the ancient world. How much the splendid Derek Jacobi resembled the historical Claudius is open to doubt. What is certain, however, is that Claudius was no girl's idea of a handsome and virile husband. He was tall, thin, foamed at the mouth when angry, stuttered and had a head tremor. He had been married twice and twice divorced, and nobody could have believed that Claudius, at fifty years of age, would marry a girl of sixteen. She was Valeria Messalina, daughter of his cousin Barbatus Messala, and was reputedly a woman of great beauty, but she was also possessed of a fierce temper and a vengeful nature. Nevertheless, she achieved something that her predecessors had failed to do, which was to bear the Emperor children: Britannicus and Octavia. It was as mother of his children as much as the wife of his bed that Messalina captivated her husband, and she soon felt confident enough of his adoration of her to begin affairs with younger and more potent lovers. Ancient writers portrayed Messalina as a nymphomaniac and if only half the things of which she is accused are true, she was a woman of insatiable passion.

With the Greek actor Mnester acting as her pimp, Messalina participated in a famous 'love-contest' against a woman from the Guild of Prostitutes. With Claudius away on his successful invasion of Britain, she decided to liven things up by competing against the prostitute to see which of them could 'wear out' the most customers. The prostitute, as a professional, demanded payment for each client. Messalina, on the other hand, was merely indulging in her hobby, for which she did not charge. It is said that Messalina won the contest easily. So shocking was her behaviour that nobody in Rome, not even the Emperor's ministers and closest friends, dared to tell him what his wife had been doing. In fact, most Romans assumed that he must know and condone what otherwise would be capital crimes for an Emperor's wife. But Claudius did not know, for he was infatuated with Messalina's beauty and would hear no wrong spoken of her.

However, when Claudius returned from Britain, Messalina realized that her torrid affair with one of the handsomest men in Rome, Caius Silius, would have to be ended. But her nature rebelled at the loss of her lover and she decided instead to divorce the Emperor and marry Silius. This was a desperate thing to do, and Silius knew it. It was quite likely that the Emperor would have them both killed. But Messalina believed her foolish old husband would never harm her, so, while Claudius was at the port of Ostia, some miles from Rome, she sent a serving-man to the palace to announce her intention to divorce the Emperor. She then married Silius and invited all her friends to a Bacchanalian orgy to celebrate. It was a sensual affair, with wine-presses set up and half-naked girls frolicking in great panniers of grapes, while men dressed as satyrs indulged in every type of excess. Silius, drunk on wine and danger at the same time, lay at Messalina's feet, crowned with ivy. It seemed as if they had succeeded.

However, at Ostia, the Emperor's freedmen, Pallas and Narcissus, were at that moment telling the Emperor that his wife had divorced him and taken a new husband. Claudius was both shocked and baffled. But as his befuddled brain took in the enormity of his wife's crime, Narcissus took command, collected troops together and took Claudius on to Rome. Back at the orgy, the wine was flowing like perspiration on the bodies of the revellers. Then one of the guests, looking out towards the coast, uttered the fatal words, 'There is a fearful storm over Ostia.' He was right. Messalina was about to pay the price of cuckolding 'that old fool Claudius' in his own palace. The orgy ended in uproar, with all the guests fleeing for their lives. But many were caught by the Emperor's soldiers and killed. Silius took his own life when he saw there was no hope, but Claudius could not bring himself to order his wife's death. Finally, while he was dozing, Narcissus persuaded him to sign a death warrant for Messalina and it was instantly carried out. Claudius's marriage to Messalina, a union doomed to failure from the start, was over. An old man's lechery had outrun his wisdom and a young woman's appetites were finally sated. But to prove that he had learned nothing from his blunder, Claudius now married his niece Agrippina, mother of the future Emperor Nero, who could claim – if indeed any woman could – to be even more depraved than Messalina. This time Claudius was outmanoeuvred. Agrippina poisoned him and then Nero became Emperor (see p. 22).

Bringing water to the eyes

The Byzantine Emperor Heraclius is one of the great figures of medieval history. His personal heroism made him a paladin for medieval writers of chivalry and his exploits in saving Constantinople from the Avars, overthrowing the Persian Empire and recapturing the True Cross made him a legendary hero for all Crusaders. Yet in his choice of wife, Heraclius made a blunder which was to torment his private life and inflict on his people all the evils of civil strife and religious schism.

Heraclius became Emperor in 610, at the age of 36, and took as his wife Fabia-Eudocia, who bore him two sons. We do not know if he had been married before but certainly there were no other children from any earlier union. However, after two years Eudocia died in childbirth and Heraclius decided to marry his niece Martina. This caused great controversy in Constantinople on the grounds that the Orthodox Church regarded the marriage as incestuous. Had anyone but the Emperor tried to marry a niece or a nephew they would have fallen foul of the civil law, on the charge of consanguinity. But Heraclius set himself above the law and flaunted his wife in the face of her critics, lavishing attention on her and taking her with him on his great military campaigns.

The inhabitants of Constantinople came to believe that their Emperor, who had been divinely blessed for returning the True Cross to Jerusalem, was, by remaining married to Martina, committing a sin against God's law. They feared that he would bring down destruction on himself and the city. As evidence they pointed to the fact that of the nine children born to Martina and the Emperor, four died in infancy and two others were mentally or physically disabled. But still Heraclius refused to put Martina aside. In fact, he even decreed that on his death her sons should rule equally with his children by Eudocia, his first wife. He further said that Martina should be regarded as 'mother and Empress' of Byzantium.

Twin disasters struck Heraclius in old age, both personal and political, and these were attributed by the people to his incestuous marriage. In the first place, most of the Emperor's lifetime achievements were overthrown by the Arab invasions of the 630s. Also, Heraclius was struck by both mental and physical afflictions in his old age. Shaken if not broken by the loss of Jerusalem and the Holy Land to the Muslims, Heraclius began to suffer from a curious phobia – fear of water. Returning from Syria to Constantinople, the Emperor found that because of his sudden and overwhelming fear of water he dared not cross the Hellespont. Even to drink water became a trial to him. He was eventually only able to return to his capital when a great bridge of boats was assembled, and a roadway of sand laid across them for him to ride over. Even then every yard of the bridge was guarded by a soldier with raised shield, guarding the Emperor's eyes from the tiniest glimpse of the sea.

As if this was not bad enough, he developed an agonizing disease of the urinary tract, probably dropsy or a related affliction. As a result, as the historian Nicephorus tells us, 'Every time he voided water, he was obliged to lay a board across his stomach to prevent its spurting in his face.' The problem with his penis was taken by the faithful everywhere as a sign that God was punishing him for his incest with Martina by destroying the symbol of the crime.

God's wrath was not assuaged even by the Emperor's death. Martina, who duly became co-ruler with Eudocia's sons, was almost immediately overthrown. She and her eldest boy were both mutilated – she had her tongue cut out, he had his nose cut off, and they were both banished to Rhodes, where she died shortly afterwards.

Weight watchers

In the kingdom of Karagwe, on the western shores of Lake Victoria, King Rumanika liked his wives to be well rounded. When explorer Richard Burton visited Rumanika's capital of Bweranyange in 1860 he found that the King had his own particular approach to the problem of women and their diets. Rumanika kept a harem of wives who were so fat that none of them could stand up. All they could do was roll about the floor or lever themselves forward on their huge forearms. To achieve this state of beauty Rumanika fed his wives on nothing but milk, which they sucked from a gourd through a straw. The gourd was never allowed to be empty and if any of the wives stopped sucking for a moment they were whipped by guards. In Burton's opinion the fate of geese in Strasbourg stuffed to produce the French delicacy of *pâté de foie gras* was far preferable to that of these pitiful human milk sacs.

Royal Mistresses

The first four Hanoverian monarchs – all 'Georges' – had poor taste in women. If one forgets for a moment that arranged marriages were responsible for providing them with wives, in the area of free choice each George chose what one might delicately refer to as 'homely' women as their mistresses. They possessed none of the admirable taste of Edward VII, lover of Sarah Bernhardt, Jersey Lily and the beauties of the Second Empire; or of Charles II, the 'merry monarch', who filled his court and his bed with some ravishing beauties, like Louise de Kérouaille, Nell Gwynn and Barbara Castlemaine. Instead, the taste of the Georges tended towards more solid and substantial German fare than the delicate dishes of Italy or France, or even, for that matter, the British Isles. Of the four Georges, it is probably true to say that George I's taste was the most execrable of all.

The elephant and the maypole

George I made no concessions to the realm he inherited in 1714. He was a German by nature, spoke no English and never wanted to. When he arrived in his new kingdom he came ready equipped with two of the most extraordinary mistresses that any monarch, not actually blind or demented, has ever enjoyed. That they were hags goes without saying, but that they were arrogant, rapacious and intolerable as well, gives the reader a better idea of what hit Greenwich when George and his ladies came ashore. It did not take the Londoners long to sum up the King's mistresses. The short, squat Baroness Kielmannsegge became 'The Elephant' and the tall, skinny Fraulein von der Schulenburg was named 'The Maypole'. As a boy Horace Walpole once met 'The Elephant' and never forgot it: 'I remember being terrified at her enormous figure . . . Two fierce black eyes, large and rolling beneath two lofty arched eyebrows, two acres of cheeks spread with crimson, an ocean of neck that overflowed and was not distinguished from the lower parts of her body, and no part restrained by stays – no wonder a child dreaded such an ogress.' Kielmannsegge resembled a pantomime dame and when she was joined by her 'sister' Schulenberg 'the Maypole' one could hardly have bettered the pair as the ugly sisters in 'Cinderella'. But they were not just comic figures; they were corrupt courtiers and the English were not slow to recognize this. Once when a crowd surrounded her coach, the Maypole called out of the window, 'Goot pipple. What for you abuse us? We came for all your goots.' 'Yes, damn ye,' shouted a stout English yeoman, 'and for all our chattels too.'

The King's mistresses viewed England as a conquered land, fat and rich for the picking. The frugal court of Hanover was forgotten as they discovered the existence of the English court's commissariat for the royal household. Both the Elephant and the Maypole placed enormous orders for furniture, silver, china, carpets and all kinds of food and wines.

Kielmannsegge, who had a beer allowance of four gallons per month in June 1715, had expanded it to sixteen barrels a month two years later, and that excluded huge quantities of wine and sherry that the good lady found necessary to keep body and soul together. So vast were their orders for kitchen equipment and food that each mistress was granted a separate kitchen allowance of £3,000 a year. Even then Schulenburg was not satisfied, demanding extra money for the candles that she used when the King visited her at night. The truth was that sex played only a minor part in their relationship now and Schulenburg usually played paper cut-outs with the King. Of Schulenburg, Sir Robert Walpole wrote, 'She was in effect as much Queen of England as ever any was, though she would sell the King's honour for a shilling advance to the highest bidder.'

On his arrival in England George naturalized the two ladies and then hung titles round their necks like so many pingpong balls. The Elephant became the Countess of Darlington, while Schulenburg was given a series of Irish estates, making her Baroness of Dundalk, Countess and Marchioness of Dungannon and Duchess of Munster. Irish rents were hard to collect, however, and so she asked the King for something in England as well. Thus she became Baroness of Glastonbury, Countess of Faversham and, finally, Duchess of Kendal. The Maypole also managed to persuade the imperial ambassador to press the Emperor Charles VI to make her Princess of Eberstein.

Titles were nice but jewels were even nicer, and soon the two mistresses had taken it upon themselves to 'raid' the late Queen Anne's apartments and go through all her drawers and cupboards in search of loot. The next day it was clear what they had found, for they were festooned in the royal jewels. So efficient were these two foragers that at George II's coronation, his wife had to wear jewellery that her husband had rented for her, for there was nothing in the royal collection but a single string of pearls, presumably too short to go round the Elephant's neck, and too big to stay on the Maypole.

By the time of King George I's death in 1727 the two grand mistresses were in genteel decline. Schulenburg had caught religion and attended church services seven times on Sundays, though because she was reputedly living in adultery with the King – did paper cut-outs constitute adultery? – she was denied communion. Adultery being probably the only one of the Ten Commandments that she was then not currently breaking this seemed an odd reaction on the part of her priest. The Elephant went to her grave in 1725, but the Maypole lived long enough to mourn for the King when he died after eating a gargantuan meal, topped off with a large number of water-melons. When she heard of the King's tragic demise the Maypole screamed and shrieked and displayed every sign of having loved the old rogue. The new king, George II, who had hated his father and all his friends, displayed unwonted magnanimity by allowing the Maypole to return to her property in England.

Mary quite contrary

King George II had better taste in women but far poorer manners than his father. His approach to them had all the subtlety of a blunderbuss in search of a target to hit. A famous incident involving the beautiful, and prim and proper, Mary Bellenden stands as an example for royal philanderers of how not to treat a lady – or a potential mistress.

Queen Caroline's 'Maids of Honour' were a select group of young ladies of the highest moral standards, who guarded their virginity with a ferocity that seems extraordinary in view of the usual lax morals of the Hanoverian court. The most splendid of these vestals was Mary Bellenden, described by a contemporary as 'incomparably the most insinuating and the most likable woman of her time, made up of every ingredient likely to engage or attach a lover'. However, she had no intention of mixing with 'the randy old stag' who sat on the throne.

At one court occasion, George managed to get Mary alone and invited her to sit beside him on a couch. Mary replied that she was not cold and would rather stand. The King then took out his purse and, first giving her a knowing look, he began counting out guineas, over and over again. Mary stood it as long as she could and then said, 'Sir, I can bear it no longer. If you count your money once more, I shall leave the room.' Taking no notice, the King carried on counting, giving her a sly smile. Mary suddenly lashed out with her foot, kicking the King's hand and sending the coins spinning across the dance floor. She then turned and ran out. The King was surprised but not annoyed and promised the girl that she could make her own choice of husband – or lover. In fact, she made a good marriage, to Colonel John Campbell, later Duke of Argyll.

A kingfisher

Even in the reign of King George III the Hanoverians had still not learned how to treat their mistresses, or, more correctly put, the women they hoped to make their mistresses. When Edward Augustus, Duke of York, the younger brother of the King, wished to enjoy the favours of the courtesan Kitty Fisher, she charged him the usual rate of a hundred guineas. However, the next morning the duke offered her merely a fifty pound note. Kitty contemptuously placed the note on a piece of bread and butter and ate it in front of him, and then ordered him out of her house.

A crime of passion

The sons of King George III were notoriously over-sexed. The fifth of them, Ernest Augustus, Duke of Cumberland, became involved in a scandal concerning the wife of one of his servants, a Corsican named Sellis. The denouement occurred one evening when the duke was asleep in his apartment at St James's Palace. He was awoken by a sound in his room and suddenly received a tremendous blow on his head. In the light of a lamp he always kept burning he glimpsed a cavalry sabre and he put his hand up to defend himself and grasp the blade. By doing so he nearly lost his thumb but definitely saved his life. Struggling out of bed he fled next door into his page's room shouting, 'I am murdered!' His assailant cut him across the buttocks as he ran. Shouting for help the Duke was soon surrounded by servants and soldiers from a nearby corridor. When the Duke called on Sellis, his valet, there was no response. A search was undertaken and Sellis was found in his room, with his throat cut. Suicide was suspected and Sellis was assumed to have been the assailant, for a cavalry sabre lay nearby. His motive was not hard to discover, as the Duke had been regularly sleeping with Mrs Sellis without her husband's knowledge. The Duke's injuries were severe, for the cut on the head had split the skull and revealed the brain. But he survived, and in the confusion that surrounded his injury, nobody bothered to inquire too closely as to how Sellis – a left-handed man – could have administered the cut that ended his life. This probably saved the King the embarrassment of seeing one of his sons stand trial for murder for we have only got the Duke's account of what happened and 'dead men tell no tales'.

Photo finish

The ancient ritual of royal toe-sucking had not been much in evidence in modern times, so that its reappearance at St Tropez in August 1992 came as a surprise to trained royal observers. That it should be revived by Sarah, Duchess of York, came as less of a surprise. For Sarah Ferguson has brought a special quality to her six years as a member of the British royal family: naïveté and an almost puppy-like capacity to blunder about and cause mayhem. At first this was very refreshing. The Queen liked her; she was like a breath of fresh air blowing through the staid corridors of British monarchy. But soon the fresh air became a hurricane, rattling the window panes and damaging the roof. 'Fergie's' social gaffes took on a more serious aspect as they invited the press to question the standards of the royal family as a whole. Was dressing up in police uniforms and 'crashing' a nightclub really what the public expected of the Duchess of York? Was throwing bread rolls about an aircraft and putting a sick-bag on your head the right behaviour for the Queen's daughter-in-law? The Duchess's jet-set lifestyle seemed defiantly to invite criticism and was ammunition to critics of the royal family in general.

Sarah Ferguson has contributed more to the demystification of the royal family than any other single member since Edward VIII. The collapse of her marriage to the Duke

The Duchess of York, aka Sarah Ferguson, holds forth in characteristically voluble fashion. The enfant terrible of the younger generation of the late 20th-century British royals, her propensity to generate bad publicity did not endear her to the older members of the British royal family. (LF)

of York and her relationship with her financial adviser, John Bryan, forced the royal family to close ranks against her in self-defence. Sarah seemed never to know where to draw the line. The photographs of her with Mr Bryan in St Tropez revealed the Duchess sunbathing topless while Mr Bryan kissed her, lay on top of her and sucked her toes. In the background the two young princesses, Eugenie and Beatrice, were seen with their nanny, and there was also a detective present. The argument that these photographs were an intrusion on personal privacy is perfectly genuine. However, they cannot be wished out of existence. And if the Duchess believed that she could act intimately in private with another man, while her family stands by and watches, she was quite wrong. It reflected a lack of judgement of astonishing proportions.

When the photographs were published worldwide the effect on the royal family was damaging in the extreme. Prince Andrew wondered if his wife had been drugged so that the photographer could get his scoop. Princess Anne wanted to 'throttle' her sister-in-law. The Duchess of York, on the other hand, thought only of the intrusion on her privacy. She did not understand the damage she had caused. Probably the only previous topless royal had been the insane Princess Caroline in the early nineteenth century (see p. 102) and who wanted to identify with her? It was Sarah's last gaffe. She was too much of a liability for the royal family. Henceforth she would no longer be known as 'Her Royal Highness' the Duchess of York. Her royal days were over.

Edward the Caresser

If the Hanoverians were bunglers when it came to matters of sex, the self-appointed expert in the field was Bertie, eldest son of Queen Victoria, the future King Edward VII. Yet Bertie had his moments of mishap amidst a lifetime of devoted adultery. So devoted was he to his mistresses, in fact, that at his coronation a special place in the Abbey was reserved for them, which was referred to by a wit as 'The King's Loose Box'. When Edward died his long-suffering wife, the charming and beautiful Queen Alexandra, remarked, 'Well at least now I'll know where he is.'

Providing for the future of the royal family was the acknowledged task of the Prince and Princess of Wales, and with five children, both Edward and Alexandra felt that they had carried out that task. As a result, Alexandra retreated into a sexless fantasy world with her young family, while Bertie ignored the little blighters and set off in pursuit of everything in skirts. Paris became Bertie's second home and *les grandes horizontales*, as the best courtesans were known, provided him with all the sensuous enjoyment he needed. From the vulgar La Goulue, who once welcomed him to the Moulin Rouge with the words *'Ullo Wales! Est-ce que tu vas payer mon champagne,'* in a voice that could strip the bark from the trees, to the snobbish but spectacular Hortense Schneider, Bertie was in heaven. When he was once introduced to Giula Barucci, 'the greatest whore in the world', Giula curtsied and then dropped her clothes to the floor, standing naked in front of the prince. Her companion reprimanded her for her forwardness, but Giula replied, 'But you told me to be on my best behaviour with his Royal Highness. I showed him the best I have and it was free.' Other famous ladies who occupied Bertie's bed included the actress Sarah Bernhardt and the grand courtesan La Belle Otero. Prince Albert's halo would have melted at the sight of what Bertie reputedly saw on a silver platter one day. It was a naked Cora Pearl with a sprig of parsley in her navel.

Mrs Alice Keppel, last and probably favourite mistress of Edward VII of Britain, photographed in 1906. Queen Alexandra invited her to sit with the royal family around Edward's deathbed in 1910. (ME)

But while Bertie loved plump young flesh, like the delectable Lily Langtry – 'Jersey Lily' – he found his greatest consolation in the arms and the beds of more mature women, notably the wives of his friends and courtiers. Mistresses like Daisy Brooke, Countess of Warwick and Mrs Alice Keppel, gave him the confidence that he had always lacked as a result of his mother's failure to satisfy his emotional needs. Queen Alexandra understood the role of such women and even became friendly with some of them. When Bertie was dying in 1910, the Queen notified Alice Keppel and asked her to sit with the family during the King's last moments.

If Bertie was a bounder, he was also sometimes a blunderer. In 1874, during one 'visit' to the beautiful Princess de Sagan, at her home in the castle at Mello, outside Paris, Bertie fell foul of the jealousy of one of the Princess's sons. The boy, apparently, entered his mother's dressing room only to find a man's clothes lying all over the carpet. He was outraged at his mother's conduct, so he collected up the garments, took them outside and threw them into a fountain. A few minutes later, the Princess's bedroom door opened and a naked Bertie came into the dressing room looking for his clothes! Even in 1874, Bertie was more portly than the average barrel of beer. Trousers were eventually found for him, but they were bursting at the seams and heaving at the waist when he arrived back at his hotel in Paris.

Sex was one of the only democratic activities to which Bertie would lend his name. He was not a snob in bed and enjoyed the company of the cockney whore, Rosa Lewis. Deprived of a trysting-place, Bertie once went for a very long drive in a closed hackney coach with Rosa. At the end of the journey, Bertie gave the cabbie a shilling. 'What's this bleedin' bob for?' asked the cabbie, who did not recognize the Prince of Wales, and was not best pleased. 'It's your fare, my man,' said Bertie. 'A bleedin' bob for two hours' drive and ten miles?' the cabbie yelled. Luckily, at this moment Rosa leant forward and gave the cabbie two sovereigns. This changed his tune. 'I knowed you was a lady as soon as I seen you,' said the driver to Rosa, 'but where d'you pick 'im up.' The future King of England loved this story and often told it against himself.

During a luncheon party in Biarritz, attended by King Edward VII, a Portuguese duchess picked up the place card of the man next to her and said in a loud voice, 'Keppel . . . Keppel . . . How very odd of you to have the same name as the King's mistress.' She was, in fact, sitting next to Alice Keppel's husband George.

A BUTTERFLY SET IN AMBER: EMPRESS ELIZABETH OF AUSTRIA

When she was a little girl Elizabeth of Wittelsbach, the future Empress of Austria, was told by her father, Duke Maximilian, that he did not want her to 'strut like princes' or drag her feet 'like common mortals' but to move like an angel 'with wings upon your feet'. Elizabeth never forgot these words and they stayed with her throughout the long years of her tragic marriage to the Emperor Franz Josef. Frankly, it was not the best advice to give a girl born to be a royal bride, but it was typical of Maximilian, who was more of a troubadour than a prince. He was a poet – a poor one – and an artist, but his greatest gift was in playing the zither – a peasant instrument – and performing tricks on horseback. He might be described as something of a wastrel, but he loved his children even though he neglected them and they adored him for his charm and open-heartedness. He pursued an amorous career of great variety if little

discrimination throughout the Middle East and North Africa, siring numerous offspring on compliant peasant girls of all races, colours and creeds, playing his zither on top of the pyramid of Cheops and buying four little Negro boys whom he brought back to Munich and had baptized. Of all his children it was Elizabeth who was most like him, for good or ill.

Elizabeth – the future royal beauty – was a complex child, highly strung and moody. With her father she could be lively, even dare-devil, and Maximilian made no concessions to her youth or sex, teaching her to swim and ride bareback on her pony, as well as play barefoot like the gypsy children, at an age when in royal courts throughout Europe her peers would be learning to act like princesses and future royal brides. In fact, until her early teens, she was not regarded as a beauty, being

Elizabeth of Austria. A Bavarian princess of great beauty with a lively artistic temperament, she found the protocol of court life in Vienna increasingly irksome. Her life of growing frustration and unhappiness was ended by an anarchist's knife in Geneva in 1898. (P)

'as round-faced as any little peasant girl'. Elizabeth was happiest playing with her little menagerie of animals, which included guinea-pigs and rabbits, and giving no thought to her future except in the general terms of handsome princes and fairy-tale castles.

While Elizabeth played with her pets, her husband-to-be, Franz Josef, had just come to the throne of the Habsburg Empire at the age of eighteen. Only after he had established peace in his realms, with the collapse of the Hungarian revolt, did his mother, the Archduchess Sophia, decide it was time for him to marry. She wished him to choose a princess from her own family, the Wittelsbachs of Bavaria. Sophia's choice for a bride was her sister Ludovica's eldest daughter, Helen. But, as fate would have it, when Ludovica took Helen to Vienna to meet Franz Josef, Elizabeth was allowed to travel along with her sister. Once the young people met it was apparent that Franz Josef was not attracted to the elder sister but had eyes only for Elizabeth. Was love blind? Well, in this case it must have been. All the two young people could see was a scene from a pop-up book of fairy tales in which a handsome young prince sweeps a beautiful young princess off her feet. It was romantic but it made no sense, as both the Arch-

duchess Sophia and Elizabeth's mother understood. Yet the legacy of Duke Max and his zither were impossible to erase and so the two women blessed the union and the wedding took place (see p. 68)

But after the wedding there was no honeymoon. For both bride and groom it was straight back to work. At her first great reception Elizabeth found that she had to stand for hours and was pleased when she had found some comfortable shoes. Unfortunately, for the next reception she was told that she could not wear the shoes as the Empress *never* wore the same shoes twice. It was symptomatic of how she had lost control over her own life; she was not even allowed to choose her own shoes.

Thus Elizabeth began to settle in to the numbing regime of a Habsburg empress. Her own thoughts were made clear by the lines she wrote at that time:

> Now in a prison cell I wake
> The hands are bound that once were free
> The longing grows that naught can slake
> And freedom thou hast turned from me.

If Franz Josef had been able to read these words he would have wondered whether he had married the right girl. She had already told her father, 'I do love him, if only he weren't an emperor.' But it was not just the Emperor that worried her, it was the Emperor's mother, her aunt Sophia, whose nagging and fault-finding were depressing her free spirit. Angels with wings on their heels have little time for earthbound spirits. And Sophia were earthbound from experience if not inclination. She had learned through harsh experience the value of common sense and due attention to court protocol. Elizabeth, like a nervous, unbroken horse, still dreamed of freedom. Sophia knew that she would only achieve a measure of relief when she came to her senses and accepted her situation. She was an empress and a Habsburg, and that entailed sacrificing herself to the position. Her new responsibilities left no room for 'adventures' and 'freedom'. Her duty now was to her husband, her people and her Church. Elizabeth petulantly referred to her aunt as 'Madame Mère' or, to her closest friends, 'that bad woman', while Sophia responded by labelling the new Empress 'that Bavarian provincial'.

The birth of Elizabeth's first child, Sophie, in March 1855, marked a further step in the breakdown of the marriage. At this, supposedly the moment of greatest joy for a young couple, the cracks began to appear. Elizabeth suffered severe post-natal depression and was greatly disturbed at the effect the birth had had on her figure. For a while she denied the Emperor her bed and rumours spread that he was sexually too rough for her. What must be understood, however, is that, at sixteen, Elizabeth was still immature, physically and emotionally. It is doubtful if her romantic view of marriage had included the physical act of lovemaking, and she was by nature, perhaps, too much in love with herself and her beauty to leave room for anyone or anything else, even a husband. For example, each time her hair was washed, twenty bottles of best brandy were used along with dozens of egg yolks. She made a fetish of her hairdressing, ordering her ladies to count every single hair that she lost. Elizabeth preferred to be adored, set on a pedestal and admired, even worshipped. But, as she later admitted, she 'loathed the whole business of child-bearing'.

Her view of child-bearing must have been coloured by the treatment she received after the birth of her daughter. The baby was taken away from her soon after the delivery and put in the charge of her mother-in-law, who promptly selected the baby's name and all the nurses, maids and so on who would be responsible for the child's upbringing. Elizabeth's reaction to this high-handed treatment was unusual, though perhaps merely a compensation for unfulfilled maternal instincts. As soon as she felt well enough, the Empress began exercising her body rigorously and, to the horror of the Archduchess, riding again. Sophia had assumed that this madcap daughter of Duke Maximilian would soon give up her mania for physical exercise and the 'outdoor life' and become a fulfilled Habsburg, content to breed quietly and efficiently, and decorate her husband's court. But she was wrong. For Elizabeth it was the rigmarole of court life that was unreal; life was to be lived, in the open air, with hair streaming and a horse galloping beneath her. She was depressed by the gloomy Hofburg palace, with every door guarded by soldiers, as if she were in a prison. But most depressing of all was that she had to make appointments to see her own daughter, who was kept on a different floor of the palace. When the mother arrived to see her baby, she was always surrounded by fussing nurses and ladies-in-waiting, so that she never got a chance to develop a close relationship with the little girl on a one-to-one basis. She even suffered the heartbreak of having her child cry when she picked her up and scream until she was returned to her nurse. When her second child, Gisela, was

born the same thing happened again and Elizabeth could see that her children much preferred their grandmother Sophia to their own mother, whom they saw so rarely.

It was jealousy that fuelled the first tragedy of Elizabeth's life, jealousy of her mother-in-law and the influence that she exerted on the two little girls. Franz Josef and Elizabeth were scheduled to undertake a royal visit to Hungary. Against the advice of the Archduchess and the royal doctors, Elizabeth insisted on taking the children with her, even though the climate in Hungary was thought to be unsuitable for the young princesses. But Elizabeth was adamant for a change. Free from Vienna and her mother-in-law, she would make the Hungarians love her and her children. Dressed in Hungarian national costume Elizabeth entered Budapest in a glass coach, with her little girls chattering excitedly next to her. It was the stuff of romance and she was deliriously happy. But after only a couple of days in the city Gisela fell ill, followed by Catherine. Both had a high fever but Sophie's condition seemed far worse than her younger sister's. Nevertheless, the royal doctor, Dr Seeburger, told the Empress that it was just teething trouble and she need not worry. As a result, the itinerary of the visit continued unchanged with the royal couple leaving their children behind in Budapest. While visiting a town in the south of Hungary they received a telegram from Seeburger in Budapest: Sophie was very ill. They hurried back to Budapest but arrived only to find that the little girl was dying. Franz Josef telegraphed Vienna with the news: 'Our little one is an angel in heaven. We are utterly crushed.' Elizabeth bore a double burden: the loss of her first child and a sense of guilt for having brought her, against all advice, to an unhealthy climate. For a while Elizabeth seemed to lose her mind but her husband, strong and unemotional as he was, brought her back to a sense of royal duty. When she asked him to dismiss Dr Seeburger he refused, arguing that the man had done his best and then crassly insisting that his wife remain under his care. It was typical of Franz Josef's generosity but also of his inability to understand his wife.

Elizabeth had none of the resilience of her husband who, as part of a dynasty that had ruled central Europe for six hundred years, was accustomed to death and was able to grieve impersonally and then pass on to the next item on the agenda. It was the Habsburg way and Elizabeth was increasingly demonstrating that she could never be part of it. She became depressed and refused to eat, talking of suicide. Seeburger, concerned to defend his public reputation, made it known that he thought Elizabeth 'unfit to be a mother', claiming that she had 'persistently ignored his advice'.

The birth of her third child and heir to the throne, Prince Rudolf, should have been the highpoint of the marriage, but Elizabeth seemed curiously uninterested by the whole affair. As before she was refused permission to feed her own baby, a task that was immediately allocated to a sturdy peasant girl, selected by the Archduchess. Again Elizabeth was being alienated from her own child and in her mind she heard, over and over again, Seeburger's poisonous accusations that she was unfit to be a mother. She was even denied a part in Rudolf's education. The Archduchess had convinced her son that she and not the boy's mother was the person best equipped to train the next emperor. After all, had she not prepared him, Franz Josef, for the throne?

By 1859 the marriage was as good as over as far as Elizabeth was concerned. Even though she admitted that she still loved Franz Josef the man, she could not face the Emperor Franz Josef – even less his mother. The Emperor was baffled at how far things had declined. His wife was still a very young woman, just twenty-two years old, yet he was denied her bed. Consequently, Franz Josef looked for solace elsewhere and found it in the arms of a beautiful Polish lady-in-waiting to the Archduchess. Elizabeth's latent paranoia made her wonder whether her mother-in-law had planned the whole thing. Unlikely as this may be, Elizabeth had to face the fact that, however beautiful she was, her husband was preferring another. Did she care enough to do anything about it?

The Wittelsbachs of Bavaria had been cursed by the shadow of mental illness for generations. Elizabeth's brilliant cousin King Ludwig II was only just setting out on his long tragic descent to madness and suicide (see p. 53), and Elizabeth herself was undoubtedly a victim of paranoia if not of full-blown insanity. News of her husband's infidelity, on top of everything else, brought about a partial nervous breakdown in 1860. There were physical symptoms too, like swollen wrist and knee joints. Elizabeth, not trusting the diagnoses of her own doctors, sought a second opinion from a noted Viennese specialist. Heavily veiled and using a false name, she visited his surgery in the city. What he told her was

shocking. The Emperor, apparently, had contracted a venereal disease and had passed it on to her. The romantic world of the little girl was shattered. She would always love her husband, perhaps even understand how it had happened, but she could no longer be a wife to him.

Elizabeth now felt that she had to get away, far away from the stifling atmosphere of the Hofburg Palace. Her physical health was giving cause for alarm. She had a nervous cough that would not leave her chest and the royal doctors feared she had a serious lung infection. Had they known the Wittelsbachs better they would have recognized the affliction for a *cri de coeur*, a psychosomatic disorder. Elizabeth's mother wrote her a letter drawing words from her own long experience of a disappointing marriage to that incorrigible child, Duke Maximilian. In fact, Ludovika had been so disappointed with Max's antics that she had locked him in a closet on their wedding night. Ludovika wrote: 'You don't know how to live or to make allowances for the exigencies of modern life. You belong to another age, the time of saints and martyrs. Don't give yourself too much the airs of a saint or break your heart in imagining yourself to be a martyr.' Wise words, perhaps, but it was far too late for them to be of any use. Why had her mother not seen that a marriage between Elizabeth and the Habsburg Emperor must end in disaster? Why had Franz Josef's mother not seen that Elizabeth was an unsuitable match for her handsome, worthy, but deadly dull son? And why was the irresponsible Duke Maximilian allowed to bring up his daughter like a princess in a fairy story, unaware of her duties as a future wife and mother? All of these questions remained unanswered, even unanswerable. But through the blunders of their parents, two young people – the butterfly princess and the dutiful prince – were forced to endure a tragic marriage that brought both nothing but distress.

News of the young Empress's serious illness caused deep concern in all the royal palaces of Europe, and when it was known that she wanted to visit Madeira to recuperate, but lacked a suitable vessel to take her, Queen Victoria put at her disposal the royal yacht *Osborne*. Once aboard the British ship Elizabeth seemed to come alive again. In treacherous seas, and with all her ladies seasick below, she ate not with the other passengers but with the English crew, thoroughly enjoying herself. From Madeira Elizabeth moved on to Corfu, where her insistence on swimming in the sea alarmed her doctor, but did wonders for her recovery. She was still diagnosed as being consumptive, but she did not behave like a sufferer, sitting out at night by the sea, swimming and exercising hard. Franz Josef sent forlorn messages from Vienna asking her to return but Elizabeth was not prepared to sacrifice her newly won freedom. Eventually, in the summer of 1862, she did return to Vienna, but almost immediately her doctors reported her old symptoms returning. In addition, the Empress was now suffering from an eating disorder which, to modern ears, sounds like anorexia nervosa. She began to starve herself, convinced that she was losing her figure, even though she was still only in her mid-twenties. A visit by her mother revealed just how far Elizabeth's mental health had declined. Her only activity during these grim days in Vienna was collecting paintings, drawings and photographs of beautiful women. Austrian ambassadors throughout the world had been ordered to supply her with pictures of local beauties and even the ambassador to Constantinople, risking life and limb by inquiring about the Sultan's harem, kept her provided. What her motivation was for this has never been explained. Partly sapphic, partly narcissistic, Elizabeth seemed to be studying these rival beauties to reassure herself that in truth she was 'the fairest one of all'. Fortunately her mother persuaded her to return to Bavaria for a holiday and there a doctor who had known her as a child diagnosed not tuberculosis but anaemia. She needed complete rest at a spa resort and a good, healthy diet. Her youth and natural strength would do the rest.

But her mind was troubled as much as her body. Each time she returned to Vienna her behaviour became a little stranger. Cured of her lung complaint, Elizabeth succumbed more and more to the ravages of anorexia. Instead of an evening meal she frequently made do with a glass of beer or milk, and a thin soup of beef extract. But this never seemed to affect her riding. She often practised the circus tricks that she had learned from her father, with just her dogs – 'Shadow', 'Mohammed' and 'Plato' – as an audience. When Franz Josef tried to distract her from her melancholia by offering to take her to places of interest she replied that there was a place she wanted to visit: the state lunatic asylum. The Emperor indulged her whim and she enjoyed herself talking to the inmates and questioning their doctors about the treatment they received. At Christ-

Crown Prince Rudolf, only son of the Emperor Franz Josef and Elizabeth of Austria. His life – and that of his mistress Maria Vetsera – ended in the desperation of suicide at a hunting lodge at Mayerling. (AR/IS)

mas in 1863 Franz Josef asked her what she would like as a present and she replied, either a tiger-cub from the Berlin zoo, or, best of all, her own fully equipped lunatic asylum. Their marriage had now reached the stage at which Franz Josef lived only for his children, whom Elizabeth saw rarely, while she lived only for the time that she could spend in the sunshine of the Mediterranean, far away from Vienna.

Elizabeth was now an absentee-Empress, seen by her people so rarely that few could be certain to recognize her. Even the death of the Archduchess Sophia in 1870 came too late to save her marriage. Elizabeth's heart was no longer in it and she lived the life of a free spirit, or perhaps of a pampered, overgrown child who had never really grown up. She loved to travel to England, where she found the hunting set and the gentry much closer to her heart than the aristocrats and courtiers who reminded her of home. In England she felt able to be free, and she also discovered, in Captain Bay Middleton, at least temporarily, a lover who could share her thoughts. Franz Josef found in the actress Katherina Schratt a mistress and a companion for his declining years, but Elizabeth, like the legendary Flying Dutchman, seemed unable to find any rest. She rarely returned to Vienna, or even saw her children, and spent much of her time 'travelling in the realms of gold' in ancient Greece. But tragedy was never far away. In 1889 her son, Crown Prince Rudolf, committed suicide with his mistress at the hunting lodge of Mayerling.

In the last years of her life Elizabeth seemed to be driven by some inner demon. Setting out in a boat once from Dover in a storm she ordered herself to be lashed to the mast, like Odysseus, and withstood an eighteen-hour beating in storm force winds and crashing seas, while all her ladies were below decks praying and being seasick. And even in middle age nobody, neither her young manservants nor her ladies, could keep up with her as she walked and climbed the rocky coasts of Greece. She read Shakespeare and Heine, and learned Greek from a handsome young homosexual named Chistomanos. So effective a teacher was the young man that Elizabeth was able to translate Heine into ancient Greek and Shakespeare's great plays *Hamlet, King Lear* and *The Tempest* into modern Greek. It was all a far cry from the captive life of the butterfly set in amber that had been her lot in Vienna.

Elizabeth's death in 1898 was as much a mistake as her marriage had been: she was assassinated in place of another (see p. 150). She was in the wrong place at the wrong time. And that had always been the problem for Elizabeth. Franz Josef was not a cruel man, nor a bad emperor, he was just the wrong man for Elizabeth. Nor was the Archduchess Sophia a bad woman. She was the mother of an emperor and it was her duty to help him to choose a wife and to train the girl for the duties that an empress had to carry out. The task of being wife to an emperor and mother, not just to one man but to an empire of many millions, was one that was simply beyond Elizabeth's capabilities. Her upbringing was flawed. She was too immature to be a wife, let alone an empress and may even have had a lesbian nature. Certainly her narcissism was so pronounced that it is difficult to see how she could ever have raised a family successfully. The death of her son Rudolf was not her fault alone, but she had failed to provide him with the love and affection that might have saved him from the desperation of suicide. Ultimately, the marriage of Franz Josef and Elizabeth was a royal blunder that imposed suffering on two handsome young people who appeared to have the world at their feet. Its failure was a tragedy for Austria–Hungary which, as a result, lacked the confident leadership of a ruler with a happy home life behind him. After a day struggling with the enormous burden of ruling the Dual Empire, the Emperor could not return to a loving wife and happy children. All that was left were the memories of what might have been.

PRINCE GEORGE AND THE DRAGON

In the last decade of the eighteenth century, with the country embroiled in war with Revolutionary France and an old and insane king on the throne, England had little to look forward to from the Prince of Wales, George III's worthless son, George Augustus Frederick. At thirty-two years of age, the Prince was an elegant spendthrift with so little interest in the future of his family on the throne of England that he had already come to an agreement with his younger brother, the Duke of York, that while he redesigned Brighton in the style of St Basil's Cathedral or the Taj Mahal, Frederick would marry and have children, who could carry on the Hanoverian line. But the Duchess of York had proved barren and the people now looked to the bachelor prince to provide a new heir to the throne. He had already contracted a secret marriage with Mrs Maria Fitzherbert. Unfortunately, because of the Royal Marriages Act of 1772 – something his father had thought up in one of his more cantankerous moments – no offspring from a marriage to a commoner could succeed to the throne. So George really would have to gird his loins and get hitched to some foreign craft – Protestant certainly, German probably, pleasing most improbably.

George was not very dynastic by outlook. In fact,

the future of the monarchy in Great Britain was of somewhat slighter interest to him than the problem of his debts. By 1794 he was so enormously in debt that tradesmen were beginning to refuse his custom and the prince's creditors were appealing to Parliament to force the royal family to face up to their obligations. In the red as he was to the tune of something approaching a million pounds, only the Prime Minister, Mr William Pitt, could bail him out. And Pitt and his colleagues were proving decidedly sticky about helping him while he refused to play the part of a good Prince of Wales and beget sundry offspring by some appropriate princess from the land of Sauerkraut and lederhosen. If he wanted the money, there was nothing for it but for him to hold his nose, unharness his girdle and think of England. It was therefore to the King's considerable surprise when he heard from his son that he was prepared to marry. Anyone would do, as long as she was German and fertile. Unfortunately it was a poor time for German princesses, so when someone suggested the King's niece, Caroline of Brunswick, George readily agreed, without even seeing her. In November 1794 Lord Malmesbury was sent to fetch her. What he found when he got to Brunswick was not the stuff of fairy-tales.

Caroline of Brunswick was nobody's idea of a beautiful princess. She was said by one observer to resemble a pudding. Her head was too big for her body, her neck was too short, her face was always red and she dressed in the poorest taste. Furthermore, she talked incessantly in a coarse and uncouth voice, and was always laughing, though for reasons not immediately apparent to her companions. What was worse was that there had already been warnings about Caroline's conduct, particularly with the opposite sex. It was rumoured that her governess had been given strict orders by her mother not to allow Caroline to leave her side at dances and certainly not to talk to young men. Apparently, Caroline's unbridled passions had already led to 'indecent conversations and conduct'. British travellers in Germany had reported the news at court that Caroline was 'very loose'.

On his arrival in Brunswick, Malmesbury discovered that Caroline's family were no more free of the taint of insanity than most of the princely houses of Germany. In fact, two of Caroline's brothers were already maniacs, confined for their own and the public's safety. Malmesbury cringed at the thought of an alliance between this tainted family

A 1795 caricature by Isaac Cruikshank showing the future George IV gazing fondly at a portrait of his mistress Lady Jersey. A miniature of Caroline of Brunswick dangles disregarded from his left hand. (ME)

and a son of King George III, who was already subject to bouts of insanity himself. Nevertheless, he had his orders. He was to do what he could to 'improve' the young lady and then take her back to her Prince Charming in England.

Malmesbury was noted as the foremost British diplomat of his day but rarely had he faced such a challenge. Securing the marriage treaty was child's play compared with moulding Caroline into a queen of puddings. His first and most pressing task was to persuade the young lady to wash – 'all over'. He achieved this delicate task by prevailing on one of Caroline's ladies to explain the need for cleanliness. Next he proceeded to explain the necessity for changing her clothes occasionally, notably her underclothes and her stockings. While the idea of hygiene was taking root in Caroline's mind, Malmesbury next tried to persuade her to stop talking so much, and to think about what she was going to say before she said it. Caroline promised to try. She then had a tooth extracted and sent it down for Malmesbury to see: his lordship was unimpressed, thinking it 'nasty and indelicate'. The problem was that Caroline had 'no judgment', and – though not bad at heart – was tactless and indiscreet. With a strong, caring husband she might have done well but with a selfish hedonist like the Prince of Wales she had no chance at all. Nevertheless, Malmesbury stuck to his task. Next he told her she must show no jealousy at the Prince's mistresses and for the first six months in England she should remain perfectly silent on every subject. With this ominous piece of advice but partly absorbed, Malmesbury set out to lead Caroline and her entourage across war-torn Europe to rendezvous with an English vessel on the coast in Belgium.

After a tiring journey Malmesbury and Caroline arrived in England on 5 April 1795 to find that, not surprisingly, George had not bothered to come down to meet them. Instead, maliciously, he had sent his current mistress, Lady Jersey, who was to be Caroline's chief lady-in-waiting. Lady Jersey arrived deliberately late so as to keep the princess waiting and then set to work to undermine her confidence. Caroline, not noted for her dress sense, had arrived wearing a blue satin dress and a black beaver hat with feathers. Lady Jersey declared herself 'very much dissatisfied with the Princess's mode of dress'. She prevailed upon Caroline to change into a white satin dress, with a green mantle, but the princess insisted on wearing her black hat. Lady Jersey, studying Caroline's florid cheeks, now persuaded her to add rouge, until the princess resembled a circus clown. Thus apparelled, Caroline set off for London to meet her prince.

The meeting of Caroline and Prince George may not have the epic quality of Stanley's and Livingstone's at Ujiji, but it has become the stuff of legend. Upon arriving at St James's, Malmesbury took the Princess up to an ante-room and waited for the Prince to enter. When he did, Caroline clumsily knelt before him and he raised her up and embraced her. The shock was palpable. George stepped backwards without a word and signalled to Malmesbury, saying, 'I am not well. Pray get me a glass of brandy.' The diplomat suggested water might be more suitable, whereupon the Prince turned away and said, 'I will go directly to the Queen.' Without another word he stalked out of the room. When he had gone Caroline turned to Malmesbury and said, 'My God! Does the Prince always behave like that? I think he's very fat and nothing like as handsome as his portrait.' Caroline had good reason to complain: George now

weighed in at seventeen stone. His waist was as round as a Wensleydale cheese and his face as florid as a fine claret.

At dinner that evening Caroline began to show all of the faults that had so worried Lord Malmesbury back in Brunswick. She chattered away to all and sundry and made coarse comments about Lady Jersey, who was sitting nearby. The Prince sat in stony silence and it was apparent that he despised his wife-to-be. Caroline's attempts at wit were leaden and the more she tried the more he hated her for it. In fact, apart from the king, every other member of the royal family took the Prince's side and treated Caroline with disdain. But Lady Jersey could not resist taunting her new rival, later reputedly putting evil-smelling substances into Caroline's hair, Epsom salts into her food and lacing her wine with strong spirits. At the next night's dinner, the Prince pointedly drank from Lady Jersey's glass to show Caroline how matters stood between them. Not to be outdone, Caroline seized the pipe of a gentleman nearby and blew smoke in the Prince's face. Lady Jersey thereupon retaliated by spreading rumours that her new mistress was 'utterly destitute of female delicacy, did not know how to put on her own clothes and put on her stockings with the seam before or the wrong side outwards'.

The wedding – almost certainly the most ill-omened in the history of the monarchy in Britain – took place on 8 April, in the Chapel Royal at St James's. Caroline, dressed in an enormously heavy dress, stumbled up the aisle, liable to fall at any moment and desperately hanging on to the arm of the Duke of Clarence, who was to give her away. Nevertheless, whether through nerves or natural inclination she chatted away to the Duke as if she was attending a cattle market rather than a wedding. When the Prince attempted to walk up the aisle it was soon apparent that he could not do so unaided and had to be supported on either side by the Dukes of Bedford and Roxburghe. He had been drinking heavily and seemed dazed and in an alcoholic stupor. Observers remarked that his face looked like that of 'a man doing a thing in desperation' or even 'going to his execution'. He constantly looked around until he found Lady Jersey, who smiled supportively at him. The royal dukes who stood by him later said that they had the greatest difficulty in stopping him making a break for it or bursting into tears. The drama intensified when, during the wedding ceremony, the Archbishop of Canterbury reached the point when he was obliged to ask if anyone present knew any reason why the couple should not be joined in holy matrimony. In fact, virtually everyone present, including the Archbishop but excluding the bride, knew of the Prince's prior commitment to Mrs Fitzherbert. The Archbishop, in fact, laid down the book from which he was reading and looked pointedly at both the Prince and the King. Neither responded. Twice more the Archbishop repeated the question but nobody spoke and all the Prince could do was to burst into tears. The service continued and George and Caroline became man and wife. As the couple left the chapel Lady Maria Stuart memorably observed, 'What an odd wedding.'

The Prince's drunkenness carried him through the official reception and intensified as the wedding night approached. In fact, the meeting of the two lovebirds that night was even more ridiculous than their previous encounters. George was apparently so drunk that when he entered the bedroom, where his new wife awaited him, he tripped over and fell into the fireplace, where he spent the whole night snoring. Only at dawn was he sufficiently recovered to climb into bed, but by that stage Caroline was fast asleep herself. Hearing of this, Lord Malmesbury reflected, 'It is impossible to conceive or foresee any comfort from this connection, in which I lament very much having taken any share.'

The honeymoon period was a nightmare for Caroline. Two weeks were spent at Kempshot Park in Hampshire, where Lady Jersey was in constant attendance. According to Caroline the rest of the company consisted of the Prince's drunken companions, so that the house resembled, in Caroline's words, 'a bad brothel more than a palace'. Nevertheless, to general astonishment, by 26 June, when the couple moved to Bognor, the Princess of Wales was able to reveal to the Queen that she was pregnant. For a few months everything was forgiven and Caroline enjoyed the only popularity with the royal family that she experienced during her whole marriage. Even the Queen was kind to her, so desperate was she to see a new heir to the throne. As Caroline went into labour, the Prince played the part of the expectant father to perfection. After all, for him a lot was riding on this child. If Caroline produced a healthy heir to the throne he would have done all that was required of him dynastically and he could abandon this mockery of a marriage and get back to what really mattered in

life, like mistresses and high living. After a twelve-hour labour on 7 January 1796, Caroline gave birth to 'an immense girl', and as far as George was concerned, that was it. He was off.

However, the Prince soon realized that he had put himself to the trouble of marriage and fatherhood to no avail. Although William Pitt had raised the subject of his debts in the House of Commons, leading Whigs under Grey, Fox and Sheridan refused to countenance an increase in his grants unless measures were taken to reduce the Prince's enormous debts. George was furious and now looked for every opportunity to insult his wife, removing all the best furniture from her apartments at Carlton House and taking back the pearl bracelets he had given her as a wedding present and giving them instead to Lady Jersey, who wore them publicly to irritate the new Princess of Wales. Nor was the Queen any kinder to her new daughter-in-law, taking her son's part in every dispute. Never a mistress of tact, Caroline wrote home to Brunswick, describing the Queen as 'Old Snuffy' or 'de old Begum'. We know these last details because Lady Jersey intercepted Caroline's letters and passed them on to the Queen herself. Meanwhile, George abandoned Caroline at Carlton House and rented a house in the country, where Lady Jersey had a bed made up in the prince's dressing room.

The birth of his daughter, Princess Charlotte, seems to have prompted the Prince to sit down and write his will. In it he bequeathed everything to 'his beloved and adored Mary Fitzherbert'. His new daughter was to be left in the custody of the King and Queen. The mother of the child, 'called the Princess of Wales', was to be denied any part whatsoever in the education or care of the child. He described Caroline as entirely lacking judgment and insisted that every effort should be made to prevent 'the child falling into such improper and bad hands'. Vindictively he insisted that everything he had ever given Caroline, notably jewellery, should instead be given to his daughter. To the Princess of Wales herself he bequeathed a shilling.

Caroline fought back by writing to George asking to be excused from dining at the same table as Lady Jersey, 'a person whom I can neither like nor respect and who is your mistress'. The Prince replied, indicating that he wanted an immediate separation. For this he needed the King's permission but George III was unwilling to give it, in spite of his son's description of his wife as 'the vilest wretch this world ever was cursed with'. The chances for a reconciliation did not seem strong.

The sudden and dramatic collapse of the royal marriage was soon public knowledge and the general view was that the Prince of Wales was in the wrong. Who could blame Caroline? After all, she had come to marry a prince and found that he was already married, hated the sight of her and much preferred to live with his mistress. Even after Caroline had borne him a child, the baby was taken away from her and brought up separately. It was a lot for a woman to bear.

For the next quarter of a century the 'disastrous marriage' of the Prince of Wales and Princess Caroline of Brunswick continued in name only. Caroline suffered every kind of humiliation and yet, as Malmesbury had found on first acquaintance with her, she was her own worst enemy. In the first few years of her separation she lived at Blackheath, where her indiscretions were legion and her lovers only slightly fewer, including some famous names like Admiral Sidney Smith and Lord Canning. She was even accused of bearing an illegitimate child and was forced to undergo an investigation by the Privy Council, known as 'The Delicate Investigation', which acquitted her of that charge. Unfortunately, it opened a Pandora's box of other scandals and indiscretions instead. Tired of England, Caroline undertook a continental tour beside which the peccadilloes of the House of Windsor in the 1990s look tame in the extreme.

Accompanied by a few lady friends and a veritable League of Nations of extraordinary hangers-on, Caroline wandered from town to town like part of some travelling circus. She was obviously the main attraction: part clown, part bearded lady. At each stop her behaviour grew more eccentric. At a ball in Geneva the now matronly Caroline appeared as Venus, bare to the waist, 'displaying a bosom of more than ample proportions'. Thus clad – or unclad – she apparently danced the night away. In the company of her chamberlain – and lover – one Bartolomeo Bergami, a tall, dark-haired Italian waiter or ice-cream seller, with vast moustachios, she lived a life of gay abandon. At Genoa, it is said, she was dressed like 'Little Bo-peep' with pink booties and was drawn through the streets in a carriage pulled by her young admirers, while at Baden she attended the opera in a head-dress so tall that her ladies needed a step-ladder to comb it, and was later seen riding beside the Grand Duke with a

pumpkin on her head, claiming that it was the 'coolest sort of coiffure'. In Athens she danced naked to the waist with a band of gypsies, while in Turkey she slept in a tent and Bergami rode across the desert sands to join her in a night of unparalleled pleasure. During a visit to Jerusalem, she appointed Bergami Grand Master of the Order of Caroline. It would all have been harmless fun except that she was still married to the Prince of Wales. One English visitor abroad, Lady Bessborough, who saw Caroline at a ball, found the sight humiliating:

> I cannot tell you how sorry and ashamed I felt as an Englishwoman. In the room was a short, fat, elderly woman, with an extremely red face (owing I suppose to the heat) in a girl's white frock-looking dress, but with shoulder, back and neck, quite low (disgustingly so) down to the middle of her stomach; very black hair and eyebrows, which gave her a fierce look . . . I was convinced she was mad.'

By 1819 the Prince of Wales's rather cautious legal advisers had at last decided that he could file for a divorce on the grounds of adultery between Caroline and Bergami, plus a list of others named or otherwise, running to several volumes. The whole matter took on an added urgency when King George III died and the Prince of Wales succeeded him in 1820.

Caroline of Brunswick was still George's wife. Did that mean that she would become queen? It was an issue of great constitutional importance, in view of Caroline's numerous sexual indiscretions. The great fear was that she would try to return from the continent in time for George's coronation. And that is precisely what she decided to do. On her return Caroline found that she was enormously popular with the masses, who loathed the new king as no English monarch before. George was now advised that Caroline should be put on trial before the House of Lords to answer charges of 'scandalous, disgraceful and vicious conduct'. But when asked by learned counsel if she was guilty of the charges of adultery, Caroline, who was nothing if not game, answered that she had only committed adultery once and that was with Mrs Fitzherbert's husband. It brought the house down. In a sense, of course, she was right. It was her husband who was the adulterer; she was merely the victim of his bigamy.

After the trial had dragged on for some three months it became obvious that Caroline's popularity would prevent any verdict of 'guilty' being acceptable to the House of Commons and so the

TRIAL OF HER MAJESTY QUEEN CAROLINE.

Explanation.

A. The Queen.
B. Mr Brougham Attorney General to Her Majesty.
C. Mr Denman Solicitor General to Her Majesty.
D. Dr Lushington.
E. The Marquis of Spinette Interpreter.

F. The Attorney General (Sir R. Gifford.)
G. The Solicitor General (Mr Serjt Copley.)
H. Mr Maule Solicitor to the Treasury.
I. Theodore Majochi First Witness against Her Majesty.
K. Mr Gurney the Short-hand Writer.

L. The Lord Chancellor.
M. The Throne.
N. The Treasury Gallery.
O. The Opposition Gallery.
P. The Judges.
Q. The Bishops.

Published Oct. 1. 1820. by H. Rowe, 2 Amen Corner.

The trial of Queen Caroline in the House of Lords in 1820 was the culmination of her disastrous marriage to George IV. The latter's attempt to divorce Caroline for adultery ended in defeat and only served to increase his unpopularity. (H)

case was dropped. For three nights London reverberated to the celebrations of Caroline's victory. But if it was a victory it was a hollow one. Government supporters penned these lines addressed to the King's wife:

> Gracious Queen, we thee implore:
> Go away and sin no more.
> Or, if the effort be too great,
> Go away at any rate.

But Caroline had no intention of going away. She was planning to attend the King's coronation and intended to be crowned herself as was her right. What followed stands as one of the most embarrassing scenes in England's long history. George knew Caroline well enough to realize that if she said she was going to attend the coronation she would have to be taken seriously. Consequently, all porters and doormen at Westminster Abbey were put on the alert, with the instruction that under no circumstances was the queen to be admitted.

On 19 July 1821 Caroline, accompanied by Lord Hood and a number of her friends, set out for the Abbey at eight-thirty in the morning. As she was driven through the London streets crowds of well-wishers stood and cheered, shouting 'The Queen! The Queen for ever!' But when she arrived at the abbey she found that the doors were guarded by two ex-prize-fighters hired by the government. Lord Hood took charge of the situation and told the doorman, 'I present to you your Queen.' But the doorman was in no mood to recognize anyone without a ticket. Caroline then addressed the man, 'I am your Queen, will you not admit me?' He refused. Hood produced his ticket and gave it to Caroline. The boxer said, 'No transfers.' Hood was by now losing his temper. 'Am I to understand that you refuse Her Majesty admission?' That was about the size of it. Collapse of stout party. Hood and Caroline stepped back, apparently flummoxed. There was a derisive cheer and then the fickle crowd began to laugh at their Queen, while others armed with tickets pushed past her and went into the abbey. As she returned to her carriage the crowd variously cheered her or called out, 'Go home, you common disturber' and 'Go back to Bergami!' Before she drove home she made one last attempt to break into Westminster Hall, where the coronation banquet was to be held. Here she was stopped by the sentries, who crossed their bayonets and refused to let her pass. Caroline was almost beside herself with humiliation, bellowing, 'I am your Queen; I am Queen of Britain.' But she only stirred the Lord Chamberlain to march up portentously and order the servants, 'Do your duty, shut the Hall door.' The door was slammed in Caroline's face. After some desultory hammering on the door with an umbrella, Caroline turned away, thoroughly defeated. Within a week she was dead, not of a broken heart but of an obstruction of the bowels. It was a curious way for the 'disastrous marriage' – as it was known – to end finally, 'not with a bang but a whimper'.

In 1935 the Prince of Wales, soon to be Edward VIII, addressed a meeting of the British Legion with the following words, 'I feel that there could be no more suitable body or organisation of men to stretch forth the hand of friendship to the Germans than we ex-servicemen who fought them and have now forgotten all about it and the Great War.'

THE WOMAN I LOVE: EDWARD VIII AND MRS SIMPSON

Edward VIII is the only British sovereign to have abdicated in five hundred years, which should give some idea of how unusual and shocking the act must have appeared to the people of Britain and its Empire in 1936. And yet those who knew the Prince well might have suspected that David (Edward was always known by the seventh and last of his forenames) was the sort of man who could abdicate. The real problem was that David viewed himself as a prisoner of his birth, chained to a destiny that others had chosen for him. In the early 1920s he wrote, 'The idea that my birth or title should somehow or other set me apart from and above other people struck me as wrong. I suppose that, without quite understanding why, I was in an unconscious rebellion against my position.' These could be the thoughts of a progressive young royal, attempting to adjust himself to the changing needs of his country in the twentieth century. But they are not. David was only dimly aware of social problems. He might visit the disadvantaged, but he did not stay long. And he had forgotten what he said to them by the time he had poured himself his next drink. His feeling for democracy was a thin veneer. Had he realized that people only respected him because of his title, rather than for his own qualities, he might have been a better man. And had he been prepared to surrender the advantages he was so quick to condemn – the servants, the palaces, the money, the social life and the compliant women – then perhaps people would have been more prepared to listen to him whining about his lack of freedom. David was a dissatisfied traveller on the richest of all gravy trains. Yet he had only to get off!

Starved of emotion as a boy, David learned nothing about love from his parents (see p. 141). He was given a thorough grounding in sex, not as in previous centuries by a compliant young peasant girl, but instead by a Doctor of Divinity, who ran through the basic facts, skipping any reference to 'love' or enjoyment and laying the emphasis on the duty of a prince to procreate. It was a disastrous

The former Edward VIII and Mrs Simpson in Paris in 1937. Edward abdicated in 1936 after the British government and representatives of the dominions had expressed their strong opposition to his intention of marrying the American divorcée. (P)

failure. Later, during his service in France in the First World War, his equerries, either on their own initiative or through orders from above, tried to improve on this by taking David to a brothel in Calais. He later described the whole experience as 'perfectly filthy and revolting'.

For a dozen years after the war David's round-the-world trips made him as famous and, in some eyes, as exciting and attractive a figure as the latest Hollywood stars. He was the first royal figure to dominate the newspapers by his public activities and his high living. He became a socialite who moved with the 'fast set' and his constant exposure to publicity laid him open to any sniff of scandal. It was the Jazz Age, and the Prince of Wales was a part of it. Sir Frederick Ponsonby, courageously answering

a throw-away question by the Prince as to how he was doing as Prince of Wales, replied, 'I think there is a risk of making yourself too available. A Prince should not show himself too much. The Monarchy must remain on a pedestal.' But David had no intention of being a statue. His Private Secretary, Alan Lascelles, was even blunter about his royal master. 'I can't help thinking that the best thing that could happen to him, and to the country, would be for him to break his neck.'

David's irresponsible approach to his duties was becoming more and more obvious. He wrote in his diary, 'What a rot and a waste of time, money and energy, all these state visits are!' But he was quite prepared to enjoy all the privileges of his office without submitting to the discipline of doing his duty. While on safari in Kenya in 1928, he received a telegram from the Prime Minister requesting his return as King George V was seriously ill. David was put out and told Alan Lascelles there was nothing in this scare about his father and that it was 'just an election dodge of old Baldwin's'. Lascelles lost his temper: 'Sir, the King of England is dying and if that means nothing to you, it means a great deal to us.' David sullenly agreed to return home. Yet this did not prevent him seducing the wife of the local commissioner the same night, and boasting about it to Lascelles the next morning.

After his slow start in the sexual stakes, David made up for lost time with a whole string of affairs, many with married women. Most prominent was Freda Dudley Ward, in whom David found the 'loving mother' he had been seeking for so long. King George referred to her scornfully as 'a lacemaker's daughter', but she was a good and loyal friend. Yet even after a sixteen-year friendship, she got no loyalty from David, who was too shy to tell her their friendship was over and instead instructed the royal telephonist not to connect her calls any more.

He had already passed on to Thelma, Lady Furness, an American socialite, whose nickname was 'Toodles', and whose twin sister had married a Vanderbilt. But this affair was not fated to last long for in January 1931 Lady Furness invited David to a weekend house party where he met for the first time Mr and Mrs Ernest Simpson.

The pressure on the Prince of Wales to marry had been growing during the 1920s, and by 1931 both the King and his subjects felt that David was shirking his duty. His brother Albert, the Duke of York, was already married and had two charming daughters. But David insisted on playing 'fast and loose' with the field. He revelled in the popularity that newspaper coverage had brought him and felt genuinely 'loved' for the first time in his life. The danger in marriage, as he saw it, was that he would have to share this adulation with someone else and also lose his independence at the same time. He much preferred nightclubs, casinos, beach parties, the best restaurants and his pick of the ladies to boring court ceremonies, flag-raising and reviewing the guard. The Conservative politician Stanley Baldwin sized up the Prince of Wales well when he observed, 'He is an abnormal being, half child, half genius. It is almost as if two or three cells in his brain had remained entirely undeveloped.' Alan Lascelles cer-

tainly thought there was something wrong with David's mind. He said in the 1940s, 'For some hereditary or physiological reason his mental and spiritual growth stopped dead in his adolescence.' Harold Nicholson put it more poetically: 'The king was like a child who has been given every gift except a soul. He hated his country since he had no soul and did not like being reminded of his duties.'

In Wallis Simpson David believed that he had found, even more than in Freda Dudley Ward, the mother-substitute that he had been seeking since early childhood. It is doubtful if Queen Mary would have been flattered by the comparison. Still, in many ways, the fault was hers. In any case, David was content that he had found the woman he wanted to marry. Unfortunately, he had overlooked an important fact: she was married, and had been divorced once before already. Was Wallis Simpson the sort of woman the British people would welcome as their next Queen of England? It was not a question David was interested in answering, but it was one that the Church of England hierarchy and the British establishment insisted on asking.

So much has been written on Wallis Simpson that it ought to be possible to answer the question of her suitability, at least according to the mores of the time. But, in fact, the real Mrs Simpson lies hidden behind smokescreens spread by the violently pro- and anti- factions that grew up after the Abdication Crisis and have continued to do battle ever since.

The real Wallis Simpson is an elusive character, as much so as the real King Edward VIII. What we do know is that Wallis was born in Baltimore in 1896 and, at the age of nineteen, married the handsome, hard-drinking naval pilot, Earl Winfield Spencer, almost certainly for his money. Only later did she come to realize that she had married a drunk, and a sadistic one at that. In 1921, Wallis walked out on him, vowing to get a divorce. She now moved in on the smart set in Washington, where she had an affair with Mussolini's ambassador, Prince Caetani, and later met and fell in love with the Argentinian attaché, Don Felipe Espil. Her affair with Felipe did not last long and Wallis was soon back with her husband, who had promised to kick his drinking habit. Wallis then spent some time in Hong Kong, where British Intelligence and American Naval Intelligence took an interest in her activities. With Winfield she went to some high-class brothels in Hong Kong known as the Singing Houses, which

The Duke of Windsor listens with amusement to Nazi propaganda minister Dr Josef Goebbels at a party given in his and the Duchess of Windsor's honour in Berlin, 12 October 1937. The former Edward VIII spent World War II as governor of the Bahamas. (P)

were frequented by naval officers from a number of countries. The girls who worked in these brothels were highly trained in the amorous arts and in Chinese eyes were regarded as artistes rather than whores. It is alleged that Wallis learned sexual techniques from these girls. In 1926, Wallis returned to America and began filing for a divorce from Winfield Spencer. She had meanwhile begun an affair with an Anglo-American named Ernest Aldrich Simpson, the son of a wealthy New York shipbroker. Simpson had money but he was also married. Wallis apparently broke up the marriage and when Simpson's divorce came through, she married him in London in 1928. Ernest, who had spent some time in the Coldstream Guards, was accepted in the best social circles in London and this is how he and Wallis came to be at Lady Furness's party, where they first met the Prince of Wales.

At this stage one would be hard put not to view Wallis Simpson as a rapacious gold-digger, prepared to go to any lengths to get what she wanted. She was accustomed to having money but she wanted more than that and, when she was introduced to the Prince of Wales, she had her eye on a crown as well as a fortune. From now on, Ernest Simpson became a mere spectator as his wife cuckolded him in her pursuit of the Prince of Wales. As she increasingly mixed with the royals, Wallis came up against adversaries who would relentlessly pursue her to the grave rather than allow her to become Queen or even a member of the exclusive royal club. There were those who viewed Wallis as a dangerous interloper who had to be stopped.

The death of his father in 1936 was not a matter of great sorrow for David. They had never really got on, the gap between them was much too wide to bridge. The late King had regarded his son as a 'cad', quite unsuited to being monarch. With extraordinary prescience, his father had warned, 'After I am dead that boy will ruin himself in twelve months.'

David's mother, Queen Mary, was distraught at the relationship of her son with Mrs Simpson. She felt that David had simply lost his sense of proportion, and she was shocked to learn that her son was prepared to pay Ernest Simpson £100,000 to persuade him to expedite his divorce, on the grounds of his own adultery rather than that of his wife. On 28 March 1936 Ernest and Wallis Simpson were divorced, Ernest admitting adultery with the unlikely person of Buttercup Kennedy, a professional adulteress. David now announced to his mother that he intended to marry Wallis immediately. Queen Mary, drawing on all her years of experience as a monarch, reminded him of his obligations as King of England. She told him that she would never accept Wallis as his wife, nor would she ever support her as Queen. The Prime Minister, Stanley Baldwin, and the Archbishop of Canterbury, Cosmo Lang, took the same line, determined that Wallis should never be Queen as a twice-divorced woman. Baldwin even made it a matter of political confidence by telling the King that the government, elected by the British people in a general election, would resign rather than allow him to marry Wallis. The British people, in whose name so many politicians claim so much, were remarkably ignorant of what the new king intended. But David, careless of what people thought, chartered the yacht *Nahlin* and 'honeymooned' with Wallis in full view of the world. The British people were scandalized at the news that the King was conducting an open affair with an American divorcée. On his return, Edward was hissed in public and at events throughout the country ordinary members of the public refused to stand for the national anthem.

With the threat of civil disorder as a result of the government's resignation, frightening possibilities presented themselves to the King. He was warned that there was even the danger of civil war. However unlikely this was, the situation in which he was placing the country was unprecedented. Edward was told that if he fought to keep Wallis it could lead to the collapse of the monarchy. The strength of the opposition to Wallis as a person and as a potential Queen took Edward totally by surprise and rather overawed him. On 10 December 1936 King Edward VIII signed a document of abdication. As he said, 'You must believe me when I tell you that I have found it impossible to carry the heavy burden of responsibility and to discharge my duties as King as I would wish to do without the help and support of the woman I love.'

If the British public had known the sort of relationship that existed between their King and the woman that he loved they would have cheered his abdication to the rafters. David had never really grown up at all. Freda Dudley Ward, who was always kind to him, wrote later, 'I could have dominated him if I had wanted to. I could have done anything with him! He made himself slave of whomever he loved, and became totally dependent on her. It was his nature: he was like a masochist. He liked being humbled, degraded. He begged for it.' This is a devastating view of the son of a powerful king, King George V, a man after whom battleships were named. Yet it is true. A friend of the royal family once saw Wallis force David to go down on all fours and beg like a dog when he asked for a cigarette. It could have been a game, but it wasn't. Wallis wore the trousers and Wallis would have worn the crown too. One of David's servants gave notice the day he saw him, his sovereign, kneeling at Wallis's feet and painting her toe-nails. Frankly, David was not cut out to be King. Abdication probably saved him from shameful deposition during the darkest days of the Second World War. A nation 'fighting on the beaches' cannot afford to have as its ruler a man of straw, who sought the domination of a woman to help him with his own childish inadequacy. As with ill-fated 'Eddie', Duke of Clarence, perhaps it was better that King Edward VIII chose 'love' rather than duty (see p. 137).

In 1939 Neville Chamberlain, the prime minister, was twice forced to prevent King George VI writing to Adolf Hitler from 'one ex-serviceman to another' in an attempt to stop the war.

CHAPTER 4: ROYAL CHILDREN

Births and Baptisms

One would imagine that the births of royal children would be events of joy and deep satisfaction to both parents and their subjects. Unfortunately, in Hanoverian England, this was rarely so. As with Christmas in some families, royal births brought out the worst in the 'Georges' and were the cause of deep and bitter feuds that influenced the political health of the country.

Hard labour

On 2 November 1717 Princess Caroline, wife of George, the Prince of Wales, gave birth to a son. King George I came down to the birthing chamber to congratulate his son on the birth of the child. He found that the Prince of Wales was in the process of selecting godfathers for the baby's christening, and was duly asked if he would stand along with his brother, the Duke of Cumberland. For some reason best known to him, at the last moment the King decided to replace Cumberland with the Lord Chamberlain, the Duke of Newcastle. Unfortunately the Prince of Wales and Newcastle were political opponents and all through the christening ceremony the Prince was seething with indignation at what his father had done. When the ceremony ended the King took his leave, but no sooner had he gone than the Prince rushed up to Newcastle, treading on his toes, and said in his thick German accent, 'Rascal, I find you out.' Newcastle, being slightly hard of hearing and a coward into the bargain, thought the Prince had said, 'I fight you.' He rushed off in terror to tell King George that the Prince of Wales had challenged him to a duel.

The King was nonplussed. In his view the Prince of Wales was guilty of mutiny, for which the penalty was death. Tsar Peter the Great had killed his son for less, and the Prussian King Frederick William had imprisoned his for a similar offence. What was he to do? He decided to call an emergency council meeting. Lord Stanhope told him, 'It is true that he is your son, but the Son of God himself was sacrificed for the good of mankind.' The Earl of Sunderland suggested asking the Royal Navy to carry the Prince off and leave him in the remotest part of the planet. Fortunately, other more reasonable views prevailed.

Meanwhile, the Prince was being questioned as to what exactly he had said, but he was hardly more lucid than before, saying, 'I said I would find him, and I will find him, for he has often failed in his respect for me, particularly on the late occasion by insisting on standing godfather to my son when he knew it was against my will.' When someone reminded him that the choice of Newcastle had been at the King's instigation, the Prince refused to believe it.

Back in the council the King had reached his decision. The Prince would be placed under arrest and confined to his wife's quarters, and the doors would be guarded by two

George I, King of Great Britain and Ireland and Elector of Hanover, thoroughly disliked his adopted country, spending as little as possible of his time there. Having divorced his wife Sophia Dorothea in 1695 he ruled without a queen, but enjoyed the favours of numerous mistresses, of which the most notorious were the 'Elephant' and the 'Maypole'. (ME)

Yeomen of the Guard, with crossed halberds. The poor midwife returning to tend the new baby had a halberd poked in her ribs.

The general opinion was that, as usual, the King had overreacted. King George, who had imprisoned his wife Sophia Dorothea in a castle for thirty years, was inclined to do that. It was felt that, being a German and ignorant of English law, he would be unaware of the existence of Habeas Corpus. His ministers felt it might be embarrassing – and dangerous – for a judge to send a court order demanding the release of the Prince of Wales. In this way they persuaded the King not to incarcerate his son in the Tower of London and throw away the key.

While all this was happening, Princess Caroline was aware that faces were growing longer everywhere and tears and groans rather than laughter seemed to have been reserved for her happy day. The King sent her word – not very reassuringly – that she could stay with her three young daughters and the new baby, provided she made no attempt to communicate with its father. Prince George now sent a note to the King agreeing to leave the palace forthwith, taking his wife with him. The King agreed but insisted that all the children, including the baby, must remain behind. Princess Caroline fainted and had to be carried out. The King asked his ministers if he could change the Act of Succession and cut his son out.

The Prince and Princess of Wales now set up house at Leicester Fields, where they became an immediate focus for political opponents of the government. King George made it plain that anyone who visited his son would no longer be received at court. However, as time passed this sanction was seen as an empty one, the King, after all, was an old man who might die soon. The Prince of Wales gathered more support as the 'coming man'. Leicester Fields, in fact, became a centre for aspiring politicians like Walpole and Townshend, and the home of an unofficial 'opposition' faction. The King did try to exploit the fact that he kept the three little princesses and the baby as virtual prisoners at the palace but he was increasingly seen as an ailing tyrant whose days were numbered. The schism between King George I and his son established a pattern for the next hundred years, in which ruling monarchs and their eldest sons became personal and political enemies.

Queen Anne was a most unfortunate mother. None of the seventeen children she bore her husband George of Denmark survived infancy. Imagine her thoughts when at her coronation the Archbishop of Canterbury expressed the hope that she would 'leave a numerous posterity to rule these kingdoms'.

Like father, like son

And what a difference a generation makes! For King George I read King George II; for Prince George read Prince 'Fred'; and for poor suffering Princess Caroline read nasty, vicious Queen Caroline.

King George II's eldest son, born in Hanover in 1707, was known to everyone as 'Poor Fred'. His parents hated him bitterly. Perhaps it was because the elderly King George I loved him that his parents felt they had to loathe him. Perhaps the fact that he was entirely educated in Germany, away from them, may have cut the ties of natural affection. Whatever the reason, 'Fred' was unloved by his parents and when he came to England for the first time in 1728, nobody was sent to meet him. He was a Prince of Wales entirely unknown to the people of England, but their dislike of his father – generally known as 'King Gruff' – served to make 'Fred' immensely popular. As his mother commented, 'Fretz's popularity makes me spew.' The Queen was also responsible for spreading stories that her son was impotent. When rumours from certain ladies suggested she was wrong she ordered Lord Hervey to ask Lady Dudley, as 'she had lain with half the town as well as Fretz'. Hervey delicately declined.

When 'Fred' eventually married Princess Augusta of Saxe-Gotha the Queen insisted that there was no chance of them ever having a baby. However, some months after the wedding, 'Fred' proudly told his mother that Augusta was pregnant. The Queen was furious. She had no wish to see a son of Fred's as heir presumptive to the throne. And she still insisted that if Augusta was pregnant, which she doubted, Fred was not the father. The Queen declared that she must be present when the baby was born or else she would not believe in it. It had been known for babies to be smuggled into the birthing room in warming-pans. She expected her son was quite capable of doing something like that and passing off some trollop's brat as his own. Fred, on the other hand, was determined to stop his mother attending the birth, if for no other reason than to spite her.

On 31 July 1737 the royal family, including Fred and Augusta, was at Hampton Court. At 1 a.m. in the morning Queen Caroline was awoken by one of her ladies with the news that Princess Augusta was beginning labour. Caroline casually told her to 'fetch her nightgown' and that she would come down presently. The lady told her that she would need more than a nightgown, perhaps a travelling cloak. For Princess Augusta was in labour at St James's Palace, fourteen miles away! The King now awoke and began shouting at his wife: 'This is all your fault. There is a false child will be put on us, and how will you answer it?'

During the previous evening Princess Augusta had begun to feel labour pains and so, waiting until his parents had retired for the night, Fred, aided by a dancing master and one of his equerries, carried the princess downstairs and into a coach, accompanied by Lady Archibald Hamilton and a midwife.

Once the coach was loaded they all set off at top speed for St James's Palace, away over bumpy and broken roads. Augusta went through agonies and spent much of the journey

George II was no fan of English literature. As he once asked, 'Who is this Pope that I hear so much about? I cannot discover what is his merit. Why will not my subjects write in prose! I hear a great deal too of Shakespeare, but I cannot read him, he is such a bombast fellow.'

screaming, while Fred, with 'all the cheerfulness of a toothdrawer or an executioner, assured that it would soon be all over, plied handkerchiefs under her petticoats and extinguished the lights so that passers-by should not see'. They reached St James's just in time. As the Princess was placed in bed, she gave birth to 'a little rat of a girl, about the bigness of a good, large toothpick-case'.

The Queen did not arrive at the palace until some hours afterwards. Her attitude towards the new baby was scathing. As she said, she had no doubt that the little scrap was Fred's. 'If instead of this poor, ugly little she-mouse, there had been a large, fat, jolly boy, I should not have been cured of my suspicions.' Fred, meanwhile, was the talk of Hampton Court:

His sister said: 'I wish that he may die, and that we may all go around with smiling faces.'

His mother said: 'I hope in God that I shall never see that monster's face again.'

His father said: 'My dear first-born is the greatest ass, and the greatest liar, and the greatest canaille, and the greatest beast, in the whole world and I most heartily wish him out of it.'

'Fred' pondered his open breach with his father and, with 'opposition' politicians flocking to join him at Carlton House, reflected that history has a way of repeating itself.

In 1935 King George V met the author John Buchan and told him, 'I don't get much time for reading, but when I do I enjoy your books, The Thirty-Nine Steps *and so on. Now before you go, the Queen would like to have a word with you.' Buchan soon met Queen Mary who told him, 'The King does not get much time for reading but when he does I'm afraid he reads the most awful rubbish.'*

Royal christenings

Historians are not well supplied with details of the numerous royal baptisms that have taken place. Nevertheless, three christenings in particular are memorable for the mishaps that occurred. In 742 the Byzantine Emperor, Leo III, died and was succeeded by his son, Constantine, who bore the unpleasant soubriquet 'Copronymous'. Apparently he acquired this name as a result of an unfortunate incident at his christening in 718, when baby Constantine defecated in the baptismal font.

In 965, the christening of Ethelred, son of King Edgar of England, and later known as the 'Unraed', was marked by an incident which boded ill for the future. Baby Ethelred urinated in the font and defiled the holy water. This was taken as a sign that he would be unlucky, which has to be one of history's great understatements.

A much more modern christening, one that took place in Belgrade in 1923, also involved a significant mishap. George, Duke of York, was standing as sponsor for the new Prince Peter, son of King Alexander and Queen Marie of Yugoslavia. During the ceremony, the duke was forced to rescue the baby from drowning after the Serbian

Patriarch carelessly dropped him into the deep end of the font, head first. The baby was unimpressed and drowned the singing in the church with his cries while the embarrassed future George VI tried to dry him with an embroidered nappy.

Heirs to the Throne and How Not to Treat Them

Far from being the great hope for the future, many heirs to the throne have been viewed by their parents more as 'the enemy within'. This was certainly true of many princes born in Germany, Britain and Austria during the eighteenth and nineteenth centuries, and even later. The results were almost universally disastrous, leading to tragedies of suicide and mental disturbance.

A grim prospect

The madness that affected the Spanish Habsburgs may have been responsible for the afflictions suffered by King Philip II's son and heir, Don Carlos, though there is substantial evidence to suggest that the boy may, in fact, have suffered brain damage after a difficult birth. Apparently when his mother went into labour with him all the experienced midwives were off enjoying an *auto da fé,* and so his delivery was bungled and his mother died just four days later. So Carlos began life at a considerable disadvantage, being motherless, a Habsburg and mentally disturbed. Even worse, his father was the obsessive and fanatical Philip II.

Carlos was an unlovable boy who spent his childhood in a state of almost permanent anger. He liked having little girls whipped and roasting their pet rabbits alive. If anyone failed to do what he required he had them beaten on the soles of their feet. He took pleasure in maiming horses – as many as twenty-three of them had to be destroyed after receiving Don Carlos's attentions. His waking hours were spent threatening people: even a cardinal escaped his dagger only by a hair's breadth. He once ordered boots of a large size so that he could carry pistols in them. But, acting on his father's orders, the boot maker delivered a regular pair, thus inciting Don Carlos to a fury in which he ordered the wretched man to cut up the boots and eat them. Passing a house one day he was drenched by water carelessly thrown from a balcony. He sent soldiers to arrest the family who lived there and ordered them to be executed, leniently allowing them to receive the last rites of the Church before they died.

Exactly what went on in Don Carlos's mind is beyond anyone but a psychiatrist. Deprived of maternal love by the early death of Maria of Portugal, he gained little affection from his father, Philip, who grew to hate and fear his own son. Significantly, after his death, a paper was found in the boy's handwriting listing his friends and enemies. His father was at the head of the list of enemies.

At the age of seventeen Don Carlos tripped on a stairway and fell heavily on his head. The head injuries he suffered were so severe that it was thought he would die. As a last resort, the corpse of a holy friar, long since dead, was laid alongside the prince in his bed.

Miraculously, Don Carlos began to recover. But now, to add to his problems, his mentality regressed to that of a seven-year-old and his brutality, if anything, seemed to have increased. Even before he left his bed he was making murderous swipes at well-wishers with his dagger. His father, the King, all too aware of his own mortality, despaired of what would happen after his death. Was it possible for Don Carlos ever to marry? Surely he would murder his wife after their first disagreement. There was talk of a marriage to the beautiful and recently widowed Juana of Portugal, but what had she ever done to deserve such a fate? Anyway, the poor girl quailed every time she saw the boy. And would Don Carlos be able to father children, in view of his problems? In order to test his son's potency, King Philip arranged for a young woman, heavily bribed and presumably intoxicated, to be introduced into his son's bed. She must have felt like Andromeda on the rock. She survived the night alive and intact, so nothing much was learned.

Meanwhile, Don Carlos was insisting on going to fight in the Netherlands, which was in revolt against Spain. He demanded that the King's commander, the Duke of Alva, take him with him. Alva refused, whereupon Carlos drew his sword, shouting, 'You shall not go to Flanders without me or I shall kill you.' Alva easily disarmed the boy but news of the incident alarmed the King so much that he steeled himself to make a decision that had been tormenting him for months. He would have to confine his own son and heir for the safety of the kingdom. Don Carlos seemed to sense this for he kept swords, daggers and pistols by his bedside and devised a system whereby should anyone try to enter his room while he was asleep a weight would fall and crush them.

Don Carlos was now a danger to everyone. At confession he told his priest that he had murder on his mind, and the confessor refused to grant him absolution as he was not repentant. Questioned further about his hatred, he admitted that it was his father he hated and wanted to kill.

Philip was faced with a most desperate choice between his son and his country. A Habsburg to his fingertips, he knew that there was no choice. His son and heir must be sacrificed. On 18 January 1568, wearing armour under his robes, the King, accompanied by soldiers and courtiers, forced his way into the prince's apartment. While the soldiers nailed up the windows, a tragic scene was played out between father and son. Carlos asked his father to kill him rather than put him to such shame. When Philip refused, Carlos said he would kill himself and tried to throw himself into the blazing fire. As Philip's soldiers restrained the desperate boy the King told him, 'If you kill yourself that is the act of a madman.' Carlos broke down in tears, saying that he was not mad but despairing at his father's cruel treatment. Philip's response was icy: 'I shall not treat you as a father henceforth.' Carlos was interned in the same castle that had held Juana the Mad's insane grandmother Isabella of Portugal. As a keeper Philip gave him the same cruel man who had watched over his own mad grandmother, Juana. Don Carlos tried to kill himself many times, once swallowing his ring in the belief that diamonds were poisonous. He went on a hunger strike but his father replied, 'When he is really hungry he will eat.' Ironically it was gluttony rather than starvation that killed him just a few months into his captivity. He died of a surfeit of partridge paté and iced water, either of which could have been fatal in a Spanish midsummer.

True to form, Philip II saw it as a sign from God. As he told the Pope, 'For my sins, it has been God's will that the prince should have such great and numerous defects, partly mental, partly due to his physical condition, utterly lacking as he is in the qualifications necessary for ruling.' Philip had taken the supreme political decision but it had come too late. Don Carlos should have been removed from the succession many years before when it was clear that he was little more than a psychopath. By deferring the decision for so long Philip ensured that his actions would be openly criticized and the sudden death of Don Carlos attributed to murder. As Philip II was to learn, painful decisions grow no easier by delay, and there are as many blunders of omission as of commission.

The staff of death

Tsar Peter the Great shared more with his predecessor, Tsar Ivan the Terrible, than merely a terrible temper and a brutal streak. The two tsars shared the unenviable record of having murdered their eldest sons and heirs to the throne. Far more than the rational Peter, the lunatic Ivan could at least plead the excuse that he was deranged at the time. Whatever the truth, both men imperilled the future of their kingdoms through their actions and seriously undermined the solid achievements of the earlier parts of their reigns.

Ivan the Terrible had loved his first wife, Anastasia Zahkarina Koshkina, and by her had two sons. The eldest, Ivan, seemed to embody the more positive aspects of his father, but the younger son, Feodor, was a simple-minded cripple. The two Ivans seemed to be on the best terms and when, in 1581, the Tsarevitch's third wife, Elena, became pregnant,

Tsar Ivan the Terrible was an assiduous reformer in his early years, but from 1564 embarked on a reign of terror, partly as a result of his deteriorating mental condition. In 1580 he killed his son and heir in a fit of rage (shown here). He was to spend the rest of his life in penance. (P)

everyone rejoiced in the hope of seeing the succession secured. But by ill-chance the pregnant Elena encountered the Tsar in one of his rages. He screamed at her for her lack of modesty and when she tried to defend herself he struck her in the stomach with the butt end of the steel-tipped staff he always carried. Elena fell to the ground and miscarried. When the news reached the Tsarevitch, he rushed up to his father protesting at the ill-treatment of his wife. In a frenzy the Tsar lifted his staff again and stuck the steel point in his son's forehead, killing him instantly.

Only later did the full consequences of his action strike Ivan, who was overwhelmed with guilt and roamed around the palace, moaning at his loss. Aware that his second son was unworthy of the throne, he tried to persuade his boyars (nobles) to overturn the succession and choose a stronger man instead. But the boyars mistrusted Ivan, believing he was trying to trick them. As a result, when Ivan died in 1584, it was Feodor who became Tsar. He ruled for fourteen years but left no heirs, marking the end of the house of Rurik, which had ruled in Russia for seven hundred years.

A judicial killing

Tsar Peter the Great's murder of his heir, Alexis, is perhaps less sheerly brutal than Ivan's atrocity, though no less tragic. Peter had married Evdokia Lopukhina, Alexis' mother, in 1689 and the boy had been born in February 1690, but the Tsar had never loved his mother and had abandoned her before his son was born. It was with the Lithuanian peasant woman, Marfa Skavronska – later to be Empress Catherine I – with whom he lived from 1703 that Peter found real happiness. He had four sons by Marfa and hoped that one of them would succeed him and carry on his work. But three of the boys died and by 1717 only the two-year-old Peter Petrovich remained. Peter was growing old and he knew that if he were to die his baby son could never take the throne, which would almost certainly go to Alexis, now 27 years old and a married man himself. But Peter could not bring himself to love this fruit of his first, brief marriage. He knew that Alexis had been brought up by his mother to oppose everything that he had achieved in Russia. He feared that, after his death, Alexis would set the clock back. Peter had tried to have Alexis educated to love ships and war as he had, but the boy was religious and loved the life of contemplation. This was enough to drive the Tsar into paroxysms of fury at the thought of his life's work being wasted.

In 1715 Peter wrote to Alexis a document entitled 'A Declaration to my Son', warning him to mend his ways and prepare himself for government. There was an unveiled threat at the end. If he did not improve, Peter warned him, 'I shall cut you off like a gangrenous limb.' Alexis was terrified and sent back a grovelling reply, admitting he was unworthy of the throne and begging to be relieved of the burden. This only made Peter even angrier. What sort of son was he to sign himself 'Your must humble slave and son'?

Peter was suspicious. He could not understand why anyone would willingly give up the chance to be Tsar. Alexis must be tricking him, planning to retire to a monastery until his father died and then emerging to take the throne by force from the tiny Peter Petrovich. Peter now sent Alexis an ultimatum: either mend your ways or become a monk. Failing this he would regard his son as a criminal and punish him as such. Alexis panicked and wrote to the Holy Roman Emperor, Charles VI, asking for asylum. He told the Emperor that his father wanted to kill him. As yet there had been no such threat, but

Peter's patience was growing thin. Before receiving any reply from the Emperor, Alexis fled to Vienna, where he was able to go into hiding. Peter did not want to face the embarrassment of asking the Emperor to return his son. Adopting methods that were to become typical of later Russian regimes, he sent secret agents to kidnap Alexis and bring him back to Russia to face charges.

In July 1717 Count Peter Tolstoy and Captain Alexander Rumianstov managed to locate Alexis and showed him a letter from his father promising that he would suffer no punishment if he returned but would enjoy his father's love. Tolstoy cunningly told Alexis that the Emperor was planning to send him back anyway, which was untrue. Alexis was thoroughly taken in and agreed to go with the two agents. Once back in Russia he was placed under arrest and taken to the Kremlin in Moscow for interrogation. In spite of his father's promise he was tortured and then forced to renounce the throne in favour of his half-brother, the three-year-old Peter Petrovich. Under torture he implicated a number of his friends in plots against Peter and the enraged Tsar had his own son sentenced to death. But so harshly had Alexis been treated that he cheated the executioner, dying on 26 June 1718.

Ironically, Peter gained nothing from this judicial murder. The succession to the throne became even more complicated when, just a few months after the death of Alexis, young Peter Petrovich also died. The Tsar was no doubt able to convince himself that he was acting in the interests of the state when he killed his son, but that has been the cry of tyrants throughout history. He was eventually succeeded not by a powerful young man, eager to continue his policy of westernization, but by a series of foolish and self-indulgent Empresses, more intent on indulging their fantasies with lovers or pursuing crackpot schemes than governing their country well. Half a century was to pass before Peter's Russia resumed its progress towards civilization and the modern world in the hands of an able ruler – Catherine II, a woman and a German.

The silken bowstring

Sultan Suleiman the Magnificent's murder of his son and heir, Mustafa, in 1553, was one of the worst of all royal blunders, with disastrous long-term consequences for the Ottoman Empire. Suleiman had come to the throne in 1520 and during his reign he took the Ottoman state to the apogee of its fortunes. His first wife, Gulbehar, 'Rose of Spring', had borne him a son named Mustafa, who was a brilliant young man, apparently destined to succeed his father and build on his work. But Suleiman fell in love with a Russian slave girl of enormous ambition, named Roxelana, and she also bore the Sultan a son, this time called Selim – the future Selim the Sot. Roxelana now set out to oust Gulbehar as 'first lady' and to secure the succession for Selim by turning Suleiman against his eldest son. So intoxicated did Suleiman become that he eventually agreed to marry Roxelana, something no Turkish sultan had done for six hundred years. This unprecedented event seemed to place Roxelana above all the rest of Suleiman's harem, and she moved from the women's quarters and took up residence in the Grand Seraglio, where Suleiman conducted his affairs of state. But Roxelana constantly found her progress blocked by the young Prince Mustafa, who was immensely popular both with the people and with Suleiman's ministers. By 1553 Suleiman had reached sixty and Roxelana knew that time was running out if she was to achieve her life's aim. She therefore told the sultan a wild tale that Mustafa was plotting to murder him. Suleiman feebly accepted her story and consulted his religious adviser as to what course of action to take. He was told that his son deserved to die and Suleiman therefore summoned Mustafa to his tent. By this time Mustafa was a man in his prime and had a large following of friends who advised him not to go to his father. But Mustafa had a noble nature and answered that, 'If he was to lose his life, he could wish no better than to give it back to him from whom he had received it.' Mustafa went fearlessly into Suleiman's tent, only to be confronted by the five deaf mutes who were to carry out the murder, holding the traditional silken bowstring. Mustafa fought furiously but was eventually overcome and strangled. His father, hidden behind a curtain, witnessed the killing.

As soon as the body had been removed, Suleiman began to lament for his lost son, though with none of the genuine conviction of the deranged Ivan the Terrible. At Mustafa's funeral, the lamentations were contrived and – in a disgraceful example of royal hypocrisy – even the horses that pulled the funeral car had had their eyes treated to make them weep. After Suleiman died on campaign in 1566, the Ottoman Empire began to experience the baleful consequences of Roxelana's ambition and Suleiman's mendacity.

The rule of Selim II, Roxelana's son, was a turning-point in Ottoman history. Until that time the house of Osmanli had produced an astonishing succession of powerful rulers, statesmen of note and generals of genius. Mustafa had seemed to be made in that mould but his murder had put a brake on the rise of the Ottoman Empire. Under Selim the Sot, the state began its long decline into degeneracy. Among the twenty-five sultans who succeeded Selim hardly one matched the great sultans who preceded him. Selim's swollen drunkard's face little resembled Suleiman's and his abilities were so far inferior that the suspicion must remain that he was not Suleiman's son and that Roxelana had deceived him. Whatever the truth the damage was irreversible. In killing Mustafa

Suleiman the Magnificent rides to prayers in procession with his bodyguards. Suleiman was the greatest of the Ottoman sultans, but in old age he was persuaded by his Russian concubine, the ambitious Roxelana, to murder his eldest son and allow her own boy, Selim the Sot, to succeed to the throne. (PN)

Suleiman had slain not only his but his country's posterity. Selim ruled for just eight years and then tripped in his bath after a drunken bout, cracking his head open. Selim's son, Murad III, fathered 103 children, leaving him little time to do anything else. The die was cast.

A Royal Upbringing

For most royal couples the only experience they ever have of bringing up children is by enduring the parenting skills – or otherwise – of their own parents. On this scant evidence they often decide to subject their own children to more of the same. Duty, discipline and service are frequently the themes that receive most attention, notably among British royals of the last 150 years, and no attempt is made to educate rather than to train. Until relatively recent times, young princes have been subjected to a degree of brutality in their childhood that must have been frowned on in lower levels of society. As most were destined for careers in the armed services this was considered a character-forming experience.

Bringing up Rudolf

The Austrian Emperor Franz Josef and his beautiful Bavarian wife, Elizabeth, were notably inept in the upbringing of their eldest son Rudolf. At the tender age of seven, Franz Josef decided that his son and heir must be taught by a military tutor. The man chosen, Count Leopold Gondrecourt, was a martinet of the worst kind, a graduate of the school of Prussian drillmasters, who was inspired by the dictum, 'It is not working if it is not hurting.'

With the sanction of Rudolf's parents he behaved towards the young boy as a sergeant-major to a particularly obtuse recruit. Rudolf's otherwise gentle mother agreed that Gondrecourt could torture her son by creeping into his bedroom while he was asleep and firing a pistol next to his ear, or locking the young lad behind the gates of the wild game reserve and shouting over the fence that a wild boar was going to attack him. The boy's screams sound a warning down the ages to every parent who ever thought to make their son more manly by frightening him.

The fact was that Rudolf never recovered from these early traumas and was a physical coward even before moral cowardice reared its ugly head in adolescence. The Empress Elizabeth only came to realize just how brutal was Gondrecourt's treatment of her son when she was awoken early one morning by Rudolf's cries. It was midwinter and the snow was thick. Looking out of her window she saw her son being marched up and down by Gondrecourt, in the bitter cold, without even a greatcoat. Almost hysterical, Elizabeth ran to her husband and presented him with an ultimatum: either Gondrecourt goes or she would leave him. Gondrecourt was dismissed but the damage was done. How close could Rudolf ever feel towards a father who had inflicted such misery on him? Rudolf's eventual suicide at Mayerling in 1889 owed much to the misery of his childhood and his fear of parental rejection (see also p. 101).

Bringing up Fritz

The suffering of young Rudolf of Habsburg was relatively slight when compared with the education and upbringing of Prince Frederick, son of the Prussian King Frederick William I. Frederick William, the 'Sergeant-Major' king, was obsessed to the point of madness with all things military (see p. 14) and he was determined that his son should grow up to be just like him. Most of all he feared that Frederick might become a 'cissy' as a result of his mother's – Queen Sophia Dorothea's – interest in music and literature. Thus each morning the young prince was awoken by the sound of cannons firing just below his window. This was merely the signal for the commencement of a daily round of supposedly 'improving' Spartan rigours, including cold baths or showers, long runs, and general discomfort. By the time he was five years of age young Frederick had learned by heart the entire Prussian drill code and, driven on by his elderly military tutor, was drilling a company of 131 cadets. But Frederick's heart yearned for the culture he could only find with his mother and her friends. He was a talented musician and at an early stage learned to play the flute to a high standard. But such activities served only to infuriate his father, who frequently beat his son for dereliction of duty. Once, when he found Frederick studying Latin, he had the boy whipped, and on another occasion when he found him reading a novel he thrashed him mercilessly and made him kiss his boots. A girl who played on the harpsichord while the young prince played his flute was flogged by the public executioner.

Frederick hated his father. So appalling was the regime under which he suffered that in 1730 he ran away, hoping to reach England with his friend, Hans von Katte. Frederick William declared that the two runaways were deserters and would be executed when they were recaptured. When news of the King's decision reached other European courts there was a general outcry. The idea of a king executing his son was anathema to the more enlightened eighteenth-century monarchs and letters begging the king for mercy poured in to the Prussian court. At last Frederick William relented, but while he agreed to pardon his son, he insisted that von Katte must die and that young Frederick must witness the execution. Frederick was made to stand by his open window while his best friend had his head cut off with a sabre. Frederick fainted at the moment of decapitation. It was a low point in the history of father-son relationships.

A Turkish misogynist

Mothers do not always know what is best for their sons. When Murad IV became ruler of the Ottoman Empire in 1623 at the age of only ten, his mother ruled for him until he reached his majority. Knowing the dangers that she might face if her son should take a fancy to one or more of the harem beauties she tried to encourage Murad to be homosexual, showing him only beautiful boys and keeping him away as far as possible from girls. But the plan misfired badly. Not only did Murad have an insatiable lust for women but he was subject to jealousy so intense that it verged on madness. And with jealousy came unbelievable cruelty, much of it directed at the feminine sex which he believed had deceived him all his life.

When a Venetian trader named Zanetti built an extra floor on his house Murad convinced himself that he had done so only to peer over the palace walls into the harem.

In spite of the impossibility of the Venetian seeing so far, Murad had Zanetti hanged by his own shirt. And when a French interpreter arranged a secret meeting with a Turkish woman to improve his grammar he was impaled by the sultan. In order to defend the harem Murad would lie in wait with his arquebus, shooting at least ten passers-by each day in case they were intending to look into the harem. He objected strongly to noisy women. When he chanced to encounter a group of women enjoying themselves in a meadow he ordered all twenty of them to be drowned for disturbing his peace. It was not safe for women to travel in parties near the palace. When a boat-load of ladies came too close to the walls of the Seraglio, Murad ordered his gunners to sink their boat, drowning them all. And when he rode out from his palace, armed with his bow, he liked to practise his aim on any passing women. On these outings he was followed by his executioners who were sometimes called upon to cut off the hands or feet of women who had annoyed him, or sometimes to blind them with ground glass.

When a lighter mood was on him he liked to simulate killing his harem girls. He would force them all to jump naked into a pool he had built and then fire harmless pellets at their bodies, leaving behind coloured marks. Once he had tired of this he filled the pool to a depth so that none of the women could touch the bottom and then waited to see how soon they drowned. If he lost interest in the game he would let the survivors return to the harem, but if he was in a sullen mood he would wait until the last head went under. So Murad IV avenged himself on women for the harm that his mother had done him.

The skeleton in the cupboard

Prince Alfred Alexander William Ernest Albert was born to be a skeleton in the cupboard. His father, Alfred, Duke of Edinburgh, was weak and ineffectual. His rabidly anglophobic mother, the Grand Duchess Marie of Russia, was odd in the extreme. So odd in fact that she insisted on ordering special boots from St Petersburg that fitted either foot as she thought it silly to have left and right shoes. With a start like this in life, Alfred reached his nadir swiftly and then sank.

Alfred was born at Buckingham Palace in 1874, eldest son of Queen Victoria's second son, the Duke of Edinburgh. His future was already mapped out for him, or so it was supposed. The plan was that he would eventually succeed to the Duchy of Coburg. In order to prepare him for what would be a German future, he was given a thoroughly German education by a fiendish Hun named Dr Wilhelm Rolfs – a pompous martinet and a disciple of the Marquis de Sade. Alfred's mother was delighted with Rolfs, believing that he would inject German *Kultur* into the little fellow and erase every trace of his Englishness. Alfred was not an intelligent boy. In fact, few of Victoria and Albert's descendants were. But the Grand Duchess considered that as her son he must be different. If Dr Rolfs had to beat knowledge into him then so be it. With the support of the boy's mother, Rolfs proceeded to make Alfred's life a misery, bullying him and trying to turn him against the land of his birth. From the age of nine Alfred was subjected to a regime of humiliation. Deprived of motherly love and with a distant, unemotional father, Alfred grew up to be a deeply disturbed young man.

As an appropriate preparation for adult life Alfred joined the German army in a Prussian Guards regiment stationed at Potsdam. Here he reacted against the restrictions of his home life by sowing his wild oats with the prostitutes who frequented the barracks and eventually contracted a venereal disease. As his health deteriorated he began to drink too much. It was perhaps during a drinking bout that he 'married' an Irish woman named Mabel Fitzgerald. Although the marriage could not be considered legal as it contravened the Royal Marriages Act of 1772, and although his parents resolutely refused to accept Mabel Fitzgerald as their daughter-in-law, there is evidence to suggest that she bore the prince a daughter. In 1982 a woman named Irene Victoria Alexandra Louise Isobel Bush died in Miami. She claimed to be Alfred's child by Mabel Fitzgerald, having been born Lady Irene Fitzgerald Coburg in Ireland in 1899. However, attempts to verify this story are doomed to failure as the whole affair has been the subject of a successful 'cover-up'.

In the last year of his life Alfred's relations with his mother notably worsened. After one particular bitter argument he tried to commit suicide by shooting himself, gravely wounding himself in the process. The incident coincided with the Edinburghs' – now the Coburgs' – silver wedding celebrations at the palace of Schloss Friedenstein in 1899. While the merrymaking took place on an upper floor, Alfred lay grievously ill in a bedroom on the floor below, suffering, as the story went, from 'nervous depression'. His mother had ordered him to be taken out of the palace and sent away to recover, but the doctors told her that if he was moved he would die. But the daughter of Tsar Alexander III knew best – she *always* knew best – and poor Alfred was taken to the Tyrol to recuperate. Within a fortnight he was dead. Only now did Marie realize the extent of her error and her grief was overwhelming. But Alfred's father never forgave her, blaming her for the tragedy, and ensuring that he never spent another night in her company. He began drinking heavily and he too was dead within a year.

This sordid little tragedy, so typical of the minor royal courts of Germany in the nineteenth century, became the subject of a 'cover-up' because it came too close to the throne of England. The young prince was, of course, Queen Victoria's grandson and his father 'dearest Affie', Victoria's second son. Suicides were not the stuff of the Victorian legend; hypocrisy and touched-up sepia images of domestic bliss were always the preferred way for the family of Victoria and Albert. Since 1899 every book but one – the *Memoirs* of Lady Walburga Paget published in 1924 – have obediently followed the 'royal line' that Prince Alfred died of 'consumption' – an unusual euphemism for a bullet.

KIBOSHING THE KAISER:
THE BIRTH OF PRINCE WILLIAM OF PRUSSIA

Few of Britain's 'Old Contemptibles' who marched off to war in August 1914, singing that 'Belgium put the kibosh on the Kaiser', can have realized who they were singing about. In the first place the ruler of Imperial Germany was half-English by birth, a grandson of Queen Victoria, and spoke perfect English as well as holding the honorary rank of Admiral in the Royal Navy. While Queen Victoria had lived she had only to wag her finger at him for

a remorseful 'Willy' to hang his head and ask forgiveness. But when his uncle, King Edward VII, became king in 1901, everything changed. 'Willy' had a love/hate relationship with his uncle. He admired 'Bertie' as the 'head of the royal firm' and as an 'English Gentleman', but despised him as a debauchee and for not being a military man. But most of all he hated 'Bertie' for being 'Edward the Encircler', King of the the country that hemmed

Victoria Adelaide Mary Louise, eldest and favourite child of Queen Victoria and Prince Albert, with her children by Frederick III of Germany. The birth of the future Kaiser Wilhelm II was a difficult one, causing permanent damage to the child's left arm. (ME)

Germany in and prevented her achieving her destiny to rule the world. William was a megalomaniac. And the root of his megalomania was the compensation he sought for the injuries he suffered during his disastrous childbirth.

Rarely has a royal birth been as mismanaged as was that of Frederick William Victor Albert, son of the Crown Prince Frederick of Prussia and Queen Victoria's eldest daughter, Vicky, on 27 January 1859. Vicky had observed her mother's numerous pregnancies and felt confident as her confinement drew near. Queen Victoria, not trusting German doctors, had insisted on sending some of her own choice. Her personal physician, Dr James Clark, who according to Lord Clarendon was 'not fit to attend a sick cat', was packed off to Germany to examine Vicky and report on the work of the Germans. In addition, the royal midwife, Mrs Innocent, was sent to help, as well as a Doctor Edward Martin, another protégé of the Queen. The German medical fraternity was outraged. When he arrived in Berlin, Doctor Martin was deliberately allocated accommodation at some distance from the palace. The German doctors, notably the royal

doctor Wegner, were determined to keep British interference to a minimum, even if that meant that the patient suffered. And without anaesthetics and with the baby in an awkward position, Vicky certainly suffered. When she went into labour in the early hours of 26 January Wegner decided to inform Martin. He wrote him a note but, instead of having it delivered by hand, he posted it. As a result, it was not until thirty-six hours later that Martin heard that Vicky was in labour. By this time it was almost too late. Martin grabbed his instruments and rushed to the palace only to find that Wegner and his assistants had mishandled the birth, had given up hope for mother and baby and were simply sitting at the bottom of the bed waiting for the end. The Crown Prince was holding his wife in his arms but Vicky was too exhausted to make any further effort. As Martin entered the room Wegner called out to him in English that there was no hope left of saving either mother or child – hardly a reassuring diagnosis for the patient. Ignoring the hysteria of the Germans, Martin set about proving them wrong. Producing first chloroform to ease Vicky's pain, he then extracted the baby with forceps after a terrible struggle. Both mother and child would live – but only just.

Outside the royal bedroom chaos reigned. Rumours of the Princess's protracted labour had reached the press and throughout Berlin editors were preparing her obituary for the later editions. However, in the snowy streets outside the palace, the crowds of onlookers were ignorant of the drama taking place within and were waiting for the artillery salute – one hundred and one guns – for the birth of a prince. During the afternoon the guns burst into action, the crowds cheered, Field Marshal Wrangel punched a hole in a window in his delight and the baby's father rushed off to a reception planned by the beaming grandfather.

But what of the baby? In the royal bedroom everyone was so concerned with the health and welfare of Vicky that nobody seemed to notice that the baby was a remarkably quiet one and an odd colour at that – blue, in fact. Fortunately Mrs Innocent took matters into her own hands. Picking up the baby she set about trying to make it cry – or move. For half an hour she rained smacks on to the royal buttocks, but to no avail. It seemed that the new prince was dead. Then, at last, came a whimper and then a series of bawling complaints at this early demonstration of English aggression.

It was not until the following morning that Mrs

Innocent presented the baby to Doctor Wegner with the observation that his left arm was blue and lifeless, with a dislocated elbow joint. The Crown Prince was summoned to see his new son but he decreed that the news of the deformity should be kept from Vicky until she had recovered her strength. Ironically, a telegram had just arrived from the baby's grandmother, Queen Victoria, inquiring 'Is it a fine boy?' Dr Wegner felt that the paralysis of the arm would improve with massage and when the baby was older special exercises would strengthen it. But it would never be normal. And there lay the problem for the parents, for the baby himself and, worst of all, for an unsuspecting world.

Ironically, it was Willy's mother – the English princess – who was going to set the young boy on the path of paranoia and megalomania. Vicky re-garded Willy's injured arm as a challenge and so she drove him relentlessly to overcome the deficiency of a weak and shortened left arm. Aware of his inferiority to other men, William developed an aggressive masculinity, which made him bully those less able than himself. Vicky arranged for him to undergo apparently endless gymnastic exercises to strengthen the arm and she forced him to learn to ride well, regardless of the humiliation he faced in falling off so often. Whenever he succeeded in any activity Vicky praised him inordinately and it soon became apparent that there was little of his father's gentle personality in the boy. Willy was entirely a product of Vicky's elitist mentality. The Kaiser, great warlord of Germany, was moulded by the fire of a woman's guilt at having given birth to a deformed child.

CAPTAIN CAREY'S BLUNDER: THE DEATH OF THE PRINCE IMPERIAL

After losing office in the aftermath of the disastrous Zulu War of 1879, Conservative leader Benjamin Disraeli reflected on the remarkable qualities of the Zulus, a people who had not only driven him from power, but had defeated Britain's generals and put an end to a great European dynasty. The death of Louis Bonaparte, the Prince Imperial and only son of the Emperor Napoleon III and his Spanish wife, the Empress Eugénie, marked the end of Bonapartism in France. Just what Prince Louis was doing in Zululand in 1879 is the subject of this case study.

The collapse of the Second Empire in France swiftly followed defeat in the Franco-Prussian War. With the Emperor Napoleon III a prisoner of the Prussians, his wife, the Empress Eugénie, and her son, the Prince Imperial, had to escape from a Paris that was seething with republicanism and a hatred of the imperial family. Cries of '*A bas l'Impératrice! A la guillotine!*' were increasingly heard in the streets. Unable or unwilling to trust the future of France to a Frenchman, the Empress looked for help to an American dentist named Evans, who helped mother and son to escape to England, where they were later joined by the Emperor, now an old man broken in health. The family settled at Chislehurst in Kent and lived quietly until Napoleon III died there in 1873.

It was now left to Napoleon's son Louis to restore the fortunes of Bonapartism in France. This could only be done by his becoming a soldier, even if this meant the 'unthinkable' – becoming an English soldier.

Louis trained as an artillery officer at the Royal Military Academy at Woolwich. The other cadets, far from overawed at having a French prince in their midst, promptly threw him into a pond. His friend, Louis Conneau, who had followed him into exile, leaped into the pond alongside him, anxious to share this affront by English philistines to the grand-nephew of Napoleon Bonaparte himself. Never-theless, Louis did well at Woolwich and was soon accepted by the other cadets for his swordsmanship, his riding ability and his quaint Anglicisms, like 'What the divel 'eapened?' His only weakness was in military history, where his views on such battles as Crécy, Agincourt and Waterloo clashed with traditional English versions taught at Woolwich and turned the classrooms there into battlegrounds as murderous as Hougoumont or Blenheim village. Louis' mother, the Empress Eugénie, visited him at the Academy, pleased at his progress even if a little alarmed to see the Prince Imperial of France playing cricket. The Empress, a true daughter of Spain, proudly ignored signals not to walk behind the bowler's arm and was nearly decapitated by a cricket ball arriving at high velocity.

Louis passed out seventh out of 34 cadets, finishing first in fencing and riding but – embarrassingly – only second in the French class, beaten by an English cadet. News of his progress in England brought a harsh response from the Republican press in Paris, which referred to Louis as Napoleon III½ or the 'Imperial Baby'. Yet he grew to be immensely popular in England and he was even spoken of as a suitable match for Princess Beatrice. But Louis was not interested in the idea of marriage. He was restless for glory and he had no intention of mouldering away into a comfortable obscurity.

The war in Zululand in 1879 brought the Prince Imperial the chance he was looking for. All his fellow cadets were going to South Africa and he had no intention of being left behind. He pestered his mother to put pressure on the Commander-in-Chief, the Duke of Cambridge, to send him, while Eugénie even appealed to Queen Victoria herself. The Empress was convinced that Louis could come to no harm and would immeasurably strengthen his chances of returning to power in France in the future if he could gain some experience of war. Under the twin assaults of monarch and mother, Cambridge gave way and contacted Lord Chelmsford, commanding the British troops in South Africa, with the news that he was to have the French Prince Imperial foisted on him. Fresh from his disastrous defeat at Isandhlwana, this was the last thing that Chelmsford needed, particularly as Cambridge saw fit to warn him that Louis was sometimes 'too plucky and go ahead' for his own good.

Public opinion in France was shocked. The Prince Imperial, *fruit sec* as many people thought him, was still heir to the French throne, even in the eyes of the most ardent republicans. He had no business joining an English army and going off to war under the cursed Union Jack. Imagine it, a French prince obeying the orders of the most menial of English subalterns.

None of this bothered Louis. He was a young man embarking on an adventure. On arrival at Durban, unfortunately, he found that the two horses he had shipped from England had died and he was forced to buy replacements locally. Here he let his heart rule his head with fatal consequences. Spying a civilian in Durban riding a magnificent grey he decided that he must have it. Even though the owner warned him that the animal could be skittish, Louis had eyes only for the splendour of its lines and its magnificent head.

Louis was taken on to the personal staff of Lord Chelmsford, though with no official rank. It was intended that he should observe rather than become involved in any more dangerous tasks. Yet observation was no task for a Bonaparte. He had a name to live up to and this tended to make him show off. He always vaulted into his saddle and challenged men to throw potatoes at him so that he could slice them with the sabre that his uncle, the great Napoleon, had carried at Austerlitz. He was playing at war, as his uncle would have been the first to tell him. But the young hero would not listen. His mind was already far away, in distance and in time. The naked Zulus of South Africa would be the best substitute he could find for the Russians, Austrians and Prussians his uncle had butchered on battlefields the length and breadth of a continent.

Chelmsford, meanwhile, found Louis a safe billet with Colonel Harrison, Acting Quartermaster-General, responsible for transport and scouting for the British Second Division. In turn, Harrison found the prince a 'nanny' in the shape of Lieutenant Jahleel Brenton Carey, a far from inspiring officer, proficient only in his command of the French language. Carey was as careful as Louis was carefree, as earthbound as the prince was ethereal. They were a fatal match, but nobody could have guessed that at the time.

In England, the Empress Eugénie would hardly have been reassured if she had heard that rather than keeping the Prince safe and sound, Lord Chelmsford had actually allowed him to accompany a patrol deep into Zululand. During this operation Louis justified the Duke of Cambridge's warning that he was 'too plucky and go ahead' by riding out in front of the rest of the column and chasing a Zulu straggler as if he was coursing a hare. The Zulu escaped, and so did the prince – this time. Commanding the patrol, Redvers Buller, a man of almost insane courage himself, regarded the prince as a lunatic and wanted to rid himself of the responsibility of harbouring such a person. Oblivious to Buller's verdict, Louis was delighted with himself and went about camp singing French martial music in a loud and discordant voice, revelling in the fact that the British troops had nicknamed the hill from which the Zulu fled 'Napoleon's koppie'. It was not quite the Pratzen Heights at Austerlitz, perhaps, but it was

Prince Louis Napoleon and his party resting in the Zulu kraal before the catastrophic incident that cost him his life in 1879. (PN)

a start. On his return to camp, Buller made an official complaint to Chelmsford about the Prince's behaviour and the C–in–C ordered Harrison to keep him safely in camp at all times, *unless he was accompanied by a strong escort.*

As a result, Louis found himself confined to duties that involved sketching the ground the column was due to cross. Bored with this, he asked Harrison if he could extend the area of his sketching. Believing that the area for ten miles ahead of the camp was free of Zulus, Harrison agreed, delegating six troopers and six of the mounted native contingent to ride with the Prince. But was this the 'strong escort' that Chelmsford had insisted on? In the event, just seven men accompanied Louis, though at the last moment Lieutenant Carey was given permission to ride with the Prince. With his small terrier dog running alongside him Louis seemed to be in his element, free of the burden of command and without specific orders – he could tilt his lance freely as the mood took him. As he rode out of the camp on 2 June 1879, an officer shouted to him, 'Take care of yourself and don't get shot.' Scarcely turning in his saddle Louis called back, 'Oh, no, Carey will take very good care that nothing happens to me.'

Around midday the patrol dismounted for Louis to make his sketches. It was then that they noticed a deserted Zulu *kraal* (village) a mile or two ahead and the Prince decided to search the huts for fuel so that he could make a fire and boil some coffee. Carey was uneasy, pointing out that the *kraal* was surrounded by tall tambookie grass that could conceal the enemy. But Louis was not listening. He ordered the men to mount up and they rode towards the *kraal*, with Carey trailing behind. They entered the village and Louis demonstrated to Carey how foolish had been his reservations – a few dogs, that was all, scrounging around the empty huts. That was the extent of the enemy. The soldiers dismounted and soon had their coffee brewing. Nobody gave any thought to setting a guard and soon Louis and Carey were engaged in their favourite pastime: arguing about the campaigns of the great Napoleon. Two or three hours passed during which their horses wandered off to graze. Just then one of the Natal natives informed Carey that he had spotted a Zulu on a piece of rising ground. Louis ordered the men to get their horses in a hurry, but it took a further ten minutes before they could bring them all back into the *kraal*. As Louis gave the order to mount there was a sudden outbreak of firing from the long grass, and forty Zulu warriors suddenly burst into the open. The British soldiers somehow managed to mount their horses, but the Prince's magnificent grey was terrified by the sound of gunfire and shied, making it difficult for Louis to get astride his back. As the horse bucked and then began to gallop off, Louis seized hold of the leather holster and held on as he was dragged for more than a hundred yards. Then the leather tore apart and he was thrown beneath the feet of his horse. All around him the other British riders were in retreat.

Louis struggled to his feet and looked around for his uncle's sword – the Austerlitz blade – but it had gone. Now, armed just with a revolver, he faced seven Zulus armed with assegais (spears). The Zulus, who over broken ground could run almost as fast as the fleeing riders, soon overtook the prince and their leader, Langalabalele, speared the prince in the thigh. As he sank to the ground a second man, Zabanga, stabbed Louis in the shoulder. He fired his revolver twice but was overcome by the pack of stabbing warriors. It was the death he would have chosen, with all wounds to the front and against overwhelming odds.

Carey and the surviving British troopers reined to a halt after a few minutes. They must have known by then that the Prince stood no chance and the sight of his horse galloping wildly towards them confirmed their fears. Was there any point in risking more lives in going back to collect the Prince's body? It was the proper thing to do, Carey reasoned, but was it the most sensible? He decided not and with his mind in turmoil he rode back towards the British camp. He had the misfortune to meet Redvers Buller, to whom he told the story. Buller's response was predictable: 'Where's the body?'

Carey could only point distractedly over his shoulder.

'Where are your men, sir?' shouted Buller.

'They're behind me.'

'You ought to be shot,' Buller exclaimed, 'I could shoot you myself.'

Buller refrained from doing so, however, and the miserable Carey was allowed to carry his dreadful news back to Harrison. The whole camp was shocked. When Chelmsford was told it was as if he had suffered the dreadful massacre at Isandhlwana all over again. He slumped at his desk with his head buried in his arms.

The end comes for the Prince Imperial in 1879. Failing to mount his fleeing horse, Louis was overwhelmed by pursuing Zulu warriors and stabbed to death. (ME)

The next morning a French journalist accompanied the party sent to fetch the Prince's body. He expressed outrage that Louis had been allowed to ride out the day before with just seven companions, while today a thousand men were being spared to fetch his dead body. It was unforgivable: someone had blundered.

The Prince's body was found where he had fallen. It had been stripped but not mutilated as was the normal Zulu custom, and bore seventeen stab wounds, all to the front. Chelmsford's first thought was to bury the body immediately with full military honours, but some of his staff officers who had known Louis insisted that it would have to be returned to England to lie alongside his father, the Emperor Napoleon III. This was easier said than done. The camp doctors did the best they could to embalm the Prince's remains before placing them in a deal casket, packed out with straw and sand. They could not guarantee that it would survive the long journey back to England from the Cape aboard H.M.S. *Orontes*. The surgeons' fears proved justified. When, more than a month later, the casket was opened for the body to be identified, the face had decomposed so as to be unidentifiable. The grieving Empress had been spared this horror but the prince's old valet, Xavier Uhlmann, who drew the short straw, fainted before he could identify his master. The job was finally accomplished by the American dentist, Dr T.W. Evans, who had rescued the Empress Eugénie in 1870, whisking her from under the noses of both the Prussians and the French Republicans who had wanted to execute her.

Afterwards the body was placed on a gun carriage and taken to Chislehurst in Kent, where the Empress Eugénie was living. Here it was interred alongside the Emperor Napoleon III after an impressive ceremony attended by Queen Victoria herself and four royal dukes. It was the least the British could do in the circumstances. It is estimated that a crowd of forty thousand, many of them having travelled from London, attended the prince's funeral.

All that was left was to apportion blame and then close the book on this tragic episode. Captain Carey – who, ironically, heard of his promotion while he was awaiting the outcome of Lord Chelmsford's investigation of the affair – was found guilty of misbehaviour in the face of the enemy and was cashiered from the army. This was a less severe verdict than cowardice and it was concluded that he had basically 'lost his head in the crisis'. But Carey was no villain. In a sense he was as much a victim as Prince Louis, whose search for 'la Gloire' inevitably placed himself and all those around him in danger. Carey's blunder was only the last – and the most visible – in a whole series of errors.

In 1880 the Empress Eugénie undertook a pilgrimage to Zululand to visit the place where her son died. Accompanied by Sir Evelyn Wood, she travelled to the *kraal* where the fatal skirmish had taken place and purchased the site from a chief named Sobuza. Incredibly she even expressed the wish to meet the warriors who had killed Louis and was introduced to Zabanga, Langalabalele having been killed in the war. Zabanga told her of 'the white man who fought like a lion'. It was a fine compliment and must have eased a mother's heart. The Austerlitz blade was never returned. No doubt the Zulus found a use for it – perhaps to hoe their fields.

BRINGING UP 'BERTIE': THE EDUCATION OF EDWARD VII

The deplorable behaviour of George IV as Prince of Wales stood as a salutary lesson on how not to prepare a prince for kingship. So awful had Prince George been that he had undermined the whole institution of monarchy in Britain. When Queen Victoria gave birth to a son on 9 November 1841, Prince Albert and his mentor, Baron Christian Friedrich Stockmar, were determined that the boy would be brought up and educated according to the most modern and scientific German principles. He would be a philosopher-king and a model of moral excellence for his people. For the queen this meant just one thing: baby 'Bertie' must grow up to be as like his father as possible. In the event, this experiment failed more completely than anyone can have imagined possible. Bertie grew up to become a *bon viveur*, a notorious womanizer, and a scandalous example of unrestrained privilege. Baron Stockmar, who had been responsible for grooming the Prince Consort for greatness, prepared his son only for moral turpitude.

The problem facing baby Albert Edward – apart, that is, from his parents – was that he was born to be king. Every part of his education would be geared towards producing a suitable occupant of the throne of Great Britain. What made it worse, however, was the fact that his mother was a single-minded obsessive, who saw him as a miniature version of that ideal person – her husband Albert – while Albert – an arrogant prig if there ever was one – doubted whether his son could ever achieve his own high standards. Nevertheless, if baby 'Bertie' could not be the 'ideal constitutional monarch', he could be the closest thing to it. As a result, each childish error that Bertie made was seen as a flaw in the character not of a child, but of a future king.

Bertie's relationship with his mother was never entirely free and loving. He was not allowed to forget who she was and she made a point of reminding him by signing notes, 'Your Mama, V.R.' Nor could she ever allow him to be himself. As she wrote to her uncle Leopold, 'You will understand how fervent are my prayers to see him resemble his angelic father in every, every respect, both in body and mind.' The fact that he was, in Stockmar's words, 'an exaggerated copy of his mother' never occurred to her. She lived for her husband and her brilliant eldest daughter 'Vicky', not for her dull, plump, disappointing little 'Bertie'.

At the age of six, the Prince of Wales began his formal education, and 'formal' was the word. Prince Albert and Stockmar assumed overall responsibility for the young prince's education. Though the Queen later wrote that 'no-one gave us better and wiser advice on the education of our children', the baron was intensely unpopular with the Queen's English advisers. Gladstone called Stockmar 'a mischievous old prig', while another contemporary critic opined that he 'nourished the weeds and destroyed the choicest plants'. Stockmar and the Prince Consort based their approach on thoroughly Teutonic ideas. Even though some of his tutors warned that the boy was suffering from mental exhaustion, his Germanic taskmasters insisted that 'all work and no play' was the right approach.

Education consisted of ramming as many facts into as small a space as possible – and in the case of Edward's brain it was a very small space indeed. Understanding was secondary to knowledge, and the pupil was merely putty in the hands of the teacher, to be moulded as he wished. As Bertie slaved away at his good German education one wonders if he ever chuckled at the thought of things that he would see in the future – like Cora Pearl naked on a silver tray – and which would have melted Baron Stockmar's monocle.

While Prince Albert strove as mightily as Mary Shelley's Doctor Frankenstein to create life as he knew it in young Bertie, what stirred in the Prince of Wales was below the waist rather than beneath the furrowed brow. Even though the Queen's earliest mentor, Lord Melbourne, had warned her that education might attempt to mould character but could never change it, Victoria still relied steadfastly on German methods to transform her wilful and lazy son into a great 'Teutonic' king. Ironically, it had taken nearly a century for the Hanoverian 'Georges' to come to terms with being British. Now Victoria was turning the clock back by relying on a man who proudly boasted, 'I am German and I shall stay a German until my death.'

It never occurred to Prince Albert to send Bertie to an English school, like Eton or Harrow, where he might have mixed with the children of the aristocracy. Albert was prejudiced against the English school system, believing that it encouraged loose morals. Yet the system of home tutoring he adopted for the Prince of Wales hardly served to strengthen his sense of moral values. As a result, until the age of seventeen, Prince Edward never met with or talked to boys of his own age and social class. In later years he observed sadly, 'I never had a boyhood.'

Edward's first tutor was the Rev. Henry Birch, a young man who had taken holy orders and who had lately taught at Eton. The timetable Birch followed was an extremely heavy one and left the prince few moments for relaxation. Six-and-a-half hours each day were given over to formal lessons, with additional time spent on languages and virtually no time given to exercise. The English obsession with team games was not shared by Prince Albert and Stockmar, who presumably felt the playing fields of Eton suitable for providing cannon-fodder in wartime but inappropriate to the intellectual development of a king. All recreation was intended to be of an instructive nature. Books were to be read for 'improvement' not enjoyment. Birch was forbidden to use any textbook that had not been personally vetted by Prince Albert. For Bertie it was a soulless existence. Even Birch appears to have felt the pressure of this cheerless routine. On the only occasion that he was given a fortnight's holiday he observed that he felt like a prisoner released from detention.

The lonely Bertie formed a close attachment to his young tutor. However, this sign of human weakness was enough for Prince Albert to dismiss Birch and bring in someone capable of imposing a more severe regime. F.W. Gibbs, Fellow of Trinity College, Cambridge, came from a legal background and was prepared to implement Stockmar's plan to the letter. Disappointed at the dismissal of Birch, Bertie was uncooperative with the new tutor and, as a result, received a sound flogging from his father, which was much applauded by his mother. But when this failed to effect an improvement, the royal couple called in a phrenologist, who delicately tried to inform the royal parents that Bertie was not well-endowed intellectually. While the German educational plan hovered on the brink of failure, senior political figures in England were growing alarmed at the damage that was being done to the heir to the throne by these well-intentioned blunderers. Lord Granville bluntly told the Prince Consort that he was doing the Prince no good by cramming facts into his head. Instead, Edward should be allowed more exercise and more companionship with boys of his own age. Even *Punch* joined the fray, printing the following warning:

The dear little Wales – sure the saddest of tales
Is the tale of the studies with which they are
    cramming thee
In thy tuckers and bibs, handed over to Gibbs
Who for eight years with solid instruction was
    ramming thee.
Giants indulging the passion for this high pressure
    fashion
Of Prince training, *Punch* would uplift loyal warning.
Locomotives, we see, over-stoked soon may be
Till the supersteamed boiler blows up one fine
    morning.

At one stage Edward came close to a nervous breakdown and even Gibbs warned his father that he needed a relaxation of the pressure. Instead, Prince Albert showed everyone the time-table Stockmar had prepared for his own studies when he was Edward's age: a daily regime of full-time study from six in the morning until eight-thirty at night.

Edward, Prince of Wales as an army cadet in 1860. His one-night stand with Nellie Clifton was said by his mother to have caused the death of his father Prince Albert. In reality the early demise of the Prince Consort probably had rather more to do with insanitory plumbing at Buckingham Place. (AR/IS)

If the Prince of Wales wished to be the man his father was he must do the same. Edward would almost certainly have rather been a boot-black than the man his father was. After all, his father was a German and Bertie was beginning to realize that almost all his relations were as well.

Stockmar's educational plan foundered on taking too little account of the character and ability of the student. Edward was not 'bookishly' intelligent and would never make a scholar. But Stockmar refused to accept this and never veered from the path he had set for the Prince, even when there were clear signs that things were going wrong. Edward often reacted violently to the tedium of his existence, making faces and spitting at his tutor, swearing and throwing things about the room. These obvious cries for help were regarded merely as confirmation that more of the same was needed. During the prince's visit to the Great Exhibition in 1851, he had shown a natural boyish interest in the sensational story of the Indian assassins known as the 'Thugs', which was part of the East India Company's stand. For this he was roundly criticized by Stockmar. Such matters were not worth the attention of a Christian prince. Any sign of frivolity was stamped out mercilessly. After all, Edward's duty would be to rule his country, not enjoy himself.

When Edward reached eighteen it was decided

that he should have his own household, at White Lodge in Richmond Park. In essence, this meant that he would have new 'keepers' to save him from the temptations of the flesh. Queen Victoria had told him that his father's iron self-discipline had made it easy for him to resist the siren calls of the opposite sex. Edward could well understand that. Meanwhile, officers of unimpeachable character, two with recent VCs from the Crimean War, were selected as the Prince's equerries. For their instructions they had only to turn to Prince Albert's 'Code of Conduct', which lay down details on how Edward should behave in every situation. It covered a range of matters from not slouching in armchairs to avoiding playing practical jokes. The equerries ensured that Edward followed the code every minute of the day.

On Bertie's eighteenth birthday he received two special gifts from his parents. The first was a memorandum beginning 'Life is composed of duties...' It was nothing less than a sermon on how he should conduct his life. He was informed that he was to have rooms in future allotted for his sole use. But these were not for entertaining girls or drinking and playing cards with young men. In fact, they were not even intended to give him privacy. They were instead to enable him to occupy himself unaided by others and to help him use his time in a profitable manner. This meant solitary study. The second present was a large, bewhiskered, 45-year-old 'Governor', one Colonel Robert Bruce, who was to replace his tutor Gibbs. The current joke was that Bruce was Edward's 'Chief Warder'. The prince's equerries were to take orders not from Edward but from Bruce. In fact, Edward was free to do nothing without Bruce's permission. Prince Albert was pleased to have found a kindred spirit in Robert Bruce, a man obsessed with nit-picking and report-writing. Except for his name he might almost have been German, constantly frowning and clearing his throat prior to barking out some order or complaint. No sooner had he met his charge than he reported to the Prince Consort that his son was interested in nothing more worthwhile than clothes.

Colonel Bruce allowed no young people to visit the Prince's new establishment. Bertie took every meal with the colonel himself and at least one of the three equerries. Conversation was restricted to re-fighting past campaigns and comparing old wounds. The only woman Edward ever met at this time was his great-aunt, the Duchess of Cambridge.

During this period of his education Edward was being crammed for the army examination. Naturally he passed, but he was refused training as an officer since the life of the heir to the throne could not be endangered. Instead, Prince Albert decided that Bertie should enjoy a taste of university education. He spent brief periods at Oxford, Edinburgh and Cambridge, though these were specially arranged to coincide with the vacations so that he would not encounter any other students. He was personally tutored by the Professor of Physical Sciences at Edinburgh University, who soon realized the prince's limitations. The Professor of Chemistry later observed that Edward could demonstrate his scientific skills by 'washing his hands in ammonia and plunging them into boiling lead'.

The weaknesses of Bertie's education were becoming evident. When he first met young men of his own age he chose his friends from a 'fast set' of drinkers, whoremasters and scoundrels, like Henry Hastings, known as the 'Wicked Marquis', Sir Frederick Johnstone and Lord Chaplin, the 'Magnifico'. In contrast with the meal set down by Stockmar for Bertie's breakfast, consisting of bread and butter and an egg, Hastings enjoyed mackerel fried in gin, caviare on toast and a bottle of claret.

When Bertie first met young women, he immediately wanted to jump into bed with them. Ironically, his first 'experience' came courtesy of Colonel Bruce. The colonel had persuaded Prince Albert to allow Edward to spend some time at the Grenadier Guards camp at the Curragh in 1861. Bruce thought it might be the making of the Prince. Perhaps it was. The young officers there smuggled a young actress called Nellie Clifton into Bertie's bed. From that moment the Prince of Wales was embarked on a career in debauchery which ranked only just behind that of Casanova. Nellie naturally boasted of her conquest and soon the story had reached the national papers. Baron Stockmar passed the news on to Prince Albert and that, as they say, was that. According to Queen Victoria, Albert's heart was broken, visions of Nellie's pregnancy haunted him and George IV appeared in his dreams like the ghost of things to come.

In the Prince Consort's tortured brain Bertie's 'fling' with Nellie amounted to little less than treason. So appalled was he that his son had reverted to the disgusting ways of his Hanoverian forefathers that that he lost all sense of proportion. He passed sleepless nights, then wrote a hysterical letter to his son accusing him of 'gross and deliberate cruelty' to his loving parents. He claimed that the news of his debauchery had inflicted on him the greatest blow he had ever suffered in his life. He warned Bertie that if Nellie got pregnant by anyone else she would still accuse him of being the father and would drag him through the courts and, before 'the greedy multitude', force from his lips the 'disgusting details of his profligacy . . . O horrible prospect . . . and to break your poor parent's hearts.' Albert's death, from typhoid fever, only weeks after the news of Bertie's 'one-night stand', was attributed by the Queen to the shock of her son's 'fall'. Medical opinion might more accurately have pointed the finger at the unwholesome drains at Windsor Castle, but Victoria would never believe that it was not Bertie's shame that had killed her husband.

What did Albert and Stockmar achieve by their educational plan? The precise opposite of what they had intended. Instead of being a copy of his father, Bertie was the exact opposite. Albert never smoked and regarded tobacco as disgusting; Bertie smoked a dozen cigars and twenty cigarettes each day. Albert took wine in medicinal draughts; Bertie simply boozed. Albert was tall and slim; Bertie short, fat and proud of it. Albert was scared of women; Bertie loved them and bedded as many as possible. Albert was an intellectual; Bertie a lovable philistine. Albert shunned society; Bertie led it. Albert was a bore; Bertie an anecdotalist's dream. Well-intentioned though he may have been, the Prince Consort inflicted an education on his eldest son which did so much more harm than good that one wonders what kind of king Edward VII might have turned out to be had he received anything resembling the normal English education of the time.

Sir Frederick Johnstone was one of Edward, the Prince of Wales's closest friends, but even he could go too far. Late one evening, at one of the Prince's parties, an inebriated Johnstone was told by the Prince, 'Freddy, you're very drunk.' Johnstone replied, 'Tum Tum, you're very fat.' Infuriated, the Prince ordered his drunken friend to leave his house.

A RIPPING YARN: THE EDUCATION OF ALBERT VICTOR, DUKE OF CLARENCE

In a meritocracy Albert Victor, Duke of Clarence and Avondale, would have found contentment as 'Eddy' the bootblack, working outside a department store in Piccadilly. But in Victorian England, this amiable dullard found himself carrying the hopes of the country, not to mention his proud parents, as 'Eddy' the heir presumptive to the throne of England. In a short and chequered career he graduated from being known as 'Collars and Cuffs' to 'Eddy the Ripper' son of 'Jack'. Nicknames accumulated around him probably because ordinary adjectives seemed inadequate to describe this curious product of royal breeding. Bearing the long neck of Denmark, the long nose of Coburg and the small brain of Hanover on his escutcheon, as well as displaying the vacant look of effete nineteenth-century royalty everywhere, he travelled the well-worn path of his forebears. First he endured a gentleman's education, playing in the nursery with Nanny, then being beaten mercilessly by his tutor. After this, it was off to sea, a flyhack at the academic life of Cambridge University and then into the nearest brothel, which turned out to be a male one. After that there was the army, in which he was able to while away the time playing cards and exterminating the fauna of the locality.

Albert Victor, always thereafter known as 'Eddy', was born two months prematurely on 8 January 1864, after his mother had been ice-skating. He was the eldest son of the Prince of Wales and Princess Alexandra of Denmark and he was a walking disaster. If one had assembled all the worst characteristics and features of his parents then one would have constructed 'Eddy'. He was thin-faced, with a receding chin, bulbous eyes and such a long neck and arms that his shirts and jackets always had to have extra long collars and cuffs, thus earning him one of his nicknames. It was clear from early on that he was extremely dim intellectually. His vacant look and weak smile only needed to be complemented by a smock and a piece of straw and his future was assured as a village idiot.

Unprepossessing as Eddy obviously was, he was the darling of his mother's eye, and she doted on him. So possessive was she that Eddy found it difficult to develop any normal relationships with women, a factor which probably contributed to his latent homosexuality. His father, however, found it difficult to like Eddy. In the first place he was jealous at how much attention the boy got from his mother, which he himself had been denied by his mother, Queen Victoria. In other ways, his father found Eddy disappointing. He was partly deaf – like Princess Alexandra – spoke with a lisp, was tall (though thin and weedy) and suffered from haemophilia. Although doctors would not have been aware of it at the time, poor Eddy may well have also been suffering from Klinefelter's syndrome, a complaint which manifested itself in an absence of body hair, and which would have made him impotent and certainly sterile. The outlook for any country dependent on poor Eddy as a future king was bleak indeed.

As we have seen (see p. 133), Eddy's father was not himself well educated, having been a guinea pig for the latest theories of Baron Stockmar and Albert, the Prince Consort. Nor was Prince Alexandra – who loved to be known as 'Motherdear' by her children and felt that smothering was the best form of mothering – ever known to open a book. Alexandra, one suspects, must have been the inspiration for Mrs Darling in J.M. Barrie's *Peter Pan*, once writing to her burly and bearded son George, who was then commanding a British gunboat, a letter ending with 'a great big kiss for your lovely little face'. It was therefore something of a surprise, especially as his tutor had declared him 'incapable of being educated', when the idiot of a family not short of them was sent to Cambridge University for two years. Removing Eddy from the company of his younger but more able brother George was regarded as a very radical step, as he was thought to need George for support and reassurance. But George was destined for a career at sea, whereas Eddy was merely destined to chase sailors. Efforts were therefore made to find Eddy a new support, and the choice for tutor fell on James Stephen, a brilliant young Cambridge academic, whose equally brilliant father had become insane. From Stephen Eddy learned little – 'he hardly knows the meaning of the word "read"', wrote his tutor. Instead, he mixed with a group of Stephen's friends at Cambridge, some of whom were homosexual and who introduced him to the notorious Hundred Guineas Club, where he was later to become involved in a scandal. Membership of the club involved one in adopting a female persona and Eddy used the name 'Victoria' when he signed in. But far worse than this, through his contacts with Stephen Eddy became a suspect in the notorious case of 'Jack the Ripper', whose murderous career took place in 1889, while Eddy was at Cambridge. Frankly, Eddy would never have had the gumption to sustain a successful criminal career but recent research has suggested that his tutor, James Stephen, who was soon to suffer a complete mental collapse and be confined to an asylum, was a possible candidate for the 'Ripper'.

On leaving Cambridge, Eddy joined the 10th Hussars, rising meteorically in rank on a tide of champagne. However, his father was not convinced that Eddy was destined for great things. So poor an officer was he that when the Duke of Cambridge suggested that Eddy demonstrate some 'elementary manoeuvres' with his men, his colonel begged the duke not to insist as Eddy had not the faintest idea of how to do it. Later, at a banquet in honour of the Commander-in-Chief, Eddy told him he knew nothing about the Crimean War and had never heard of the battle of Alma, in which the Duke had played a notable part. When not dropping clangers, Eddy was sewing even wilder oats than the Prince of Wales had done in his day. Women apparently found him irresistible. But it must never be forgotten that as second in line to the throne Eddy was at the mercy of any fortune-hunting woman. One actress claimed to have had a child by him, another that he had given her 'the clap'.

In 1890 Queen Victoria made Eddy Duke of

Edward, Prince of Wales and Alexandra with their children at Marlborough House. The three daughters were so shy that they were known as the 'Whispering Wales girls'. Albert Victor wears a high collar to conceal his extraordinarily long neck. Seated on the steps in the centre is the future George V. (AR/IS)

Clarence and Avondale, an ominous decision as it turned out. The press, alerted to some of Eddy's less salubrious activities, drew the public's attention to the fact that among the previous holders of the title, one had been drowned in a barrel of Malmsey wine, while the late King William IV had been foul-mouthed, vulgar and a positive danger to women. Eddy seemed to be living proof that the title carried a curse.

By 1891 Eddy's private life was thoroughly public and his sexual escapades were the talk of London. He was pilloried in *Punch* and the Prince of Wales decided that Eddy must be sent abroad before matters got truly out of hand. Queen Victoria, unaware of Eddy's homosexual proclivities, had suggested that he would do well to go on a European tour. Bertie, remembering his own excesses in Paris during the Second Empire, immediately booked Eddy a ticket on the next boat for Bombay.

Eddy was sent to India on the assumption that he could not get up to too much mischief there. How wrong this turned out to be could be assessed by his ailing physical condition on his return, the result of a dissipated life that would have left athletes of both sexual persuasions utterly exhausted. His most abiding memory of the mysterious sub-continent was neither the Taj Mahal nor the golden temple at Amritsar; it was his liaison with an Indian laundryman he met at Shuttadore.

There seemed to be no alternative but to find Eddy a good wife, and so the hunt began. The Queen alerted her 'beloved daughter Vicky', the ex-Empress of Germany, and she began lining up suitable princesses. Eddy, meanwhile, fell in and out of love with every shop assistant who did not immediately enter a nunnery when he hove into sight. While 'Vicky' was pressing the credentials of the splendid Princess Alix of Hesse (later to marry Tsar Nicholas II and die at the hands of the Bolsheviks in 1918), Eddy had fallen in love with Princess

Hélène, daughter of the pretender to the French throne. While he conducted a clandestine affair with this young lady, the Queen dismissed her as a French Catholic and therefore unacceptable as the wife of an heir to the English throne. Hélène was heartbroken. Eddy would have been if he could have remembered who Hélène was. Since meeting her he had had several other flings and was currently deeply in love with Lady Sybil St Clair Erskine. Eddy liked writing love letters, but with their appalling spelling and non-existent grammar, they challenged not only the decoding skills of their recipients but their willingness to take on the education of a royal half-wit. In his letters Eddy told Sybil that though he loved her deeply he was also in love with another, Hélène. Wasn't that extraordinary? He asked her to destroy the royal crest on his letters so nobody would ever know who had been writing to her. Lady Sybil, whom the Queen rejected as far too common for her grandson, naturally kept the letters, hoping they might come in useful when Eddy became King Albert the First.

At last 'Vicky' found the right girl: Princess May of Teck, daughter of the enormously fat but kindhearted Mary Adelaide of Cambridge. May was a 'brick' and far too good to waste on Eddy. She would eventually become Queen of England, but not quite in the way that was expected. May – who was always known thereafter as 'Mary' – was a mature and attractive woman, with a strong sense of duty. Only this could have convinced her to take on such a problematic husband. But her sacrifice was not, in the event, required, nor was England ever to be ruled by King Albert Victor I. Not long after celebrating Eddy's twenty-eighth birthday at Sandringham, Princess Mary learned that her fiancé had been taken ill with pneumonia. On 14 January 1892, Eddy died. The royal family, indeed the whole nation, callously breathed a sigh of relief. Through his death the nation was spared the rule of a monarch who would have been one of the worst kings in England's long history. Princess Mary was a widow before she was a bride, yet Queen Victoria and the Prince of Wales were not going to let this paragon go to waste. Mary of Teck became Queen of England in 1910, but as the wife of Eddy's brother George, now King George V. So convenient was the death of the Duke of Clarence and Avondale that there were rumours of a 'judicial killing' carried out on the orders of leading royal and political figures, but there was never any real proof of this. Eddy's father, the Prince of Wales, was griefstricken and yet, in some ways relieved. As he said, 'Our beloved son is happier now than if he were exposed to the miseries and temptations of this world.' As an epitaph it leaves so much unsaid that one wonders what other skeletons there were in Eddy's cupboard. Significantly, a television inquiry into the identity of Jack the Ripper some time ago was prevented by the Home Office from seeing certain documents that it believed had a bearing on the identity of the murderer. It would appear that the royal family even today is determined to prevent the private life of the Duke of Clarence from becoming too widely known. Yet accusations that he was Jack the Ripper lack substance. His character suggests Eddy was a vague and listless individual, idle and debauched, with none of the qualities that go to make a psychopathic killer. But Eddy *did* move in dubious circles, and it may well be that he either knew the Ripper or was too closely involved with those who did. The mystery remains, but what is certain is that the Duke of Clarence was the poorest possible advertisement for a monarchical system of government and as much a wastrel, even in democratic Britain, as any of the 'black sheep' fathered by King George III in the eighteenth century. Eddy could have put an end to the monarchy in Britain in a few brief years, whereas his brother George revitalized it and moulded it into a unifying force able to cope with the great challenge of world war in 1914.

At a cocktail party a guest was chatting to Princess Mary, sister of King George VI, without being able to remember who she was. He ventured the question, 'What is your brother doing these days?' 'Oh,' the Princess replied, 'he's still king.'

*King George V's knowledge of fishing was rather greater than his knowledge of literature.
On the birthday of the novelist Thomas Hardy, the prime minister telephoned the King
and asked him if he would send a telegram to congratulate 'Old Hardy' on his birthday.
The only 'Hardy' the king knew was Mr Hardy of Alnwick, in Northumberland,
'esteemed maker of fishing rods'. As a result, it was this Hardy who received a
telegram congratulating him on reaching an age he had not reached and on a day
that was not his birthday.*

BRINGING UP DAVID: THE EDUCATION OF EDWARD VIII

The most substantial thing about King George V and Queen Mary's eldest son was his name: Edward Albert Christian George Andrew Patrick David. He was to become a playboy prince, potentially the most dangerous King of England since James II and a liability of no small proportions to his country. That he chose the path of love rather than duty has a certain sentimental ring to it, but the truth is that he found in the American divorcée, Wallis Simpson, the mother he had lacked as a child (see p. 108). His search for a mother-substitute throughout his young manhood was a sign of a deep insecurity that made him ill-suited to ascend the British throne. The root cause of this unsuitability lay – as was the case with Edward VII – in a failure of royal parenting. The parallels, however, are much closer to the case of Prince Charles and his relationship with his parents. (see p. 143).

As Prince of Wales, King George V was a poor father. As he once said – and he meant it – 'My father was frightened of his mother: I was frightened of my father and I'm damn well going to see to it that my children are frightened of me.' And they were, notably 'David', his eldest son. Those who knew Prince George well were astounded that such a naturally kind man could be 'such a brute' to his children. With a father like that a child will naturally turn to his mother and what did he find when he did? The emotionally barren Princess Mary, the former May of Teck. She was so aware of her

dignity and her duty that she seemed emotionally disconnected from her family. What love she had within her stayed firmly locked there or only appeared when the flag flew and the troops rode past and the national anthem played. She had no idea whatsoever of how to deal with children. Writing of the two-year-old David she said, 'I really believe he begins to like me at last. He is most civil to me.' The civility or otherwise of two-year-olds has long been of concern to all caring mothers. So, if the parents were opting out, what arrangements had they made for the child's nurses or tutors? Sadly the answer is 'very bad ones'.

Both David and his younger brother Albert – later to become King George VI – were much influenced by the extraordinary nurse Mary Peters who was responsible for them in their early years. So obsessed was she with the young David that when it was time for him to be shown to his parents, the nurse pinched him hard to make him cry, so that the Princess would have to hand him back to her care. In fact, it was the Queen – Alexandra – who gave the boys the most love. Once, when the Prince and Princess of Wales were away, the two boys were left with their grandparents, the King and Queen. They had such a good time that when their parents returned they found them completely 'out of hand', so the Prince of Wales decided they needed much stricter treatment. It was typical of him: fun and enjoyment were just one step away from mutiny in

The future Edward VIII at the age of ten, photographed at Osborne Naval College with his father the Prince of Wales, later King George V. Prince George and his wife Princess Mary imposed a fiercely disciplinarian regime on their eldest son. (P)

his narrow naval mind. When their father wanted to see either of his sons he would send a footman with the verbal command, 'His Royal Highness wishes to see you.' Punishment from their tutors was severe. Prince George had given these men *carte blanche* to beat the boys' bare buttocks when they felt it necessary. Ultimately his father was so fierce a disciplinarian that he stunted David's emotional growth.

In later life, both David and Albert observed that they had never once been alone with their mother, on a one-to-one basis; there was always a lady-in-waiting or a servant present. Queen Mary did not understand the needs of young children. She spoke to them politely but without affection as if they were merely visiting her for the day. Both she and Prince George rammed home the message of 'duty, dignity and obedience!' The only things David ever

shared with his mother were the tapestries she made him help her sew.

David spent his entire boyhood starved of the company and influence of women. His tutor, Henry Hansell, was a poor substitute for a mother, or an elder sister, or a loving aunt. One wit later commented of the young prince that he had had 'too much Hansel and not enough Gretel'. At thirteen the young prince was sent to become a naval cadet at Osborne Naval College. In spite of Hansell's attentions, David was a dunce and only gained a place at Osborne because of who he was, his marks being the lowest of any candidate. The Prince of Wales had supreme faith in the ability of the Royal Navy to mould a man's character. After all, look what it had done for him. But it failed to do much for David, who was badly bullied by the other sea cadets at Osborne, on the basis that it was the last time they would ever get the chance of punching a future King of England. Once they symbolically decapitated him – shades of Charles I – by ramming his head through an open sash window and pulling the top section down on his neck like a guillotine. David graduated to Dartmouth and then undertook a three-month cruise aboard HMS *Hindustani*, the captain commenting on their return, 'I would never recommend anyone sailing a ship under his command.'

In 1910 King Edward VII died and the Prince of Wales became King George V. If it was possible for him to become more distant from and more tyrannical to his children than before, he now did so. And it seemed that Princess Mary had been elevated beyond the need for normal human relations. She had provided her husband with children – or as one wit observed, 'with a regiment' – and she saw her task as finished. Now was the time gradually to metamorphose into a bronze statue symbolizing the British monarchy at its apogee. And so David was left to get on with it at Dartmouth, and cry into his pillow. Significantly, many photographs of David as a child and as a young man show him with a sad face. He had much to be sad about. His education had been a disaster, and he was grossly deficient in subjects like mathematics and science. A few months spent at Oxford University when he was eighteen, only served to lower the boy's self-esteem even further. When he remarked that he preferred picture books to written texts, the sycophantic titters served to mask real embarrassment. On the other hand, he played golf and tennis and enjoyed hunting and beagling while he was at the varsity. His sense of priorities was truly royal.

As an adult David was dogged by feelings of rejection. Even the great event of his life, the Abdication and his marriage to Mrs Simpson, involved a form of rejection that did not entail, as he saw it, rejecting his country, but his country rejecting the woman he loved and of his family, notably his brother Albert, turning its back on him. He had experienced so much humiliation and failure as a child that he spent much of his life trying to compensate for it, pursuing older women, married women and unattainable women in an attempt to win the love he had never received from his mother. And for much of the time he still lived in terror of a father who grew more and more disillusioned with him with every day that passed.

When he was young, Prince Charles, who was sensitive about his ears sticking out, was told by his 'uncle' Lord Louis Mountbatten, 'They'll never let you be King with ears like that.'

BRINGING UP CHARLIE: THE EDUCATION OF CHARLES, PRINCE OF WALES

Perhaps Desmond Morris is the best man to explain the lack of parenting skills in the royal family over the years, notably the inability of fathers to relate to their sons, and the failure of mothers to commit themselves emotionally to their offspring. Furthermore, what *was* an appropriate education for a future King of England? Nobody ever seemed to know. The Prince Consort's ineffectual scheme of tutoring merely ensured that his eldest son 'Bertie' (see p. 133) rejected everything that he was taught and became everything that his father was not. The brutal upbringing endured by David, later Edward VIII, at the hands of his father, King George V, did much to damage his weak personality and led him to reject what his father as 'King-Emperor' represented. Some might think it too glib and too convenient to detect the same parenting errors in Prince Philip's attitude towards the upbringing of Prince Charles. Certainly, the role of the Prince of Wales in Britain has been a difficult one over the last hundred and fifty years, notably because, as heirs to the throne, the princes have been given no worthwhile jobs to perform. Instead, they have become 'princes-in-waiting'. However, it would be unbalanced to pinpoint the failings of the fathers and not those of the mothers. In the three cases I have cited – 'Bertie', David and Charles – their mothers were Queens of a distinctly authoritarian kind. Each – Victoria, Mary and Elizabeth II – were or are exceptional monarchs, two of whom were rulers, while the other set the standard by which other members of the royal family have been judged. However, those more qualified than this writer in the field of psychology have detected in these three 'strong' women a commitment to duty and the job of being a queen that left far too little time for them to be mothers. It has been claimed by some that their sacrifice of a close mother-child relationship, notably with their sons, resulted in the three princes in question growing up starved of maternal affection.

From the outset, Charles was trained for kingship. He believes himself to be the end-product of a tradition of monarchs whose duty was to sacrifice

Prince Charles greets his housemaster on his first day at Gordonstoun School, 2 May 1962. Prince Philip (far right) had enjoyed his time at Gordonstoun, but Charles later described his schooldays there as 'hell'. (H)

their own interests for their people. Unlike most of the younger 'royals' he is a mature and, in some ways, appropriately serious person, who demands the deference that goes with his rank in return for the performance that he gives as a responsible prince and future king. This stiffness of person is his idea of how an heir to the throne should conduct himself.

As a young boy Charles experienced what has been called 'long-distance' parenting or 'love at arm's length'. His mother became Queen when he was just four years old and her strong sense of duty soon overcame the maternal imperative. Her frequent visits abroad reduced her personal contact with her son and meant she often had to communicate with him by telephone. As a result, Charles was always in the hands of his nannies, developing relationships with them that have continued throughout his life, but which are not substitutes for a mother's love.

Both the Queen and Prince Philip believed in maintaining the standards of etiquette that had been set down by Queen Mary. Charles was taught to bow to his grandmother and to stand in the presence of his grandfather, unless permitted to sit. As a result, his childhood became ritualized. The severe etiquette that he absorbed has made him solemn-

natured and this has undoubtedly presented problems in making friends both at school and afterwards. Charles, of course, was the first heir to the throne to be sent to school and it involved him in what was a terrible case of culture shock. The fault undoubtedly lay with his father, the Duke of Edinburgh, who believed that the experiences that moulded him as a boy were just the ones that should help to mould his son into a future king. Unfortunately, Philip gave scant consideration to the fundamental personality differences between his son and himself. Prince Philip's success at Gordonstoun, where he became Head Boy, was not an argument for sending all three of his sons there, in disregard of their wishes or their personalities.

The Prince of Wales has been quite open recently – both in television interviews and in information he gave to author Jonathan Dimbleby for his authorized biography of the Prince – about his unhappy childhood, much of which resulted from his treatment at the hands of his father. Prince Philip may have been an all-action man, confident and self-reliant, forced to find his way in a hostile world and fend for himself without the privileges normally reserved for royalty, but, as a boy, Charles was very different. He was a gentle, insecure child, who needed the comfort of a loving home background, not the rowdy dormitory of a Scottish public school, hundreds of miles from home. In a sense he was 'softer' than his father had been, which persuaded Philip to try to 'toughen him up'. Charles was not a weakling but he was very sensitive, and shrank from his father's brusque tone, sensing rejection.

His mother, whose role was so important, distanced herself from the parenting process, leaving all the major decisions to her husband. She spoke of Charles as needing 'as normal an upbringing as possible'. Prince Philip believed that Charles's upbringing, and life at Gordonstoun, was normal. In both respects he was wrong. He could not easily bring himself to accept his son's gentle nature, and friends of the family were often aware that Prince Philip openly belittled his son, perhaps even bullying him.

As has been the case with so many young royals, Prince Charles was frightened of his father. If this was evident to friends and occasional visitors, it drew no reaction from the Queen. For her, the demands of the job came first and her family second.

Prince Charles has described the decision to send him to Gordonstoun as a 'prison sentence'. The school, located in the northeast of Scotland, based its regime on the theories of the German educationalist, Dr Kurt Hahn, and was famous for its tough 'man-making' discipline. Cold showers and cross-country running were popular ways of making boys into men. A newspaper report that Charles was entering a 'classless' society at Gordonstoun overlooked the fact that the school was anything but classless. For a start, its fees were higher than those of Eton. Perhaps by 'classless' the writer meant 'less academic'. It has to be said that the school does not provide an education that suits everyone, and many of its old boys share Prince Charles's regret at having gone there.

As a thirteen-year-old, Charles was shocked by the sheer brutality of many of the boys he met. Having experienced a sheltered upbringing, Charles found the 'short sharp shock' treatment which represented his secondary education deeply depressing. He was bullied constantly and scarcely allowed any sleep at night by the boys who shared his dormitory. On the sports field he was frequently attacked during rugby matches, paralleling his great-uncle David's experiences at Osborne and Dartmouth (see p. 141). It was the same buzz for the bullies: the excitement of punching the next king of England. The Prince's letters home simply ache with misery: 'I don't like it much here. I simply dread going to bed as I get hit all night long.' He frequently referred to his school as 'hell'. He was also ridiculed about having sticking-out ears, something that could have been corrected after he had suffered ridicule at Cheam, his prep school. One might almost say that Gordonstoun taught the Prince of Wales an important but very negative lesson: 'trust nobody' – a particularly damaging thought for such a shy and reclusive boy, with low self-esteem.

The result is that the Prince of Wales has continued to be a 'loner'. Whether his predilection for paintings of landscapes rather than those with a human presence is a significant feature of his interests is not for this writer to say, but his concern for buildings and architecture has been interpreted by some as a *cri de coeur* from someone who had endured a cold and loveless upbringing.

In spite of being Prince of Wales, Prince Charles's knowledge of the history of the principality has proved lamentable. In 1969, just prior to his investiture at Caernarfon, Charles approached a Welsh Nationalist demonstrator, pointed to his banner and asked, 'Who is Llewellyn?' The demonstrator replied, 'Llewellyn was the last Welsh Prince of Wales.'

CHAPTER 5: ROYAL DEATHS

Last Rites

Monarchs cannot die quietly. As Shakespeare wrote, 'When beggars die, there are no comets seen; The heavens themselves blaze forth the death of princes.' To a people the death of a ruler – for good or ill – is memorable. Whether it leads to celebrations or to deep mourning there is no disguising the fact that the passing of great men is something that can profoundly affect the lives of ordinary human beings. And in many cases the deaths of the great have been far from ordinary events. Even those who died peacefully in their beds have sometimes not been allowed to find much rest. One such case was William I, the Conqueror, who caused more fear to his people when dead than ever he did while alive.

No resting place

On 9 September 1087, in the town of Rouen in Normandy, Duke William the Bastard – known to history as William 'the Conqueror' – lay dying in agony of an internal injury – probably peritonitis – suffered when his horse threw him. As the cathedral bell of Rouen summoned the righteous to morning prayer William breathed his last. The man who, in his lifetime, had ruled England as well as Normandy now found in death that he did not own even a suit of clothes. No sooner had his soul passed on but his death chamber became a scene of chaos and pandemonium, like a street of squabbling stallholders. The priests who had been praying for his soul and the servants who had been attending to his earthly needs now fell upon the body and stripped it of all its rich garments, leaving it naked on the ground. All the robes and linens, plate and royal furniture were taken away until the room was as naked as its only wretched occupant – William – stark upon the cold floor.

Matters did not improve much when William's body was taken for burial to the church of St Etienne in Caen. It was a blisteringly hot day and the corpse, which had been left unattended for some days, had begun to swell. As it was lowered into a stone coffin in the crypt it was found that it would not fit in and so the priests had to bend and press the King's body this way and that so that they could close the lid. Unfortunately they pressed too hard on the swollen belly and the body split and burst open, spilling the contents of the stomach on the floor. Pus and putrefaction drenched the King's shroud and filled the coffin, and so overwhelming was the stench that issued from the body that the priests and bishops fled from the crypt, vomiting and holding their noses. The crowd, which had assembled in the church for the solemn ceremony, bravely stood their ground at first and then one by one and finally in a frantic rush they all ran screaming for air to throw the church doors open. For a while nobody dared to return to the body and when they did the remains were unceremoniously tipped into the coffin and quickly interred.

There matters might have rested had not William's tomb been opened in 1562 by

Calvinists during the French Wars of Religion. The great King's remains were now taken and scattered about the courtyard, with just one thigh bone remaining in the coffin. After the Calvinists had gone loyal Catholics retrieved as many of William's bones as they could find and reburied them. But in 1793, during the French Revolution, the tomb was desecrated again, and nothing was left behind of the body this time. Only a stone slab remains today to tell of William's far too temporary resting-place.

The grave yawns

The Empress Maria Theresa of Austria was a wonderful mother to her numerous children. However, on one occasion, she allowed religious scruples to interfere with her normal maternal instincts, with unfortunate consequences. Her daughter, the Archduchess Josepha, was due to leave Vienna to marry King Ferdinand IV of Naples and Sicily. However, before she left, her mother ordered her to go into the family vault to pray at the tombs of her Habsburg ancestors. However, the recently deceased body of the Emperor Joseph's wife, who had died of smallpox, was present in the vault, inadequately embalmed. As a result, Josepha contracted smallpox and died on the very day she should have left for Italy.

Bursting with life

The death of Caroline of Ansbach, wife of George II of Great Britain, in 1737 was not without its humorous side, in spite of the grievous suffering of the patient at the hands of the doctors. Caroline had been suffering from an umbilical rupture, as a result of a difficult earlier pregnancy. On 9 November she was taken ill with violent stomach pains and vomiting. When George's eldest son and heir, Frederick (whose unhappy relations with his father are described elsewhere) (see p. 115) heard that his mother was ill he asked permission to visit her. When the King heard he flew into a fury and said, 'I always hated the rascal and now I hate him worse than ever. He wants to come and insult his poor, dying mother. But she shall not see him. No. No.'

The surgeons now began a series of painful operations, cutting into her stomach and taking mortified pieces away. On 17 November, her bowels sudden burst, flooding the bed and the floor in putrescent matter. Alexander Pope's spiteful couplet summed up the situation:

> Here lies, wrapp'd in forty thousand towels,
> The only proof that Caroline had bowels.

In spite of Pope's jibe, Caroline showed courage and a sense of humour. Once during an operation – without anaesthetics, of course, and conducted only by candlelight – one of the surgeons' wigs caught fire and Caroline asked for the operation to be interrupted, while she laughed at the ridiculous sight. But death could not be long delayed and once she had passed on, the King's superstitious nature meant that a page had to keep watch by his bed for several nights, for fear of Caroline's ghost returning. The death of the Queen distressed the London mob, who would have preferred to have learned of the King's demise. Anonymous epitaphs included:

> O death, where is thy sting?
> To take the Queen and leave the King?

Poor Fred is dead

The death of King George II's eldest son, known to posterity as 'Poor Fred', marked a first for the Hanoverian dynasty in England. Fred suffered a thoroughly English demise, being killed by a cricket ball. As if to spite his appalling German parents, Fred became a cricket fanatic and was responsible for helping to develop the game in the south of England. He had his own cricket pitch at Cliveden, and here, playing with his children, he received a blow on his chest, from which an abscess developed.

On 20 March 1751, while listening to one of his friends play the violin, Fred felt a pain in his chest as the abscess burst, and suddenly gasped, 'Je sens la mort.' The King, hearing that his son had been taken ill, declared that he hoped it was nothing trivial. When he later heard that he was dead, he remarked, 'I am glad of it.' So bitter was his hostility to his now late son, that he refused to provide any food for the mourners at the funeral, who had to go to the local tavern. King George also decreed that the service in Westminster Abbey should be attended by no bishops or peers and that there should be no anthems. But the public was not entirely fooled. In their opinion Fred was worth the whole lot of the royal family put together, as this famous epitaph proves:

> Here lies Fred
>
> Who was alive and is dead.
>
> Had it been his father
>
> I had much rather.
>
> Had it been his brother
>
> Still better than another.
>
> Had it been his sister
>
> No one would have missed her.
>
> Had it been the whole generation
>
> Still better for the nation.
>
> But since 'tis only Fred
>
> Who was alive and is dead
>
> There's no more to be said.

Gone with the wind

If Fred's death was at least semi-tragic, the death of King George II, his father, was in the best traditions of English farce, for the king died on the privy. On the morning of 25 October 1760 the King rose early and, having drunk a cup of chocolate, retired to the privy. Moments afterwards, a loud sound was heard, followed by a groan. His valet was alarmed, the sound being somewhat louder than the royal wind tended to be, and so he ran into the privy only to find that the King was lying on the floor, having cut his face as he fell. He was carried back to his bed but was found to have died instantly. The sound that had been heard was the ventricle of his heart bursting. And so King George's family died: his wife from burst bowels; his son from burst abscess; and he himself from a burst heart. The shades of 'Poor Fred' might have wondered that he had one to burst.

Life drains away

The death of the Prince Consort in December 1861 from typhoid was a direct consequence of the faulty drains at Windsor Castle. It was ironic that Albert, a man of science and progressive ideas, who had modernized much of Buckingham Palace, should die in this way. According to the Lord Chamberlain, work on the drains connected to the water closets, sinks and baths of the castle had not been adequately done. As he explained, 'The noxious effluvia which escapes from the old drains and the numerous cesspools still remaining is frequently so exceedingly offensive as to render many parts of the castle almost uninhabitable.' This was of scant comfort to Queen Victoria as she grieved, nor, with her capacity for illogicality, would she accept it as the cause of Albert's death. Instead she blamed her son's one-night-stand with Nellie Clifton (see p. 136), which she believed had sent the saintly Albert to his grave.

Murder most foul

Some English rulers have met violent deaths by the hands of enemies or assassins, but none a more terrible death than Edward II. On the night of 22 September 1327 villagers around Berkeley Castle in Gloucestershire heard sounds so dreadful that most of them took to their beds and pulled the covers over their heads. The still night air was rent by screams, unearthly and agonized. The poor folk knew what they meant: the King, poor Edward II, was being murdered.

In order to leave no outward marks upon the body and, so it is said, as a reminder of the King's homosexual relationship with Piers Gaveston (see p. 43), the manner of execution used was that employed to kill leopards without marking their fine skins: a red hot poker inserted by the back passage. It appears that the three murderers – Maltravers, Gurney and Ogle – sent by Roger Mortimer, crept into Edward's cell when he was asleep and flung a heavy table on top of him so that he could not move. They first inserted a horn in the King's rectum and then thrust a heated poker in through the horn and burned his internal organs. It was an agonizing – and humiliating – death. When the Abbot of Gloucester came to take the body he said that the face was contorted with a terrible look of horror and pain. All the gold leaf on the coffin and the pure gold on the hearse could not conceal the vileness of Mortimer's action. Appropriately Mortimer was to die the traitor's death of hanging, drawing and quartering for his crime.

A privy secret

The death of Edmund 'Ironside', the last 'English' king, in 1016 resulted from another particularly foul crime. Edmund had been successfully fighting the Danish invader Cnut until an English traitor – one of Edmund's thanes, Edric Streona – hoping to curry favour with Cnut, arranged the murder of his great rival. There are several variants on the way the blow was struck, but there is complete agreement about the place where Edmund breathed his last.

After feasting one evening Edmund retired to the building which held the privy – little more than a deep hole dug in the ground – in order to relieve a call of nature. Hidden inside the privy was the son of ealdorman Edric. As Edmund sat down Edric's son thrust upwards with his dagger, penetrating Edmund's rectum and leaving the weapon fixed in his bowels. Another version has an even more complex method of killing. A Norman chronicler, Geoffrey Gaimar, wrote that a bow had been fixed in the privy by Edric's son so that as the King sat down he triggered an arrow which flew up and penetrated his body from beneath. Whichever weapon was used, the essential facts are clear: Edmund died by being pierced through the vitals in a privy.

But Edric did not live long to profit from his crime. He presented himself to Canute saying, 'Hail! thou who art sole king of England' and told the Dane what he had done. To his surprise Canute was angry and replied, 'For this deed I will exalt you, as it merits, higher than all the nobles of England.' He then commanded that Edric should be decapitated and his head placed upon a pole on the highest battlement.

Royal Assassinations

Royalty have always been a target for assassins. Absolute power may corrupt absolutely, but it is not always the kings and emperors who are the ones corrupted. Ostentatious displays of privilege, considered so important for royalty until the twentieth century, have provoked those who seek a public stage for their own display. Believing that only the big crimes hit the headlines, thousands of activists for one cause or another, or even those with no cause but their own, have found in royalty some of the biggest targets of all. Such assassinations rarely have a personal motive. The king or queen is killed not as a person but as a symbol pregnant with meaning for millions of people.

Death in Geneva

Luck rather than security precautions has usually been the deciding factor in the survival or otherwise of the royal target. Queen Victoria, for example, survived numerous assassination attempts. Gladstone smugly observed that whereas assassins in other countries were politically motivated, those in Britain were always madmen. Her Majesty did not make the obvious response that that was precisely the reason why she was still alive. On the other hand, while Victoria ducked and weaved as her subjects blazed away at her, the Empress Elizabeth of Austria was killed because the assassin did not have fifty francs for the train fare from Geneva to Rome, where he planned to assassinate King Umberto of Italy.

The murder took place in the Swiss lakeside city in 1898, where the Empress was about to board a steamer. An Italian anarchist, Luigi Luccheni, had selected her as a target as he could not locate the Duc d'Orléans, his original second choice. Elizabeth, now sixty years old but still startlingly beautiful, seemed an easy target and so he walked up to her and seemed to stumble. As he did so he stabbed her through the heart with a metal file. But so fine was the weapon and so minute the entry wound, that the Empress thought she had been punched and got to her feet and carried on walking. There was little sign of blood and her lady-in-waiting thought she had suffered a heart attack, but the wound was obviously fatal. Elizabeth was taken to a hotel room, where she died an hour after being stabbed through the heart. Luccheni was disappointed that he had not killed the King of Italy but, as he said, 'They're all made of the same stuff.' Yet it was a pointless act, totally without significance. Elizabeth had no political importance for Austria or for Italy. Even as a symbol of royalty she was a poor one, having ceased to exert any influence on her husband Franz Josef or on anyone else, for that matter, years before. Elizabeth died because, as usual in her life, she was the wrong person at the wrong time and in the wrong place.

Bang on target

It is not always the assassin who blunders. Sometimes the victim is an unsuspecting accomplice to the crime, as was the case when Tsar Alexander II was killed by a bomb

The assassination of Tsar Alexander II at St Petersburg, 13 March 1881. Having survived a first bomb blast (shown here), Alexander alighted from his carriage only to be killed by a bomb thrown by a second terrorist. (ME)

in St Petersburg on 1 March 1881. Alexander had survived several previous attempts on his life and must have been aware that there would be others. However, when his carriage was hit by a grenade while travelling at high speed along the Embankment beside the River Neva, the Tsar, unhurt in the explosion, alighted from the damaged vehicle to see if he could help the wounded. It was a fatal blunder. Russian assassins worked in groups and another man was waiting for just such an opportunity. Alexander stood no more than six feet away from his killer, Ignacy Hryniewicki, who tossed another grenade between the Tsar's legs. There was a blinding explosion and both victim and assassin were blown backwards. Alexander lay dying in the street, with both his legs blown off at the hip. Hryniewicki was in no better a state and both men died a few hours later.

Lady Diana Cooper was once talking to Queen Elizabeth II at a party when she suddenly remembered to whom she was speaking. She said, 'Oh, I'm so sorry, I didn't recognize you without your crown.'

A royal martyr

England has not been the scene of a royal assassination in the modern period. But one such crime in Anglo-Saxon times had such consequences for the kingdom that it can only be seen in terms of a royal blunder of surpassing importance. For a hundred years from the time of Alfred the Great England was ruled by a line of great warrior-kings, unsurpassed in quality by any other nation in European history. The only parallel is with the Ottoman sultans of the fifteenth and sixteenth centuries, whose line ended through murder and the ambition of a scheming woman (see p. 123). So, now, did the great line of Saxon kings end the same way, with the murder of King Edward the Martyr at Corfe Castle at the hands of his step-mother Elfrida, who wished to see the throne pass to her son, Ethelred, to be known in England's history as Ethelred the Unraed or 'Unready'.

Edward visited his mother at Corfe on 18 March, 978, and as it was hot he was brought a goblet of wine. As he was drinking it Elfrida's servants came up behind him and stabbed the King in the back. His horse ran off, dragging the body, the foot of which was caught in a stirrup. Ethelred, though only fourteen, was consecrated king at Kingston in 979. He was no warrior himself and had a vein of treachery that won him a reputation as a corrupt and evil king. His reign coincided with renewed Danish raids on England and Ethelred tried to buy off the invaders rather than fight them. The wealth of England was being fast diminished by the enormous tributes that Ethelred paid to the Danes and so, true to form, the King tried to solve his problem by treachery rather than courage. On St Brice's Day – 13 November – in the year 1002, Ethelred called on his subjects throughout England to fall on their Danish neighbours and slay them without mercy. A massacre took place, notably in London, where King Sweyn of Denmark's sister Gunhilda and her family were murdered. Ethelred should have realized that this cowardly act would rebound on him and, as soon as the news had crossed the North Sea

King Edward VII was a stickler for a precise dress code and once, when an admiral's daughter arrived at a party with a dress one inch above her ankles he commented, 'I'm afraid you must have made a mistake. This is a dinner not a tennis party.'

The murder of King Edward the Martyr at the behest of his stepmother Elfrida at Corfe Castle, 18 March 978 opened the way for the disastrous rule of Ethelred the Unready. (P)

to Denmark, King Sweyn and his son Cnut invaded England with a vast force of Vikings. Sweyn had not come for money this time, though Ethelred tried to bribe him to go home. He had come to conquer England and annex it to his northern empire. Sweyn died in 1014, but his son Cnut continued the fight and eventually brought England under his sway, becoming King in 1016. Between mother and son, Elfrida and Ethelred had destroyed Saxon England for ever. The last so-called 'English' ruler, Harold II, who fell at Hastings in resisting the Normans, in 1066, was no true Saxon but an Anglo-Dane by birth.

A double-crossing by sea

One of the most inept assassination attempts was committed by the Emperor Nero, who wished to kill his mother, Agrippina. Rather than spill her blood he decided that she should die by drowning and to achieve this he commissioned his chief engineer to construct a collapsible boat. The plan was that a boat would be constructed with a section that would come loose at sea, thereby hurling the helpless Agrippina into the water without warning. Her death, as a result of a shipwreck, could not be held against the Emperor, her son, who would be free to dedicate a temple to her memory. What could be more filial than that?

The trap was set and Agrippina and two of her ladies was transported in luxury aboard a splendid new ship that Nero had provided her with. It was a calm night and Agrippina was resting on a bed in her cabin when the signal was given and the crew, who were a party to the murder, released the heavy weight which was to fall on Agrippina's cabin. One of her ladies was killed at once, but as the boat capsized, Agrippina jumped overboard and swam towards the shore. Nero had overlooked the fact that in her youth, her mad brother Caligula had once banished her to an island off the coast of Africa where she had been forced to earn her living as a pearl diver. As a result Agrippina was an excellent swimmer and had no difficulty in swimming to a fishing boat, which took her ashore.

At first she was unaware that the 'accident' had been planned by her son and sent him a message to say that she was safe. But then she thought further and realized that the boat had fallen apart by sections, like a house of cards, and that on a calm night with no wind and no high seas, a shipwreck was the last thing to be expected. But it was too late to recall the messenger and, once Nero had heard of her escape, he knew that he had blundered and that he would have to kill her immediately. Troops of soldiers were sent to Agrippina's house and there they stabbed her to death, beginning, as she directed them, with her womb, from which had come her monstrous son.

Opening a park in Glasgow in the 1920s, Queen Mary told one of the proud city councillors, 'It's a beautiful park, but what a shame it's surrounded by all those nasty houses.'

CHAPTER 6: A ROYAL MISCELLANY

Valuable Lessons

There are times when royalty are almost human and make mistakes like anybody else. Unfortunately, the mistakes of the great can all too quickly become great mistakes. Things that would ordinarily be dismissed with a laugh or a shrug of the shoulders take on an importance out of all proportion. Take, for example, that genius of Victorian invention, Prince Albert – Great Exhibitions and Christmas Trees included. Albert was not the sort of man to surrender his reputation for infallibility easily. After all, as historians wiser than this writer have said, the Victorian Age should, by rights, be known as the Albertian Age. Yet when victory in the Second Sikh War brought Britain the spoils of the Punjab, including the incomparable Koh-i-noor diamond, Albert's enthusiasm got the better of him for once.

The 'Jewel in the Crown'

The Governor-General of India, Lord Dalhousie, had annexed the Punjab in March, 1849, and without receiving permission from London deposed the twelve-year-old ruler, Maharajah Dhuleep Singh. As well as placing the province under direct British rule, Dalhousie decreed that the Koh-i-noor diamond, the largest and most famous in the world, must be presented, as a gesture of goodwill, to Queen Victoria. This was little less than daylight robbery, but the Sikhs were in no position to refuse and the diamond, known as the 'Mountain of Light', was presented to General Sir John Lawrence for safe keeping. Unfortunately, Lawrence then forgot all about it until Dalhousie received a sharp note from the Queen indicating that she would like to see her new possession – the diamond, not the Punjab. Dalhousie asked Lawrence to forward the diamond straightaway but Lawrence could not for the life of him remember where it was. He had put it in a cloth and kept it in his jacket pocket. But which jacket was it in? He searched madly but drew a complete blank. Fortunately for him, and for generations of tourists at the Tower of London, his servant, not realizing the value of the cloth and its contents, took it out of his master's pocket and placed it in a strongbox. 'Do you know what was in the cloth?' gasped Lawrence. 'Yes,' said the old man, 'it was just a bit of glass.'

The 'bit of glass' was taken back to England under guard and was duly presented to Queen Victoria at St James's Palace. The little lady's eyes blazed with a light that no man ever born could have matched and no woman could have mistaken – triumph and greed. Unfortunately, Victoria, as both a dutiful wife and an obsessive personality, liked to please her husband by indulging his various whims, one of which was to know best at all times. Albert – who dares to call him a know-all? – felt that the diamond was not perfect and needed to be refined. He would find just the man for the job. Soon a master diamond cutter from Holland was at work on the Koh-i-noor diamond, improving on nature. He

THE POOR OLD KOH-I-NOOR AGAIN !

1. The Koh-i-noor.
2 2. The Dutch Artists.
3 3 3. The Requisite Machinery.

4. The "Dook" manifesting Great Interest in the Precious Gem.
5 5 5. Eminent Scientific Men watching Proceedings.

The Duke of Wellington leads the Koh-I-Noor diamond to the cutting-wheel for reshaping in a Punch *cartoon of 1852. The bungling efforts of the dotard Duke and Prince Albert reduced the magnificent stone from 187 to 109 carats. (AR/IS)*

brought with him the latest four horsepower engine, which was set up at Buckingham Palace, with both Albert and the dotard Duke of Wellington on hand to assist. A month passed, then a further week, and then the work was completed. The Koh-i-noor diamond, which had weighed in at 187 carats was now a stripling of a mere 109 carats. Prince Albert was first to inspect the gem. It was much reduced in weight; its presumption had been trimmed; its vulgar excesses were modified: it was ruined!

Prince Albert met the cost of the work: eight thousand pounds. He found the English virtue of a stiff upper lip very helpful in this situation. No lip-trembler he. The diamond was still a phenomenon and it added lustre to the Queen on state occasions. But, oh, he could have wept for the waste.

Dhuleep Singh, in the meantime, had accepted Christianity and had come to England to be educated. He was a frequent visitor at Buckingham Palace and when he came the Queen was careful not to wear the 'Mountain of Light'. Just once she did raise the subject with this very-British young Maharajah, but Dhuleep Singh was at pains to reassure her that he was only too happy for the great diamond to be in her possession. Privately, of course, he thought nothing of the sort, referring to Queen Victoria as 'Mrs Fagin' and complaining that she was, in fact, a receiver of stolen goods. As he pointed out, 'She has no more right to the diamond than I have to Windsor Castle.'

The case of the disappearing pearls

If the previous story might stand as a salutary warning to the British of the results of their depredations in India, the story of the Maharani Chimnabai's pearls gives a warning to those whose greed overcomes their generosity. The Maharani was the second wife of the ruler of Baroda, and was inordinately proud of her collection of pearls. The wife of the British Viceroy at the time, Lady Willingdon, had something of a reputation for persuading her hosts to give her gifts of whatever she might take a fancy to in their palace. When the Maharani heard that the Willingdons were coming to Baroda to pay a visit she panicked, fearing that Lady Willingdon might take a shine to her pearls. As a result, she placed her finest pearls in a velvet-lined box and had it buried in the palace gardens. The visit by the Viceroy and his wife duly passed off well, but the Maharani did not immediately dig up the box. In fact, she was so remiss that it was not until three months had passed and the rains had come that she eventually sent a servant to extract the box from the ground. What she found when she opened the now-soggy box was heartbreaking. Water had got into the box and the pearls had literally disintegrated.

And then there were none...

Pearls of another kind were the price the Rajah of Drangadhara paid for a blunder by his flag-bearer at the battle of Kuwa. Among the Rajput princes the royal standard-bearer only dipped his flag in battle in the event of the king being killed. The flag was therefore the focal point for all resistance by his warriors. As it happened the flag also served as a signal to his eight wives, who watched the battle from the roof of the palace and knew that while the flag flew high their husband and king was well. However, at one point in the battle, the flag-bearer unforgivably lowered his flag so that he could relieve a call of nature. For the wives watching from the roof it seemed that the worst had happened and that their husband and king was dead. Obedient to the law of *sati*, seven of the eight women leaped to their deaths from the roof. The eighth woman, fearing to jump, was overjoyed when she saw the flag lifted again and carried back to the town, denoting the victory of the king. But the Rajah, shocked as he was by the deaths of his wives, was far from happy to find that his eighth wife had not obeyed *sati* and so he made her jump as well. Thus the day, which had been marked by victory in battle, had ended with the unnecessary deaths of all eight of his wives.

Royal Travels

The royal family in modern Britain has many functions; not the least of these has been that of roving ambassadors, representing Britain in far-flung parts of the world. Queen Elizabeth II has become highly professional in her performance of this delicate task and has rarely been found wanting, even in some of the most frustrating situations. Nevertheless, there have been occasions when blunders have been made, far more often against the queen than by her.

During a visit to Ottawa in Canada Prince Philip told his audience, 'The monarchy exists not for its own benefit, but for that of the country. We don't come here for our health. We can think of better ways of enjoying ourselves.'

The bottom line

During the royal visit to New Zealand in 1977 the Queen entered a private room set aside for her at a restaurant and found a woman going through the contents of her handbag. The Queen politely enquired what she thought she was doing. An embarrassed police woman, apologizing profusely, explained that she had been told to 'Check the Queen's suite and don't miss a thing.'

On her trips to New Zealand the Queen has sometimes fallen foul of Maori demonstrations that claim Queen Victoria had promised that they would keep their traditional lands. As a descendant of Victoria and as head of the Commonwealth, the Maoris feel that Queen Elizabeth could do more to help them. They therefore threatened to bare their buttocks to her – a Maori insult – and greet her with 'a twenty-one bum salute'. A number of Maoris – men and women – succeeded in reversing the usual trend of smiling faces and were arrested.

A cool reception

On a royal visit to Yugoslavia in 1973, Queen Elizabeth arrived at Dubrovnik to find that there was no welcoming committee. A mistake had been made in Yugoslav circles and the dignitaries assembling to meet the Queen had rushed off instead to Titograd, believing that the royal plane had been diverted. Many stiff upper lips were in evidence, along with red faces, copious apologies, twiddling thumbs and an air of general resignation. So experienced a traveller as Her Majesty had seen it all before. She waited for some twenty minutes in the royal aircraft while a new reception committee was found and assembled on the tarmac.

On the other hand, the Queen's patience is not limitless. Rulers of the Muslim world have always found it difficult to accept a woman as head of state and when she visited Morocco in 1980 King Hassan seemed to go out of his way to be rude to her. He failed to attend a luncheon engagement in her honour, choosing to play golf instead. When he received her at his palace in Rabat he rudely ordered her two ladies-in-waiting, the Duchess of Grafton and Mrs John Dugdale, to leave the room. He then refused to confirm a dinner engagement, leaving Her Majesty sitting in her car for half an hour. When the dinner was finally confirmed, the Queen was welcomed not by King Hassan but instead by two of his children. A planned visit to Fez was cancelled by the King without explanation, and on a desert picnic near the Atlas Mountains he kept Her

Queen Elizabeth II and Prince Philip in New Zealand, 1990. The Queen's trips to New Zealand have more than once been interrupted by Maori demonstrators complaining that she has not yet made good a supposed promise by Queen Victoria to restore their ancestral lands. (RF)

Majesty waiting in a tent for half an hour while he relaxed in his air-conditioned caravan. The Queen's mood, understandably, was frosty and she began tapping her foot, a sure sign of trouble to come. The following day the British press caned the Moroccan King with their headlines. Then, to cap it all, King Hassan arrived nearly an hour late for a banquet in his honour aboard the royal yacht *Britannia*. Apparently, the Queen was as angry as anyone had ever seen her. Her aides denied that this was so, but they were aware that the Queen had undertaken the visit, begging bowl in hand, to expedite the clinching of a government steel contract with Morocco, and King Hassan knew it and took advantage of it. Lord Salisbury would have sent a gunboat but Britain in the 1980s could not afford to stand on her dignity, even when her monarch was insulted.

While visiting Xian in China, Prince Philip was asked by a Scottish student studying Chinese at the local university what he had thought of the Forbidden City, which he had been allowed to visit by special permission of Deng Xiao Ping.
'Ghastly,' Prince Philip replied.
Everyone's face dropped. The Forbidden City was one of China's most magnificent sites. The Queen hastily intervened. 'It was fascinating. I could have spent a lot of time there.'
'The Forbidden City, oh yes,' said the Prince. 'But Beijing, that was ghastly.'

In touch with royalty

In 1993, during her visit to Australia, the Queen had a disagreement with the Australian prime minister, Paul Keating. Keating's relaxed manner led him, at one stage, to put his arm round Her Majesty's shoulder. It might have been better to have pretended not to notice it, but the British press blew the incident up out of all proportion. It was just one tense moment on a tension-packed trip. Keating's expressed wish to make Australia a republic by the year 2000 had not gone down well with the Queen who is, of course, Australia's head of state.

Visiting St Petersburg in 1994, Queen Elizabeth was introduced to some Russian university students. One told her that she had been to England and had stayed at Manchester. Her Majesty replied, 'Manchester, that's not such a nice place.'

Royal Servants

Royal servants are more often perfectionists than their masters and mistresses and this weakness has resulted in some famous royal mishaps and blunders.

Too little, too late

M. de Vatel, chef to the Prince de Condé in the seventeenth century, set standards of royal service which cannot be surpassed. Famed throughout the realm for the excellency of his cooking, Vatel was a man who had never known failure and consequently lacked the humility so necessary in serving as grand a master as a prince of the blood in Louis XIV's France.

One day in 1671 the Prince told his trusty chef that his greatest moment was at hand. Within a week Louis XIV, *Le Roi Soleil* himself, would be coming to dine at Chantilly. Vatel immediately began planning for the occasion, as the King travelled with many followers and catering for such a large party was beyond most men – but not, fortunately, beyond Vatel. However, when the King actually arrived, Vatel found that there were more in his party than had been expected. As a result, he had to stretch the roast meats further than he had planned. This minor incident seemed to knock Vatel's confidence and he slept badly the night before the grand banquet, which would crown his career. Inexplicably, Vatel had grown nervous. Suppose something should go wrong? Could he cope? The next day he arose tired and feeling seedy after his poor night's sleep. Little things began to irritate him. And then he was brought news that would have disturbed the equilibrium of any man. The supplier of the lobsters, that would form the basis for the royal sauce, had not sent enough; they were two hampers short. It was a catastrophe.

Vatel never considered reducing the strength of the sauce thereby stretching it further. He simply turned to his assistants and announced, 'I shall never survive the disgrace.' He went up to his bedroom and stabbed himself through the heart. Only the callous would wish to know that only minutes later news arrived that the missing hampers had been found and there would be enough lobsters after all. It was the equivalent of the Victorian Englishman with his tumbler of whisky and revolver. Failure was not a word that was known in Vatel's dictionary.

Hanging in the royal gallery

A parallel case concerned the keeper of Charles I's gallery of paintings, Abraham Van der Voort, who hanged himself rather than admit to the King that he could not locate a picture when he was asked to find it. The picture, 'The Good Shepherd' by Richard Gibson, had not been stolen or damaged as Van der Voort in his tormented mind believed. In fact, it had merely been misplaced during restoration work.

The unkindest cut of all

When the Emperor Napoleon III and the Empress Eugénie of France visited England on a state visit in 1855, the Empress was eager to display to the dowdy English just how a daughter of Spain and an empress of France could dress. Eugénie was an extraordinarily attractive woman, unfortunate only in that her beauty was matched and even exceeded by her contemporary, the Empress Elizabeth of Austria. Otherwise, in any lesser age, she would have been a *Stupor Mundi*. To maintain her brilliant image in England, she brought with her, besides her numerous ladies and servants, her personal hairdresser Felix, a man of intense professional pride and Gallic sensitivity.

The first problem Felix encountered was with the transport as they left France. Members of the royal party were separated from each other on the boats and by a malevolent chance Felix was left behind. In fact, the royal couple had reached London before Felix had even landed at Dover. He was heartbroken and suicide must have been firmly in his mind when he met the Comte de Fleury who was boarding a train to carry him to London. Fleury noticed a dishevelled individual with a greenish hue and woebegone expression, who earnestly entreated permission to ride in his carriage. 'But who may you be?' Fleury inquired. 'I am Felix, Her Majesty the Empress's hairdresser', was the reply. 'And I am in despair at being left behind! What Her Majesty will do without me I cannot tell, but I feel like cutting my throat!' Felix droned on and on, his mind a prey to despair. 'The Empress must already be at the palace and with no coiffeur to dress her hair for dinner! What a disaster!' 'Quick, then, jump in,' said Fleury, and away the train sped. When they arrived in London, Fleury hastened to inform the Empress of the incident. 'Tell Felix not to distress himself,' said Eugénie, laughing, 'he must on no account commit suicide. We want no *affaire Vatel* here. My maids have done their best for me in his absence.' Vatel must have turned in his grave at the idea of maids making do when the great craftsman was not present. One might as well have suggested that his scullions could have made the lobster sauce while the great Vatel lay cold and dead on the floor of his room, genius draining out of him with his blood.

A touchy subject

A final 'overmighty' subject was one Norasingh, coxswain to the seventeenth-century King Surasak of Siam. Navigating the royal barge one day in high winds and on a stormy river, Norasingh allowed the boat to hit the bank. Nobody was hurt and no real damage was caused, but Norasingh went ashore and demanded to be executed on the spot. The King laughed and told him not to be so upset about such a minor incident. But Norasingh was adamant. He cited a law dating from 1450 that dealt with the safety of navigation for the royal family and decreed that careless navigators must be executed. Again the King tried to reassure him but Norasingh stood his ground and demanded, as a point of professional honour, that he should die. At last the King gave way and ordered his execution. Vatel would have understood, and Felix, and even, maybe, poor Van der Voort. Yet there have been few kings in recorded history who have deserved such loyalty and such service.

During his visit to Delhi in 1911, King George V was introduced to the two distinguished brothers, Sir Montague and Sir Harcourt Butler.
'These are the two Butlers, your majesty,' said the King's aide.
'Yes,' replied the King, 'but what are their names?'

The Royal Image

The image that a monarch portrays to his people has always been of prime importance. The strength and health of the state are mirrored in the person of its ruler and thus a monarch's public relations have always been vital even before the advent of democracy and constitutional monarchy. As a figurehead, the monarch must be above criticism. As some of the following examples show, this has not always proved to be possible.

It's a Royal Knockout, 1606

When King Christian IV of Denmark visited England in the summer of 1606 King James I entertained him with revels at Theobald's, the great house built by Queen Elizabeth's minister, Lord Burghley, and now the property of his son, Robert Cecil, Earl of Salisbury. Christian had a reputation for his feats of drinking and carousing and King James and his courtiers were determined to show him that in these activities they could hold their own with the best. All would have been well, one presumes, had not the drinking started rather earlier than planned. What followed was one of the most amusing of royal fiascoes, and far better fun than Fergie's frolics of a much later age, which came to be known by the infamous title of 'It's a Royal Knockout' (see p. 164).

Queen Elizabeth's godson, Sir John Harrington – the inventor of the water closet and a minor poet and wit – was present at the entertainment and has left us an amusing account. For Harrington the whole affair was like a scene from what he called 'Mahomet's paradise'. He seemed to see everything through a series of gauzes, which were removed from time to time to let him see more clearly. Presumably, our commentator is referring to an alcoholic haze, which he shared with the rest of the courtiers present. As he reported,

> We had women and indeed wine too of such plenty as would have astonished each sober beholder. Our feasts were magnificent, and the two royal guests did most lovingly embrace each other at table; I think the Dane hath strangely wrought on our good English nobles, for those whom I never could get to taste good liquor now followed the fashion and wallow in beastly delights.

The English ladies, according to Harrington, abandoned their normal sober ways and rolled about on the floor in a drunken state. After dinner, a masque was staged, which represented the story of Solomon and Sheba. Unfortunately the arrival of the Queen of Sheba was even more dramatic and immediate than had been planned. The lady who was playing the part of the Queen carried a basket of precious gifts, which she was going to present to the brother monarchs. However, fearing stage fright or loss of her voice, one presumes, she had lubricated her throat with copious draughts of wine, with the result that she was no longer as steady on her feet as she imagined. When she came to climb up the steps to the King's high chair, she tripped over and tipped the contents of her basket, such as 'wine, cream, jellies, beverages, cakes, spices and other good matters', into the Danish King's lap, although, Harrington believed, much of it went into his face. There was much hurrying about and confusion, but 'cloths and napkins were at hand to make all clean'. His Majesty, King Christian, was not unduly alarmed and said that he wished to dance with the Queen of Sheba; but then, when he tried to rise, he fell down and humbled himself before her. The 'Queen' was then sick and had to be carried out and left to recover in an inner chamber, where she was laid on a bed of state. King Christian's clothes were covered in the presents that the Queen of Sheba had bestowed on them, but he was not a man to make a fuss and he called for more wine.

The masque continued, unfortunately now renamed 'Solomon', in the absence of the Queen. But most of the actors could not walk straight and fell down, since 'wine did so occupy their upper chambers'. Suddenly on to the scene came the three ladies playing Hope, Faith and Charity. Hope tried to say her lines but 'wine rendered her endeavours so feeble that she withdrew and hoped the King would excuse her brevity'. Faith, finding herself alone and feeling rather unwell, 'left the court in a staggering condition'. Charity now had to hold the fort for her enfeebled sisters. She knelt at the feet of King Christian and apologized for the 'multitude of sins her sisters had committed'. Bravely speaking her lines she bowed to the stout Dane and brought him gifts, while proclaiming that there was no gift that she could give that heaven had not already given His Majesty. She then scuttled out to find Hope and Faith, who were 'both sick and spewing in the lower hall'.

To a flourish of trumpets Victory entered, dressed in bright armour, and presented a rich sword to the King. Christian did not accept it at first but put it to one side for the moment, fearing in his present condition to do damage with so sharp a weapon. But Victory did not enjoy her triumph long, for 'after much lamentable utterance' she was taken ill and was 'led away like a silly captive and laid to sleep on the outer steps of the antechamber'.

Lastly the lady depicting Peace came in and tried to reach the King. She was so drunk that when her attendants tried to hold her back for fear that she would topple over on him, she flew into a rage and ranted at her ladies so angrily and so contrary to the role that she was playing that she seemed to be more like War than Peace. When attendants tried to restrain her she 'most rudely made war with her olive branch and laid on the pates of those who did oppose her coming'.

The masque now dissolved into chaos. The great hall was strewn with drunken gentlemen and ladies, while in the corridors many of the revellers were vomiting on the rich carpets and tapestries. Yet neither King James nor his Danish guest was unduly disturbed. For Christian, Theobalds had become a home from home – it was always like that at his palace – while Robert Cecil, his nimble mind unclouded by drink, was gloomily estimating the cost of the damage to his house and its furnishings. Sir John Harrington, meanwhile, had had an idea for public conveniences.

It's a Royal Knockout, 1987

In the annals of the decline of the House of Windsor, the charity showbiz event that came to be known as 'It's a Royal Knockout' holds a special place. Masterminded – if that is not too strong a word – by Prince Edward, this royal version of a popular BBC television programme took place at Alton Towers theme park. There had been an earlier programme known as 'Three Quarters of a Royal Knockout', held at Ascot racecourse, and starring Prince Edward, Princess Anne and Sarah Ferguson, when Prince Andrew had been absent on naval duties, but the Alton Towers event, in the ruins of a real castle, was to be the *pièce de résistance*. The previous evening, as the guests took dinner at a nearby hotel, Fergie was in top form, pelting Prince Andrew with 'One over the Eight' mints. In fairness, the event was held to raise money for charity, yet in its denouement it was hardly charitable. The next morning the competitors, divided into four teams each led by one of the royals – Anne, Edward, Andrew and Sarah – assembled in medieval costumes in front of the cameras and more than four thousand onlookers. The 50 members of the press, who were going to spread Prince Edward's message to the globe, were, unfortunately, crowded together for fourteen hours in a tent, sheltering from the rain, and watching the event on a small television monitor. It was poor PR – press relations – as Prince Edward was fated to discover.

The roll of guests was an impressive one, ranging from pop star Bill Wyman to singer Tom Jones, cricketer Viv Richards, comedienne Pamela Stephenson, Superman star Christopher Reeve, racing driver Nigel Mansell and a host of others. There were just four clowns and they were all royal. The problem was that Prince Edward, fresh from his tearful farewell to the Marines, could not divorce art from life. Where Cliff Richard or John Cleese knew precisely the difference between showbiz and real life, the young prince seemed to think that the knockabout fun over which he was presiding should have some great significance for those watching beyond that of a silly but harmless game.

The royals did not actually take part in the games. They were 'non–playing captains', but the shrieking and encouragement from the Duchess of York showed that she would have loved nothing better than dressing as a giant stick of rhubarb and buffeting other vegetables. She made do instead with pelting her husband with apples and pears. Prince Edward, wearing a T-shirt with the slogan 'No, I just look like him', put on a doublet and offered to go into the stocks for £50. Eventually Fergie's 'blue bandits' were pipped at the post by the Princess Royal's more demure and efficient red team.

The event ended at 8 pm and Prince Edward now remembered that he had better talk to the press, who, at that moment, were having a whip-round to raise £50 to put him in the stocks for the night. Many had not yet completed their copy for the next day and had a long drive back to London. They had hoped to have heard from the Prince by now. Prince Edward was highly stressed when he met them and not in the best of moods. He had written a speech which he promptly read out to the press until, when he paused for a moment, ITN's Joan Thirkettle interjected a question, believing he had finished. 'I haven't finished yet,' growled the Prince. Then in a hectoring voice, with a faint hint of hysteria, he asked, 'I only hope you have enjoyed yourselves – have you?' There was no response: dumb insolence to this teacher from Wanganui.

Then in a tone uncannily reminiscent of his father, Prince Edward began to rant. 'Great. Thanks for sounding so bloody enthusiastic. Well? What have *you* been doing all day?'

The reporters refrained from telling him that they had not been watching *Hamlet*. The Prince's temper snapped and, kicking back a chair, he said, 'Right, that's it.' Then he walked out. The reporters were delighted. Here was the story they had been waiting fourteen hours to find. Prince Edward, having shot himself firmly in both feet, now reloaded and aimed a bit higher. As he left Alton Towers he passed some press photographers. He could not resist a final sally. 'One of these days you people are going to have to learn some manners,' he threatened, in his best Henry VIII manner. The photographers quaked, but continued snapping. Edward drove away, with the consciousness that he had blundered growing by the minute.

Unwelcome guests

To mangle slightly the words of the Duke of Wellington, being born in a stable does not make you behave like a horse, neither does being born in a palace make you act like a king. Some rulers have displayed such extraordinary manners when engaged on royal trips that one is left uncertain as to which of the two places was the scene of their nativity.

One such man was Nasir ud-din, Shah of Persia during the late nineteenth century, who first burst upon the European scene by visiting Germany in 1873. At the Berlin Opera, he was entertained in the royal box. First he called for a glass of water, drank it down, hawked it up and then spat on to the heads of the ladies in the seats below. Returning to the Emperor's palace after the performance, he ritually slaughtered a goat on the priceless Turkish carpets in his apartment, set up a brazier in the room and roasted it. When he left the next day, the tapestries on the wall were covered in blood and grease and the carpets were burned and bloodstained. Before returning home he visited Russia, where he was lavishly entertained by Tsar Alexander II. The Tsar was astonished when, in taking his leave, the Shah told him that he was governing his country well and had his permission to continue to do so.

In 1889, the Shah returned to Europe and was entertained by Queen Victoria at Windsor Castle. During the royal banquet, the Shah insisted on spitting cherry stones at the guests sitting opposite. When he was later introduced to the Marchioness of Londonderry he reputedly eyed her up and down, slapped her rump affectionately and immediately offered to buy her. Even Edward, the Prince of Wales, found Nasir ud-din difficult company. Having viewed the Queen's ladies-in-waiting he told the prince in a loud voice that they were all so ugly he would have them executed and buy some prettier ones.

The Shah was by no means the only difficult and vulgar ruler who has accepted an invitation to visit England. Some two hundred years before, the young Tsar of Russia, Peter the Great, visited the court of King William III in 1698. The Tsar was travelling incognito, though at nearly seven feet tall, he did tend to stand out in a crowd. While in London he was housed at Sayes Court, the elegant mansion belonging to the diarist John Evelyn. Evelyn had been honoured to house so important a guest but by the time Peter left, three months later, his views had changed somewhat. The first intimation of trouble came when his steward wrote to him, 'There is a house full of people and right nasty.' Just how nasty Evelyn discovered three months later. The parquet floors and the carpets were so smeared in filth that they all had to be replaced. Tiles had been levered off the walls and stolen and all the brass door fittings had been taken. Almost all the windows were broken and every chair in the house – more than fifty – had been broken and most burned in the stoves. The bedding had been ripped apart 'as if by wild animals'. Evelyn's collection of fine paintings were cut to shreds, having been used by Peter's followers for archery practice. Outside, Evelyn's pride and joy, his elegant gardens, looked like a ploughed field after a cavalry charge. The lawns were trampled into mud 'as if a regiment of soldiers in iron shoes had drilled on it'. The prodigious holly hedge, renowned throughout the kingdom, which was four hundred feet long, nine feet high and five feet thick, had been flattened. Neighbours reported to Evelyn that the Russians appear never to have seen wheelbarrows before and thought they were some kind of toy. One man, usually Peter himself, sat in the wheelbarrow and others lifted the barrow and

Tsar Peter the Great tried to modernize Russia by learning modern industrial techniques from the West. Here Peter (left) – a huge man nearly seven feet in height – meets the diminutive William III (right) at Deptford. (PN)

pushed and pulled him in and out of the hedge. It was all great fun. Evelyn's bowling green, another object of his pride, was crisscrossed by the barrow wheels, presumably from races the Russians had staged. Evelyn, for one, was not sorry to see Peter leave England to wreak havoc elsewhere. Once the guests had gone, Evelyn presented Sir Christopher Wren, as Royal Surveyor, with a bill for the reconstruction of his property.

Fat Mary

Princess Mary Adelaide of Teck – a glutton, a scrounger and a bankrupt – was, nevertheless, probably the most popular of all British royal figures of the nineteenth century. She had the common touch, unlike her priggish cousin Queen Victoria. The princess, known to everyone as 'Fat Mary', was a fine performer with a knife and fork. When she was just eighteen, untroubled by youthful worries over slim waistlines or corsets, she weighed fifteen stone and had a moon face that positively shone as she polished it with greasy dishes. Unfortunately, there was a down side to Mary's life. Kind and popular as she was with the working classes, Mary was never likely to find a husband who would value her for her kind heart. Princes usually made their choice from mere slips of girls, none of them more than a mere twelve stone. And then, at the age of 32, Mary met the man of her dreams: Prince Francis of Teck. It was a meeting of minds. She liked eating and spending too much and so did he. Unfortunately, neither of them had an ounce of common sense.

Prince Francis of Teck was basically a penniless wastrel, who hoped to better himself by marrying into the British royal family. When the two lovebirds first moved into Kensington Palace they began to spend lavishly and live far beyond their means. They soon demolished Mary's ten thousand a year and ran heavily into debt, borrowing first from friends and then from anybody who would lend them money. Mary tried to extend her credit by honouring her suppliers with permission to print over their door: 'Purveyors to her Royal Highness the Princess Mary Adelaide, Duchess of Teck'. It impressed people at first but later became a symbol of gullibility and as much feared as the plague.

Soon the Tecks were in trouble with the Queen, who told them that their behaviour was bringing the royal family into disrepute. She therefore packed them off to Italy, where Mary could gorge on pasta. But Mary never forgot that she was a princess. Arriving in Florence she booked an entire floor of the finest hotel in the city and was soon in the same mess she had been in at home. Moreover, her husband had recently suffered a stroke, and so the decision was taken to return to England. Matters went from bad to worse. Soon every shop within travelling distance knew of the Tecks and refused to grant them any more credit. Barkers, the famous grocery store in Kensington High Street, was Mary's largest creditor. This led to an embarrassing moment for both. When Mary Adelaide was invited to open a new church hall in Kensington, to which Mr Barker had donated a substantial part of the cost, she had to make an address, during which she turned to thank him saying, 'And now I must propose a special vote of thanks to Mr Barker, to whom we all owe so much.'

In spite of Queen Victoria's reservations about Mary Adelaide, the common people never lost their faith in 'Fat Mary', whose tireless charitable work achieved more for them than the royal pontification emanating from Buckingham Palace or Windsor Castle. And fate had a last trick up its sleeve. The Princess of Teck may not have looked like much, or been good at balancing her books, but she brought up a beautiful daughter, Princess May, who was to marry Edward VII's son George. As Queen Mary, wife of King George V, Mary Adelaide's daughter was to surpass Victoria in royal qualities and take the monarchy in Britain from the stuffy petty-mindedness of the Coburgs to the magnificence of imperial power that it possessed in 1910.

While attending royal dinners in Victorian times, it was the custom for guests to stop eating as soon as the Queen herself stopped. However, on one occasion, Lord Hartington forgot himself. Partaking of a cut from a saddle of mutton Hartington turned to speak to a neighbour only to find that his plate was whisked away as Queen Victoria had apparently finished her meal. Undeterred, Hartington called out, 'Here, bring that back. I haven't finished yet.'

The battle of Flora Hastings

'Bitchy' is not the first word that comes to mind when one thinks of Queen Victoria, yet it is difficult not to use the word to describe the queen's appalling 'gaffe' in the case of her mother's lady-in-waiting, Lady Flora Hastings. In the early months of her reign, the Queen had taken an extreme dislike to Lady Flora who, apparently, had laughed when she heard that the young monarch was addicted to caraway seeds. For this serious offence, Victoria chose to believe whatever harm she could of the lady and, when she learned that Lady Flora had travelled all the way from Scotland, sharing a coach with her mother's confidential secretary, Sir John Conroy, she assumed that some impropriety must have taken place. Her suspicions were confirmed, she thought, when Lady Flora's waistline began to enlarge. Such was the hostile gossip that, in order to stop tongues wagging, Lady Flora consented to undergo a medical examination to demonstrate that she was not 'with child'. Even though the doctors found her to be a virgin, the Queen made no effort to dampen the rumours, saying 'there was an enlargement in the womb like a child' and insisted on 'cutting' Lady Flora and referring to her as 'that nasty woman' and 'that wretched Lady Flo'.

Lady Flora's brother now stepped in to clear his sister's name. He passed the story on to *The Times*, claiming that his sister was the victim of 'a depraved court'. Lord Hastings' evidence to the newspaper included a furious letter from his mother to the Prime Minister, Lord Melbourne, insisting that the 'atrocious conspiracy' be ended. Neither the young queen nor the elderly politician liked receiving such letters from angry subjects and Melbourne, with Victoria's permission, sent a damning reply, which included the following verbal swipe: 'The demand which your ladyship's letter makes upon me is so unprecedented and objectionable that even the respect due to your ladyship's sex, rank, family and character would not justify me in more, if indeed it authorises so much, than acknowledging that letter for the sole purpose of acquainting your ladyship that I have received it.'

The 'Lady Flora Hastings' case became the first scandal of Victoria's reign. When the Queen visited the opera people called out 'Mrs Melbourne' and booed her, while cheering Lady Flora as soon as she appeared. In Parliament, the Tories sniffed a chance to embarrass the Whig government and campaigned strongly in favour of Lady Flora. But just as the warring factions were manoeuvring for position, Lady Flora settled the matter by becoming dangerously ill. What had been assumed to be a pregnancy was, in fact, a cancerous tumour on her liver, and scandal was soon translated into tragedy. The Queen, no amazon in height, must have felt diminished. Her suspicions were shown to be groundless and mean-spirited. Lord Melbourne prevailed upon her to visit Lady Flora before her death and – possibly? – apologize. But even in death Lady Flora would not go away. The Queen and her ladies had by their behaviour provoked an outburst of public anger against the whole court. Even Victoria was not safe from public scorn. In the royal enclosure at Ascot, she was hissed and booed by the Duchess of Montrose and Lady Sarah Ingestre, drawing from the Queen the famous response, 'Those two abominable women ought to be flogged.'

A Victorian Andrew Morton

After the financial excesses of King George IV's reign, Parliament was very eager for Queen Victoria to keep royal spending under control. Crown finances through the Civil List needed investigating and it was hoped that the new monarch would support sensible reforms. In fact, through inexperience rather than malice, Victoria completely misman-aged the Civil List in the early years of her reign, and corruption and malpractice were almost as bad as in the worst days of the Regency. Court supernumaries were thicker than passengers on an Indian train.

At the outset Parliament gave the Queen permission to create royal pensions for 'such persons only as have just claims on the royal benevolence, or who, by their personal services to the Crown, by the performance of duties to the public or by their useful discoveries in science and attainments in literature and the arts, have merited the gracious consideration of their Sovereign and the gratitude of their country'. This was all thoroughly laudable, but what was really happening behind the scenes? The author of a book entitled *Court Jobbery or the Black Book of the Palace* was eager 'to dish the dirt' and play the Andrew Morton of his times. According to this writer, the whole royal pension system was riddled with corruption. The money went, not to those who needed it or deserved it, but to 'court butterflies and state caterpillars'. Some ex-courtiers or royal servants drew enough from the Exchequer to own a box at the opera, keep horses, carriages and liveried servants and entertain on a lavish scale – one even held a garden party for 1,200 guests at the taxpayer's expense. All this, our author explains, at a time when the widow and two children of a police officer killed during a riot received just eight pounds a year from the monarch.

The narrow horizons of the young Victoria saw hardship where there was none and knew little of the suffering of ordinary people. She allocated most of the royal pensions to those who did not need them, like her old teachers, most of whom were comfortably placed. Baroness Lehzen, the awkward old harridan who, as governess to Princess

Victoria, had made her the petty-minded prig that ascended the throne, was rewarded with £400 a year – a fortune at the time – 'for faithful services'. One of the late Duke of Sussex's illegitimate brood, Mademoiselle Augusta Emma d'Este, received a thousand pounds in 1845 'in consideration of her just claims on the royal benevolence'. The good lady was, at that moment, in the process of marrying a wealthy judge who was soon to become Lord Truro.

The author of the 'Black Book' lost control of his pen when he related the case of the elderly Sir John Newport, a 'public cormorant for fifty years', who was awarded a thousand pounds by the Queen for his 'zealous and efficient services as Chancellor of the Exchequer of Ireland'. William Wordsworth, the great Romantic poet, received £300 from the Queen. However, Her Majesty was apparently unaware that at that time the same William Wordsworth was receiving £2,000 per annum as Distributor of Stamps for Westmorland and Cumberland. The Queen insisted on honouring a number of extraordinary pensions, including £25 each per year to two men 'in consideration of the services rendered by their ancestors to King Charles II in his escape after the battle of Worcester in 1651'. The daughter of Napoleon's jailer on St Helena received £50 annually, while a man named Snow Harris got £300 for investigating electricity. An unnamed geographer was awarded £100 for 'enduring much on the north coast of America.' Six orphans of a Chief Constable in Ireland, on the other hand, received just £8 each. It was a thoroughly shoddy business and did much to confirm the British people in the view that even though there was a new monarch on the throne nothing much had changed.

Prince William's handicap

An incident in June 1991, which most parents would have taken in their stride, involved the Prince of Wales in a public relations blunder, leaving his image as a 'good father' in shreds. While at school, Prince William had apparently been accidentally struck on the head by another pupil with a golf club. The blow had been quite severe and the Prince had been taken to the Royal Berkshire Hospital, whose doctors recommended that he be taken to Great Ormond Street Hospital for Sick Children, where he could be examined by a team of neurologists. The Princess of Wales travelled in the ambulance with her son, while Prince Charles drove behind. At the hospital it was decided to carry out an operation on the young prince, who had suffered a depressed fracture of the skull. There were dangers in the operation, though these were apparently slight, and the worried parents were kept fully briefed by the doctors. Prince Charles was apparently relieved to hear that the dangers were small and decided, as a result of the diagnosis, to

Invited to attend the Scottish Women's Institute Display in 1966, Prince Philip told his audience, 'You know, British women can't cook. They are very good at decorating food and making it attractive. But they have an inability to cook.'

Charles and Diana displaying something less than complete togetherness. Their interests and temperaments were so divergent that their alliance was probably doomed from the start. (LF)

continue with his next engagement, which was to attend the opera *Tosca* at Covent Garden, where he was host to a group of European Community Commissioners.

Princess Diana stayed with her son and, during the hour-long operation, paced up and down in a neighbouring room. The operation was a complete success and the Princess was able to see her son shortly after he recovered from the anaesthetic. Meanwhile, after the opera, having ascertained by telephone that the operation on William had been a success, Prince Charles boarded a train for Yorkshire, where he was attending an environmental conference next day.

Prince William's condition was still potentially dangerous – there was a chance that he might have suffered brain damage or might develop epilepsy. While the nation waited and wondered about the health of the heir presumptive, his father was in the Yorkshire Dales, worrying about the future of the planet. It was laudable, dutiful even, but was it wise? The newspapers thought not and slated the Prince with headlines like, 'What kind of father are you?' In some ways it was a naïve question and yet, in view of the history of royal fathers neglecting their sons, it was one that was worth asking.

When Prince Charles understood the public reaction to the incident he was furious with his wife, as if she was responsible for his actions rather than he himself. This episode, emotionally charged as it was with the involvement of an injured child, was too important for the Prince to fluff. However much he felt the pull of duty, the public was bound to criticize him for leaving his son at such a time. Whether he was badly advised or acted from his own conviction, Prince Charles committed a serious public relations blunder from which the royal image could scarcely emerge unscathed.

Annus horribilis: Charles and Diana

In the Queen's 1992 Christmas message, which was broadcast from Sandringham, the fortunes of the royal family occupied her mind as never before. There was less talk about the people of the Commonwealth and more about her own suffering in the previous twelve months, which she referred to as her *annus horribilis*. During 1992, she had seen the marriages of her sons Charles and Andrew break up, as well as the divorce of her daughter, the Princess Royal. In addition, part of Windsor Castle had been destroyed by fire and she had been prompted, by the poor public response to the restoration fund, to open Buckingham Palace to the public and – a thorny issue this – she had at last agreed to pay income tax. It would have been a terrible year for any family. Yet for the Windsors, most of the damage was self-inflicted.

The break-up of the Prince of Wales's marriage was not a sudden, catastrophic event like the conflagration at Windsor Castle. It was an inevitable consequence of that tragic folly – a marriage of convenience. In 1981, the wedding of the eligible prince and the beautiful virginal princess was the stuff of fairy tale. However, after the publication of Andrew Morton's book, *Diana: Her True Story*, in 1992, there was an almost daily flood of scandal, alleging eating disorders and suicide attempts by the Princess, adultery between Prince Charles and Camilla Parker-Bowles – including the deeply embarrassing 'Camillagate' tape recording a sexually intimate conversation between Charles and his 'mistress', which, if genuine, is hardly likely to raise the stock of the Prince of Wales with the traditional royalists of 'Middle England' – and an equally unflattering picture of the Prince as a husband jealous of his wife's popularity and unable to give his sons the love they need.

These revelations challenged the notion that Charles had ever really loved Diana, even when they wed, and suggested that he had been acting under pressure to marry to ensure the succession. Evidence today suggests that Charles and Diana had virtually nothing in common when they married and that the whole affair was a marriage of convenience. Such marriages have a way of breaking up when they are no longer convenient.

Windsor Castle ablaze, 20 November 1992. Coming towards the end of a year that had seen the marriages of Prince Charles and Prince Andrew break up, as well as the divorce of the Princess Royal, the fire – which caused extensive damage – was the culmination of what the Queen later described as an 'Annus Horribilis'. (PN)

In view of the morass that Charles and Diana have dug for themselves, and the public relations blunders to which the Duchess of York and Prince Edward seem prone, many pundits are writing off the House of Windsor, claiming that rather than a case of *annus horribilis* one is in fact dealing with a *familiaris horribilis*. Significantly, the previously passive Princess Diana has recently described the British royals as the 'Leper Colony'. It is a bitter verdict on which to end a relationship, but in a way it says it all.

By the mid-1990s the image of the British royal family was in a parlous condition. Opinion polls in early 1995 suggested that a large majority of Elizabeth II's subjects did not believe Prince Charles to be 'setting a good example'. The jury was still out on his chances of becoming Charles III.

Perhaps the biggest blunder perpetrated by the House of Windsor in recent years was to have allowed their image become so dependent on a media-led PR machine in the first place. Having first invited their readers to feast daily on a wholesome diet of royal pageant and conjugal happiness, the press were unlikely then to deny them the richer and more exciting fare of rumoured adultery and imminent marital breakdown. The tabloids who raised the House of Windsor to a peak of popularity in the early 1980s mercilessly exposed its travails in the 1990s, proving that those who live by PR very often die by it as well.

There is one last salutary thought for Charles, Di and co. Princess Anne, generally considered as a young woman to have 'an image problem' on account of a somewhat prickly and un-media-friendly manner, and despite the trauma of the breakdown of her marriage to Captain Mark Philips, now commands a public respect that must be the envy of the younger royals. Energetic work on behalf of Save the Children has a lot to do with it, but she has also avoided the mistake of talking to the likes of Andrew Morton and Jonathan Dimbleby. . . .

Lese-Majesty

Queen Elizabeth I was not a ruler who would have taken kindly to the idea of appearing in a book of 'Royal Blunders'. Perhaps more than any other British monarch she cultivated her public image, emerging as 'Gloriana' and the 'Virgin Queen'. Yet, during her long reign of forty-five years, she was subjected to many cases of lese-majesty – injuries to the honour and standing of a monarch. All of these she handled with dexterity and vigour.

A clerical error

The problems for Elizabeth were twofold. In the first place, as part of the 'monstrous regiment of women' which in the opinion of John Knox, the Scottish ecclesiastic, dominated the government of England and Scotland during the sixteenth century, she was regarded as a woman in a man's world and consequently acting above her true station, which was to be as man's subordinate and helpmate. Moreover, as an unmarried woman she was even more unusual in the eyes of the chauvinistic males of the time, lacking as she did the guidance and superior advice of a man. As a result, high churchmen sometimes felt they had the duty – nay, the right – to instruct a weak and foolish woman on matters above her understanding. Archbishop Edmund Grindal felt he needed to instruct Elizabeth in 1576, when she ordered him to suppress Puritan classes, known as 'Prophesyings', which she believed were likely to undermine the teachings of the new Church of England. He wrote a letter to Elizabeth, a letter which contained the following warning:

> Remember, Madam, that you are a mortal creature: Look not only upon the purple and princely array wherewith you are apparelled, but consider withal, what is that that is covered therewith? Is it not flesh and blood? Is it not dust and ashes?

As a believer in the divine right of kings – and queens – Elizabeth was not happy to be lectured by somebody she had just appointed. It was a brave letter by Grindal, but it cost him his job. He was suspended from his office and kept under close confinement until his death six years later.

A lady surprised

Queen Elizabeth I had many favourites, but never one who was allowed to take such liberties as did Robert Devereux, Earl of Essex. Essex's mistake was to feel that he was so important to the ageing monarch that he could take her for granted. In this he was fatally mistaken. Elizabeth was not just a queen, she was very much a woman. She had

Robert Devereux, Earl of Essex, draws his sword against Queen Elizabeth I. On this occasion Elizabeth overlooked Essex's act of lese-majesty, but his failure to put down the Irish revolt and subsequent attempt to raise a rebellion against Chief Minister Cecil led to his execution for treason. (PN)

ruled the country since 1558 without a husband and she would never allow any man to take advantage of her. By the late 1590s Essex had forgotten this. During one argument Elizabeth had boxed his ears in open court and Essex had made to draw his sword against her. This was a capital offence, but for the moment she overlooked it.

However, on his return from Ireland, where he had failed utterly to suppress the revolt of the Earl of Tyrone, Essex made the sort of mistake that only an inexperienced man could make. Elizabeth's image as 'Gloriana' was a product of cosmetics and inordinate attention to detail. She was an old woman who, through paint and pigment, could still astound her courtiers and the representatives of foreign powers with her beauty. However, it took time and her secrets were shared by her ladies-in-waiting only. No man dare intrude on her privacy. She was as deadly to wandering eyes as the gorgon.

But Essex was aware of no imperative but his own and, hurrying to the Queen before news of his failure in Ireland reached her ears, he committed the crime unpardonable. Muddy and sweat-stained, he burst into her sleeping quarters before she was fully dressed, unmade-up and with her hair awry. What he saw was the woman as she really was, stripped of her finery, of her cosmetics and of her image. It was more than the humiliation of a queen, it was the exposure of a legend for the lie that it really was. No man could survive such a crime.

Elizabeth had loved Essex but he had crossed a line that everyone at her court knew must never be crossed. She dismissed him from court. It was the end for Essex and after his abortive rebellion, she signed the warrant for his execution.

A change of air

Not every event at Elizabeth I's court was fraught with such consequences. Sometimes fear of the 'Virgin Queen' was itself enough to send men packing from her court. Edward de Vere, Earl of Oxford, once committed what he believed to be a cardinal sin in front of a full court.

As he made an elaborate bow before Her Majesty he audibly broke wind. De Vere was so embarrassed that he could not bear to stay at court to face the ridicule of his peers. As a result, he left England and travelled on the continent for several years before he dared to return. When at last he plucked up courage to return to England, believing that the matter must have been forgotten, he presented himself again before the Queen. Elizabeth welcomed him home with the words, 'My Lord, I had quite forgot the fart.'

During King George VI's tour of Canada before the Second World War he noticed, while visiting a provincial town, that the mayor was not wearing his chain of office. Looking for an opportunity to present him with a gold chain, the King asked him whether or not he already had one. 'Yes, sir,' the mayor replied, 'I do.' 'But I notice you are not wearing it,' said the King. 'Oh,' explained the mayor, 'I only wear it on special occasions.'

Royal Blunders

Errors of judgement by kings and queens can have farcical as well as tragic consequences. Often the most well-intentioned can prove the most disastrous. This was particularly true of the Emperor Joseph II of Austria – one of the most famous of the 'Enlightened Despots' of the eighteenth century. Between 1780 and 1790 Joseph issued six thousand decrees, covering every aspect of life. However, his attempts to rule his domains entirely by the principles of logic involved him in a series of absurd blunders.

Paved with good intentions

His most famous error of judgement arose from an apparently wise and progressive decree: that which lifted press censorship. Unfortunately, the decree unleashed a tidal wave of new publishing. Censorship had existed in the Habsburg lands for so long that its suspension allowed the pent-up frustrations of centuries to burst on an unsuspecting world. The result was that Vienna became, at least for ten years, both the centre for progressive political thinking and a sewer through which flowed the filth of diseased minds. The Emperor and his government became a target – in fact, the only available target – for satirists, lampooners and a new gutter press. Hundreds of political agitators came to Vienna from all parts of Europe to plot the overthrow of governments and print subversive leaflets. Every café in Vienna was teeming with revolutionaries and peddlers of filth. Books appeared for sale with the sort of titles that had only ever been seen before in France, and were on sale publicly where previously they had been kept under counters and in plain covers. Joseph's new relaxation of censorship allowed such books as *Magister Hilarius' Wonderful History of an Old Virgin Who Remained Unviolated for 30 Years, told in Clean Rhymes; Bawdy Houses are Necessary in Vienna, No Matter What Herr Councillor Sonnenfels May Preach from the Pulpit Against Them; Mama Wants Me To Enter a Monastery; Concerning Chambermaids; Concerning Viennese Housemaids; Concerning Viennese Girls* to be sold openly. But it could not last. Joseph's enlightened views had not taken account of mankind's baser nature. After the Emperor's death in 1790, censorship of the severest kind was reimposed in the Habsburg Empire. It had been fun while it lasted, and the release of pressure may even have saved Austria from going the same way as France in 1789.

Joseph II had already declared war on waste and so he now turned his attention to the question of coffins. In his view ornate coffins were a sign of the superstitions so typical

The Emperor Joseph II was a musical dilettante, but this did not prevent him from giving advice to Mozart when he felt like it. After hearing a performance of the opera The Abduction from the Seraglio, *he congratulated the composer with the words, 'Beautiful, my dear Mozart, but too many notes.'*

As perhaps the greatest of the 'Enlightened Despots' of the eighteenth century, the Emperor Joseph II of Austria believed there was a logical solution to every problem. His supreme confidence even led him to advise Mozart on how to write his music. (ME)

of the Roman Catholic Church. Joseph, as a freethinker, thought it was much better to wrap corpses up in a sack and throw them in the ground without a lot of fuss. As a result, in 1784, he issued a decree ordering that coffins should henceforth only be made of soft wood and with flat covers. This apparently sensible idea was taken even further seven months later by another decree making coffins illegal and stipulating that cadavers be buried in a linen sheet or sack. He can hardly have expected the public outcry which threatened revolution in Austria. Crowds of people came on to the streets and called on the Emperor to forgo his heathen ways and return to the true church of Christ. Within six months he had to revoke the decree, admitting that he did not understand what all the fuss was about. In frustration he told his ministers, since the people 'display so great an interest in their bodies even after their death, without realizing that they are then nothing but stinking cadavers, I no longer care how they bury themselves in the future'.

Goldfinger

We have seen elsewhere that Franz Josef of Austria was unlucky in love. But in other matters he brought problems on his own head, as with the fiasco of the 'gold factory'. During the 1860s, three international swindlers persuaded the Emperor that they could turn five million guldens of silver into eighty million guldens worth of gold. So excited was Franz Josef that he allowed these men to operate from the Imperial Mint in Vienna, with the full-time assistance of professors from the Vienna Technological Institute. Absurd as it sounds the swindlers were not found out for more than two years. By that time they had got away with millions of guldens of silver. When the truth came out, the director of the Mint was dismissed and the documents relating to the case were placed in secret files in the state archives. Unfortunately for the memory of the Emperor, when the Austro-Hungarian Empire collapsed in 1918, the documents were published by republican newspapers to ridicule the imperial administration.

Where ignorance is bliss

The career of King Faustin I of Haiti was a well-intentioned saga of mishaps and blunders. Elected president of the Caribbean state in 1849, Faustin Élie Soulouque made himself Emperor Faustin I a few months later, crowning himself in the absence of a real gold crown with a gilt cardboard one instead. He was an enthusiastic man who was sometimes confused by the nature of different political systems. Having established himself as a benevolent autocrat, he addressed the crowds at his coronation with the words, 'Long live liberty! Long live equality!'

Faustin was impressed by everything French, notably the splendour of the imperial court under Napoleon I, which he hoped to emulate. He appointed one man Lord High Baker, but when the recipient asked him what were his duties, a baffled Faustin replied, 'It's something good.' As it happens the Lord High Baker was a man named Count Lemonade, which may sound odd but was a result of the new nobility taking their titles from the land or property that they had been given. Thus Count Lemonade was the owner of an area of lemon groves. The new owner of the jam factory became, naturally, the Duke of Marmalade. This system of nomenclature was as sensible as, if less mellifluous than, many titles of the French nobility, which referred to the castles or demesnes that they owned, and included such evocative names as Count Torrential Stream, Count Red Terrier, Baron Syringe and Baron Dirty Hole.

Having established a nobility in Haiti, Faustin felt that his regime needed to be consolidated by the creation of a royal guard. This impressive force was again to be based on a Napoleonic model. He commissioned splendid uniforms for the chosen men and, a stickler for detail, he ordered genuine shakos from Marseilles. These duly arrived and each was decorated with an ornamental metal insignia. However, neither Faustin nor any of his men could read and therefore nobody knew the significance of the inscription on the heroes' helmets. It was not until a French traveller came to the island and was invited to witness a military display that the inscription was translated for the Emperor. It said, 'Sardines in oil, Barton and Company, Lorient.'

In spite of her 'bloody' reputation, Queen Mary Tudor was in fact a gentle and rather naive woman. On one occasion she overheard her Lord Chamberlain flirting with one of her ladies-in-waiting, Frances Neville. As he tickled her under the chin he said, 'My pretty whore, how dost thou?' Not knowing what this meant Mary thought it a good jest to repeat it to the girl. A little later she called Frances to help her with her farthingale and as the girl knelt before her the Queen said, 'Go-a-mercy, my pretty whore.' Frances was astounded and embarrassed and complained that she never expected to hear such words from the Queen. Mary admitted she had heard the Lord Chamberlain using the phrase but Frances told her, 'My Lord Chamberlain is an idle gentleman, and we respect not what he saith or doth; but Your Majesty doth amaze me either in jest or earnest to be called so by you. A whore is a wicked, misliving woman.'

Royal Diplomacy

King Edward VII of Great Britain regarded monarchy as a club and it frequently fell to him to introduce new 'members' to the rules and regulations that applied. That all rulers should aspire to the same standards was vital if monarchs were to present a united front to the world. Unfortunately, there were occasions when the behaviour of some monarchs threatened the diplomatic equilibrium that their ministers and ambassadors had struggled so hard to achieve. Precedence at royal events was a frequent cause of trouble. Once, in London, Crown Prince Frederick of Germany was miffed at having to yield precedence to the visiting King Kalahua of Hawaii. Prince Frederick took his complaint to his brother-in-law Edward, who was then Prince of Wales. Edward explained that crown princes must always give way to kings, even kings of Hawaii. 'After all,' said Edward, 'either the brute is a king or he's a common or garden nigger; and, if the latter, what's he doing here?'

During a state visit to Brazil in 1968, the Queen and Prince Philip were invited to a state banquet in the capital, Brasilia. While there, Prince Philip was introduced to a Brazilian general, whose chest was well decorated with medals. 'Where did you get all the medals?' inquired Prince Philip. 'From the war,' replied the general. 'I didn't know Brazil was in the war that long,' observed the Prince.
'At least, sir,' replied the general, 'I didn't get them for marrying my wife.'

Outsmarting the Kaiser

Tsar Ferdinand of Bulgaria, he of the elephantine proboscis, was extremely proud of the fact that he, a minor prince of Germany, had become a tsar and was, at least in his own eyes, the equal of rulers like Tsar Nicholas II of Russia and Kaiser Wilhelm II of Germany. Unfortunately they did not see things that way and regarded Ferdinand as a parvenu. As a result, Ferdinand was very touchy on this matter and refused to allow his dignity to be impugned. He was a hard man and could be cruel, even callous, as he was to his second wife – he made her take her meals in her bedroom and insisted that these be cold so that he could not smell them in the palace corridors.

Thus he was not the ideal man with whom to joke, as the Kaiser found when, in December 1909, Ferdinand undertook a state visit to Germany. Ferdinand was hoping to combine business with pleasure, as he was looking for an arms supplier for the Bulgarian army and planned at the outset to deal with Krupp of Essen. However, at a banquet held in his honour, at the New Palace at Potsdam, the Kaiser put paid to all Ferdinand's plans as a result of a childish prank that backfired.

Ferdinand was standing by a window engrossed in conversation with some other guests. Noticing something outside that interested him, Ferdinand leant out of the

Kaiser Wilhelm II of Germany dressed as a Prussian general. For all his military bearing, the Kaiser was not above the occasional schoolboy prank, as his mischievous slapping of the Tsar Ferdinand of Bulgaria's bottom shows. (PN)

window. As Ferdinand bent forward, the Kaiser - unable to resist the acres of royal buttock, in stretched uniform breeches, thus presented - scuttled up and slapped Ferdinand's bottom with a laugh. Ferdinand swung round as if he had been shot and demanded an immediate apology in front of the guests. The Kaiser, the smile fading on his lips, explained that it was just a joke and refused to apologize. Without another word, Ferdinand stormed out of the palace, immediately cancelling his appointment at Krupps and transferring the military contracts to the French company of Schneider-Creusot.

Elephants never forget, it is said, and so neither did Ferdinand, and relations between Germany and Bulgaria remained strained for a number of years. But members of the royal profession cannot help meeting each other in the line of duty and so this smouldering disagreement broke out afresh from time to time. At the funeral in London of King Edward VII in 1910, for example, Ferdinand found himself snubbed by the German Emperor. He had been talking to ex-President Theodore Roosevelt of the United States, when Wilhelm swept up, put his arm round Roosevelt's shoulders and said, with a malicious glance at the Tsar, 'Roosevelt, my friend, I want to introduce you to the King of Spain. He *is* worth talking to.'

In 1968 Prince Philip was being driven into Amsterdam from the airport. He observed to the detective travelling with him, 'What a po-faced lot these Dutch are. Look at them.' At this point the Dutch chauffeur, who had overheard the Prince's words and understood English, angrily refused to drive any further. Only a swift apology from the Prince's detective allowed the journey to continue.

Black George's diplomacy

Prince George Karageorgeovitch of Serbia was a man who found himself at odds with the petty conventions other people seemed to find necessary to make life endurable. George was inclined to give his violent nature full rein and if this offended someone that was his misfortune. But once, in 1909, the delicate relations that existed between his country and its powerful neighbour, Austria-Hungary, were nearly broken by the prince's lack of self-control.

Dining one evening in a restaurant in the Serbian capital, Belgrade, Prince George became increasingly obstreperous as the evening went on. Finally, viewing some foreigners dining at a nearby table, he despatched one of his aides to inform them that he found their ugly faces repulsive and would be obliged if they would turn away from him and sit facing the wall. His choice of victim was unfortunate. The party consisted of the Austrian ambassador and his senior embassy staff. Observing that the insult came from Prince George himself, the Austrian ambassador stormed out of the restaurant and immediately telephoned the Foreign Office in Vienna. Within a short time the Serbian government received an official complaint from the Austrians and a demand for an apology, failing which diplomatic relations would be severed. For a few anxious hours it seemed that Prince George's foul temper might lead to war between Austria and Serbia, thereby triggering the First World War five years early.

Chosen by God?

Throughout history kings and queens have believed – or at least claimed – that they had been selected to rule by God alone. As these examples show, the Almighty sometimes 'moves in a mysterious way'.

Selectors' error

As Malvolio once discovered to his cost, 'Some are born great; some achieve greatness; and some have greatness thrust upon them.' We can be certain that Shakespeare was not thinking of the Roman Emperor Jovian when he wrote this, but it has to be admitted that the imperial crown certainly fitted him when it came his way by mistake.

In 363 the Emperor Julian led a great army against the Persians but, after some success, was killed in a skirmish. The legionaries tried to appoint the Praetorian Prefect of the East, Sallustius Secundus, to be emperor, but he refused on the grounds that he was now too old. In the confusion, a few followers of the commander of the Imperial Guard, an amiable dullard named Jovian, began shouting out his name. Ammianus Marcellinus the historian, who was with the army, tells that now a ridiculous mistake occurred. Hearing the name 'Jovianus!' being called, the troops at a distance from the imperial tent thought that the name 'Julianus!' was being called, and that the late Emperor had made a recovery from his wound. Soon everyone in the army was yelling 'Julianus'. But the men at the front were still shouting for Jovian and so he was declared the new Emperor, by public acclamation. When the truth dawned on the men at the back, that they had made the half-wit Jovian Emperor, they 'gave themselves up to tears and lamentations'.

And with good reason, for Jovian was 'not up to the job'. He immediately made a humiliating peace with the Persians, surrendering everything Julian had gained. But he did not long outlive his cowardice, dying within a year of eating too many mushrooms.

Too young to rule, too young to die

A similarly inadequate method of selecting a new king was operated in fifteenth-century Siam. The late king, Intraraja, had three sons and before his death he had decreed that his successor should be one of his two elder sons as his youngest, Baromaraja, was too young to be considered. The two sons who would contest the succession should fight a duel to the death, riding on the backs of elephants. However, when the duel began, things did not turn out quite how the old king had expected. When the elephants charged each other the two elder boys were both knocked off and trampled beneath the feet of the great beasts. Baromaraja, who was watching from a safe distance, thus found himself king by a process of elimination.

BUCKINGHAM PALACE: AT HOME WITH 'IN I GO' JONES

'In I go' Jones was a regular visitor at Buckingham Palace. In fact, he had originally come to London to better himself and soon found himself resident with Queen Victoria in her new royal palace. It was called 'making good' in Victoria's days and 'In I go' Jones went several steps further than Pip's 'Great Expectations' had taken Dickens's hero. He ate in the Queen's kitchen, listened to her meetings with her councillors and senior politicians, opened her sealed letters, spied on the Queen and her ladies, and even sat on her throne. 'But is it worth three months in a house of correction on a treadmill?' asked the Judge. 'Yes, your lordship,' said Jones, 'I'm now a national celebrity, appearing in music hall at four pounds a week – and I have become a part of the notorious history of Buckingham Palace.'

Buckingham Palace is so much the centre of the 'royal industry' in England that it is with considerable surprise that one reads of its chequered history. In fact, during the reign of King George IV its name was synonymous with graft and corruption, fraud and shoddy workmanship. George IV had envisaged the extended Buckingham House as a private residence. He hoped to dazzle the princes of Europe with a building of startling dimensions that would make Versailles and the Tsars' Winter Palace seem mere gatehouses. But George IV's imagination, always vivid, ran beyond his means, and raspberry-coloured pillars were all very well but who was going to foot the bill? You had to be a Wellington or a Marlborough for a grateful people to agree to finance a giant bronze statue of you. George IV was, unfortunately, the most unpopular king of England since Ethelred the Unready.

While George IV struggled with the question of cost, his architect John Nash underwent a crisis of confidence and decided that he had lost the knack of building palaces. His new creation was bidding fair to be a monstrosity, and a very expensive one at that. He was already under attack by jealous rivals, who accused him of cutting corners on safety and of falsifying stress calculations in order to reduce costs. In 1830 the Duke of Wellington, then Prime Minister, ordered his Chancellor of the Exchequer to 'make a hash of Nash' over the escalating costs of

the ridiculous palace, which were now four times the original costing. But so much money had already been spent that Wellington and, after the death of George IV in 1830, King William IV – 'Silly Billy' – decided that there was nothing for it but to complete the structure. Shorn of his royal defender, Nash was promptly dismissed from the project and replaced by a man of less talent but sounder credentials, Edward Blore. The King, meanwhile, was trying to find a use for the new building. When the Houses of Parliament burned down in 1834, William was the first to offer the new palace as a replacement. Members of parliament were no happier with the idea of working in the building than William IV was of living in it. The King's next idea was to use it as a barracks for his footguards. Again the idea was rejected. The palace was now scheduled to cost close to a million pounds. Let the footguards freeze, said the Treasury, they were not going to warm their toes at the taxpayer's expense.

Buckingham Palace had now become a satirist's dream. So complete a folly had never been built in England before and no self-respecting humorist was going to miss the chance of making fun of it. The dome that Nash had built to provide extra lighting, rose, as a result of a miscalculation, above the parapet designed to conceal it like a 'pimple'. It was ignominiously removed, as was the triumphal arch built in front of the palace, which was described as 'horridly ostentatious'. Worse than that, when someone at last got round to testing if a state coach could actually pass through the arch it was found, to nobody's surprise, that it was too narrow. As a result, the 'Marble Arch' was born and Buckingham Palace's loss was Oxford Street's gain. George IV's favourite raspberry pillars were pulled down on the grounds that they were 'wicked, vulgar' and made the architects feel sick.

Surprisingly, when Victoria became Queen in 1837 she actually seemed to like the palace. Like some student leaving home for the first time and finding 'her own place', Victoria regarded the unloved building as a place to 'be herself', away from the cloying presence of her mother. Even when she found the floors uncarpeted and the

Today Buckingham Palace is universally regarded as the most enduring symbol of the British monarchy. But when the palace was first built in the 1830s it was viewed as an architectural monstrosity and a folly.
(AR/IS)

rooms unfurnished, she would not be deterred from moving in at once. The only drawback she found was that she did not have a throne. Her nanny had promised her a throne when she became Queen, so she must have one. She commissioned a new design from an upholsterer named Dowbigin and ordered the bill to be sent to the Chancellor of the Exchequer. The Treasury responded by informing Her Majesty that they were unwilling to pay the £12 involved in changing the 'WR' to 'VR' on the throne at St James's and could she reimburse them for the said necessary adaptation. It was tit for tat.

However, the palace presented rather greater problems than the pattern on the Queen's new throne. Nor was it sufficient for her to declare that her pet spaniel – 'dear Dashy' – was quite happy in the garden. The building was virtually uninhabitable, particularly for the domestic servants who would live there in their hundreds. The kitchen, placed in the basement, lacked light and ventilation: 'Stygian gloom' was a phrase frequently invoked to describe its general properties. The large number of stoves needed by such an enormous building produced so much smoke and soot that chimney sweeps were on permanent call and conditions for the cooks and their assistants must have resembled those in an ironclad's funnels. Naturally, one could hardly expect the Queen to give a thought to her subterranean scullions, but one might have hoped for more intelligence from men who were supposedly qualified architects. The same observation might be applied to the complete absence – presumably an oversight – of normal kitchen stores, pantries and larders. Staff accommodation in the garrets was tiny and overcrowded, with eight or ten footmen sharing a room large enough for perhaps two or three. In addition, the lack of a bootroom meant that the staff had to clean sometimes hundreds of pairs of shoes, belonging to the Queen's visitors, in their own tiny rooms.

The list of domestic complaints seemed never-ending. Of the fifty new water closets few worked, and these only intermittently. The palace's new water system seemed to have been designed by the man who built the Hampton Court maze. Those state rooms with their own conveniences were found not to have been equipped with taps. Heating, which was supposed to have been 'state-of-the-art', was so unreliable that each room needed coal fires daily, resulting in the need to appoint hundreds of extra staff simply to cope with firelighting and coal carrying. Even when the fires were lit, they smoked abominably, forcing the wretched inhabitants to open the windows, even in winter, thereby chilling the room and producing smog in the most unlikely places. Living conditions at the palace might even have stirred the imagination of Charles Dickens and, anticipating his future novel, persuaded him to write a royal *Bleak House*.

Bearing every indication of having been designed by a committee of 'experts', the palace was administered by four separate departments of state: the Lord Chamberlain's Office, the Lord Steward's Office, the Master of the Horse's Office and the Office of Woods and Works. As a result there were frequent demarcation disputes. For example, the Lord Steward was responsible for providing fuel for a fire and for laying it. However, he had no authority to light it and that necessary function could only be undertaken once a member of the Lord Chamberlain's staff became available to do so. However, it was all change when it came to lamps. There the Lord Steward had the advantage. It was the task of the Lord Chamberlain to provide the lamps, but he had no authority to light them; that was the Lord Steward's job. Or was it? The Master of the Horse would claim that 'trimming' was the Lord Steward's job. 'Lighting' was the time-honoured task of the Master of the Horse. Meanwhile, the Lord Chamberlain was happy to clean the windows. 'Only the outside,' declared the Office of Woods and Works, for the inside of the window was their responsibility alone. And so it went on. When Prince Albert's mentor, Baron Stockmar (see p. 133), with his orderly German mind, arrived at the palace, he must have believed he had entered the wrong building and was, in fact, in Bedlam.

Amidst all the confusion, corruption was rife. The Lord Chamberlain, Lord Conyngham, who actually lived at the palace, took advantage of his situation to appoint his mistress as housekeeper. It was an important position, though the lady appeared to have no qualifications for the job, unless it was understood that she was keeping house for His Lordship and warming his bed in her secondary capacity. With the senior household offices occupied by political appointees, nobody took responsibility for supervising the domestic staff who, naturally, took whatever advantage they could of the slack administration. Servants, aware that there was no one to discipline them, were frequently rude even to royal guests. Some visiting royalty lost their way in the smoky corridors and wandered down into

what must have seemed like the heart of a volcano, blackening their faces and clothes and losing their baggage. When they did meet servants these usually laughed at their broken English and refused to direct them.

It is hardly surprising to read that numerous intruders entered the palace in its early days. As nobody seemed to know who should actually be in the building at any one time it was easy for young Edmund Jones – dubbed 'In I Go' Jones by an amused public – to roam the palace unchallenged. Another notable intruder was twelve-year-old Tom Cotton, who claimed to have spent a year in the palace, only being apprehended when he took a 'constitutional' across the lawns.

But above everything else – or at least beneath it – was the fact that the palace had been built on a conduit, which acted as an overflow for the now subterranean Tyburn Brook. Raw sewerage as well as water passed through the conduit and, horrible to relate, it was the kitchen that was built directly over this serious health hazard. The atmosphere in the royal kitchens was damp and foul and when an investigation of the building was at last carried out by the Office of Woods and Works, it was discovered that, apart from the sewer below ground, there was a dunghill piled up against the kitchen wall. When one of the department's inspectors, Sir Benjamin Stephenson, raised this matter with the housekeeper, she memorably replied that 'it was nothing to do with her'. Stephenson reported that so foul was the smell in parts of the ground floor that he felt it was virtually uninhabitable.

The arrival of Prince Albert came not a moment too soon. His reforms saved thousands of pounds a year and turned Buckingham Palace into a worthy symbol of British royalty. In concluding we should not forget our guide – 'In I Go' Jones. There have been modern Joneses, as a result of poor security, the most determined and successful of whom was probably Michael Fagan. In 1982 Fagan climbed into the Palace by an open window, found the queen's bedroom and sat on her bed and talked to her. In spite of the fact that this dishevelled and shoeless individual was sighted by a number of Palace staff nobody challenged him. Only when a chambermaid saw him with the Queen and remarked, 'Bloody hell, Ma'am. What's he doing here?' was the alarm raised. Fortunately Fagan was harmless, but the revealed inadequacy of the security systems was hardly reassuring.

INDEX